GUNS ACROSS AMERICA

GUNS ACROSS AMERICA
Reconciling Gun Rules and Rights

ROBERT J. SPITZER

OXFORD
UNIVERSITY PRESS

OXFORD
UNIVERSITY PRESS

Oxford University Press is a department of the University of
Oxford. It furthers the University's objective of excellence in research,
scholarship, and education by publishing worldwide.

Oxford   New York
Auckland   Cape Town   Dar es Salaam   Hong Kong   Karachi
Kuala Lumpur   Madrid   Melbourne   Mexico City   Nairobi
New Delhi   Shanghai   Taipei   Toronto

With offices in
Argentina   Austria   Brazil   Chile   Czech Republic   France   Greece
Guatemala   Hungary   Italy   Japan   Poland   Portugal   Singapore
South Korea   Switzerland   Thailand   Turkey   Ukraine   Vietnam

Oxford is a registered trademark of Oxford University Press
in the UK and certain other countries.

Published in the United States of America by
Oxford University Press
198 Madison Avenue, New York, NY 10016

Library of Congress Cataloging-in-Publication Data
Spitzer, Robert J., 1953-
Guns across America : reconciling gun rules and rights / Robert J. Spitzer.
  pages cm
ISBN 978-0-19-022858-3 (hardback : alk. paper)
1. Gun control—United States.   2. Firearms ownership—United States.
3. Firearms—Law and legislation—United States.   I. Title.
HV7436.S677 2015
323.43—dc23
2014041660

9 8 7 6 5 4 3 2 1
Printed in the United States of America
on acid-free paper

To Tess,
You turned my world around, when you held out your hand—

Contents

Acknowledgments

I have many people to thank for all manner of assistance, advice, and information.

My most sincere thanks to Glenn Altschuler, Cortland County Undersheriff Herb Barnhart, Erik Bitterbaum, Judge Julie Campbell, Gregg Lee Carter, John Colasanto, Saul Cornell, SUNY Cortland's University Police Chief Steven Dangler, Deb Dintino, Julie Easton, John Robert Greene, Herb Haines, Steve Handelman, David Holian, George Jennings Jr., Cortland County Clerk Elizabeth Larkin, D. Bruce Mattingly, Dave Miller, Steve Newman, Hans Noel, Raymond Petersen, Dick Pious, Mark Prus, Grant Reeher, Don Richardson, Cortland Deputy Chief of Police Paul Sandy, Daniel Shea, Henry Steck, Cortland City Police Sergeant Patrick Sweeney, and to the Cortland City Police Department, the Cortland County Clerk's Office, Cortland County Sheriff's Department, and the McGraw Sportsmen's Club. At Oxford, my special thanks to social sciences editor-in-chief David McBride, and assistant editor Sarah Rosenthal.

I extend my gratitude as well for the opportunity to present my arguments and data at several universities and other venues, including Cazenovia College, Colby College, Fordham University, Georgetown University, Jefferson

Community College, John Jay College of Criminal Justice, King's College (Britain), Manchester University (Indiana), the Monroe County Bar Association, the Pediatric Grand Rounds at the Upstate Golisano Children's Hospital (Syracuse, NY), the Sterling (New York) Historical Society, Syracuse University, and the University of North Carolina, Greensboro. This research was supported in part by a sabbatical leave from SUNY Cortland. My home institution has treated me well these many years, and I am happy to express my gratitude. Finally, my three gals, Mellissa, Shannon, and Skye, cheer me every day. And everything I do of any worth is dedicated to Tess.

Introduction

Imagine a country where the government keeps tabs on citizen gun possession—what kinds of guns, how many, and their condition—and where the government can confiscate them for offenses ranging from failing to swear an oath of loyalty to the government, to the violation of various hunting restrictions, to the failure to pay an obligatory gun tax. That country is neither a quasi-socialist European nation, nor an authoritarian nation, nor a postmodern, futuristic American leftist utopia. That nation is the American colonies and the early American nation.

The American gun narrative is familiar to most. From the colonial era through the Wild West, men mostly relied on their wits for survival, which included a trusty flintlock or pistol at their side. This heritage was enshrined in the Second Amendment's "right to bear arms," which played out most famously in the nineteenth-century American West, where stalwart men tamed the West by standing their ground—again, in the grand American tradition—against outlaws, Indians, and predators. These often repeated and widely accepted shibboleths frame the contemporary gun debate (even if some disagree about how this past should or should not inform modern gun policy) and buttress often successful efforts to make it easier for modern-day John Waynes to arm themselves, and their values, against modern-day predators of both the criminal and political variety.

This narrative, of course, is mostly wrong—not just exaggerated, but wrong. I do not suggest that I am by any means the first to point this out, but in recent years, new and important research and writing have chipped away at old myths to present a more accurate and pertinent sense of our gun past.[1] This is important not only because the truth matters, but also because modern American gun policy, more than most other policy areas, has an indisputably long and direct heritage and lineage dating to the country's earliest beginnings. That heritage, in turn, frames the modern gun debate to a degree seen in few other areas. As if to ratify the idea that modern gun policy is framed by the past, the Supreme Court's important 2008 case defining (and redefining) gun rights is one of the most history-driven (as opposed to law-driven) decisions in modern times. This past-to-present continuum has had very specific consequences, as it has been key to the concerted contemporary political drive in the last three decades by gun rights groups, and parallel marketing efforts by the gun industry, to roll back gun laws and to press as many guns into as many hands as possible.

This movement has occurred, ironically, at the very time when fewer Americans than ever own guns. This long-term trend arises from profound demographic, behavioral, and attitudinal changes that span many decades. Women, younger people, immigrants, ethnic minorities, urban and suburban dwellers, and political independents are all large or growing segments of the population, and all exhibit significantly less interest in guns than older, more rural, white males.[2] Little wonder, then, that the overarching political and financial imperative of gun interests in the last several decades has been an ever-more frantic campaign to wed guns to modern society. This gun frenzy is juxtaposed with a further contradictory trend: a multidecade continuing nationwide decline in crime. This is a welcome trend, to be sure, but it also undercuts a primary justification for gun ownership, since fear of crime is a central reason for gun (specifically handgun) acquisition.

The purpose of this book is to understand both the political framing and trajectory of the modern gun issue by drawing, in part, on newly available data, unexcavated history, and political perspectives for what is at bottom a purely and profoundly political movement. By examining the full history of gun laws in America, the Second Amendment, the stand your ground controversy, and the real world of gun politics and practices (informed, in part, by the author's own experiences in building a gun and seeking a pistol permit) in a seemingly anomalous place where guns are, by American standards, tightly regulated—New York State—this book will show that the predicates of modern American gun politics are mostly built on quicksand. One can have a legitimate debate about whether modern America should or should not have tougher (or weaker) gun laws. And that debate need not tether itself unduly to the past. After all, twenty-first-century America is a very different nation from the thirteen Atlantic Coast–hugging colonies that banded together to bravely declare their independence from Britain in the eighteenth century. But like it or not, the contemporary gun policy debate is tethered tightly to its origins, and one may not conduct that debate based on an imaginary past.

To state the matter more bluntly, America's contemporary gun culture, and prevailing gun narrative, have run amok, and it's time to set the record straight. Early Americans struggled to end violence and the threat of violence as a mode of political change; yet political violence as an alternative is extolled in some contemporary political debate. Early gun laws were tough compared to most contemporary gun policies. The contemporary framing of the Second Amendment and its consequences for recent efforts to regulate assault weapons have little to do with our actual heritage, much less what is painted as a high-stakes struggle over anything resembling gun rights. Recent state stand your ground laws bear no resemblance to the legitimate self-defense tradition and are probably causing unnecessary and unjustifiable mayhem. And even in a place in America with relatively tough gun laws, New York State, gun habits, traditions, and rights can still be meaningfully exercised and preserved.

★ ★ ★

The American gun debate is, to say the least, tightly wound. As noted, one purpose of this book is to unwind or unpack the assumptions, slogans, and glib generalities that too often deflect useful analysis and coherent understanding. To that end, Chapter 1 begins with an obvious, seemingly elementary, but rarely examined question: Why do we have government? Many of the core beliefs and assertions in the gun debate are really about the nature of governance itself and the relationship between citizens— specifically armed citizens—and the state in a democratic society. Thus, we hear endlessly that one reason many Americans want to own guns is not to hunt or for self-protection (although these perfectly sensible reasons are often expressed) but to prevent the ascension of a "tyrannical government." Really? How, exactly, does or would that work? What does this claim entail? This claim is closely related to another common assertion: that American citizens have a "right of rebellion." This chapter examines this idea, arising most directly from the British political philosopher John Locke, and, many claim, from our own Declaration of Independence. Examination of these ideas leads directly to an even more sensitive point: the government monopoly over the use of force. Is there such a thing, and is its acceptance nothing more than an endorsement of tyranny? Was American government designed to reject this very assertion?

Chapter 2 bores deeply into a subject that has only recently begun to receive careful and systematic attention: the history of gun laws in America. It is now known, at least among those who have any acquaintance with the subject, that gun laws were not uncommon in early America. Researchers and authors including Saul Cornell, Alexander DeConde, Adam Winkler, and Craig Whitney have all published important work in recent years that make clear that gun laws are by no means a contemporary phenomenon.[3] Yet even now, far too few understand or appreciate the fact that while gun possession is as old as America, so too are gun laws. But there's even more, even more than the aforementioned authors described: gun laws were not only ubiquitous, numbering in the thousands; they spanned every conceivable category of regulation, from gun acquisition, sale, possession, transport, and use, including deprivation of use through outright confiscation, to hunting and recreational regulations, to registration and express gun bans. We will see, for example, how the raging dispute over the regulation of semi-automatic weapons that began in the 1990s was actually presaged seven decades earlier, when at least seven states banned such weapons entirely—a fact that, to my knowledge, was unknown to modern analysts until now. Drawing on a vast new dataset of historical gun laws, it turns out that the first "gun grabbers" (as contemporary gun rights advocates like to label gun control proponents) were not Chablis-drinking liberals of the 1960s but rum-guzzling pioneers dating to the 1600s. An appendix to this book provides a complete list of these laws. This chapter also presents the latest and most complete assessment of actual patterns of gun ownership in America in its first 200-plus years. This analysis includes laws that predate the ratification of the modern Constitution and adoption of the Bill of Rights because our chief interest is in the extent to which America enacted and embraced gun laws dating to its beginnings. After all, the American legal tradition long predated the Constitution of 1789, just as it informed that document.

Chapter 3 turns to the Second Amendment, the role of which has now become the centerpiece of modern gun regulation deliberations, thanks to the Supreme Court's important and controversial decision establishing individual gun rights (for the first time in American history) in 2008. It, too, is based on a profoundly history-based approach to jurisprudence. The Court ruled, in part, that modern gun rights are and will be framed by its understanding of the past. Whether the Court's understanding of that history is actual or fictional is, frankly, an academic point, since the Court's ruling has indeed changed the law. Taking this as our analytic cue, the chapter then approaches the hypercontroversial matter of banning or restricting assault weapons, a step taken by the federal government after a furious political fight in 1994, but which lapsed as law ten years later. After lagging interest, the idea was brought back at the national level by control advocates forcefully, if unsuccessfully, in 2013. Yet whether such a measure is ever enacted nationwide or not (several states have adopted such bans), the idea proves to be a useful and instructive way to both unpack the individual gun right established in 2008 and to use it as a tool to disentangle the assault weapons ban's political and cultural roots. I conclude that the core argument against regulating such weapons has little to do with the Constitution or self-defense but in fact is mostly about, to put it plainly, the "fun" of such weapons.

So-called stand your ground laws are the focus of Chapter 4. Arising from and constructed as an extension of the Castle Doctrine (that one's home is one's castle), the centrality of this seemingly arcane legal principle was brought vividly to the nation's attention in 2012, when a Florida neighborhood watch volunteer, George Zimmerman, shot and killed a teenager, Trayvon Martin, who Zimmerman said had attacked him. For the first time, most of the nation learned that, in the previous seven years, half of the nation's states had enacted new, beefed-up stand your ground laws. Some states already had a more limited version of such laws in place, but these new stand your ground on steroids laws seemed, in the eyes of critics, to do little more than encourage a "shoot first" ethos. This chapter examines the evolution of this notion, beginning with the rise of self-defense from the Middle Ages, through its transformation and evolution here in America, up to and including the case of Florida, which pioneered this important change in law in 2005. Once again, despite the claims of supporters that these new laws "restored" formerly lost or neglected rights, they did no such thing. Instead, they moved states into a legal realm that would have made even nineteenth-century Western sheriffs question the wisdom of their descendants' judgment.

Finally, Chapter 5 draws its focus specifically to New York State, where contrary to American tradition (critics say), gun owners are subject to strict, and even more strict, gun laws. This has occurred at the very time when most states have moved in the opposite direction—rolling back existing gun laws, easing or even eliminating restrictions on gun carrying (and on gun use via stand your ground laws), and pressing every political hot button to spur gun sales, ownership, and use. While some may think of the Empire State as a postmodern gun owners' nightmare, this chapter confronts a matter little examined: Are gun ownership and use compatible with a strict gun regulatory regime? In part to answer this question, I have built a gun—specifically, an AR-15, the poster boy of assault weapons—that is also legal to own in New York. In addition, I applied for a pistol permit. I conclude that New York's tough gun laws pose no obstacle to the exercise of gun rights, and in fact are compatible with America's gun traditions and habits.

Like it or not, regulations are integral to America's gun ownership tradition. But like it or not, guns are an integral part of America and will continue to be a part of who we are.

CHAPTER 1

Why Do We Have Government?

Virtually every important political and policy dispute in American politics addresses, in some respect, the size, scope, and consequences of government power and its relationship to individual liberty. This is undeniably true in the ongoing debate concerning gun control and gun policy in America. Yet the gun debate extends more deeply into the far reaches of the scope of government power, as it attracts some advocates who question the nature, legitimacy, and even the very existence of government authority. And this is not a debate limited to the shadows of the American political landscape.[1] It is thus not only useful, but also necessary, to begin with a consideration of why governance exists.

At its core, the act of governance is a continual process of balancing two opposing, yet equally necessary, ideas: order and freedom. Perfect order equals authoritarianism and tyranny; perfect freedom, on the other hand, yields anarchy. In a democratic system, freedom is exalted, yet it is bounded by the power of the state. The freedom to speak is a virtue, but the freedom to kill one's neighbor is not, for not only does it extinguish the freedom of another, it also violates the moral sense of the community. Americans sometimes forget that unlimited freedom is not an unlimited good. As a political analyst from an earlier age once noted, "The State has 'the power of promoting the public welfare by restraining and regulating the use of liberty and property.'"[2] Further, "to preserve democracy we must not only love it, but sacrifice other things we love to its preservation. Democrats can only maintain democracy by renouncing some of the fruits of perfect freedom. . . . [S]ome of our desires must be altogether suppressed, and some put off to the future; that we must be content with small mercies. . . . "[3] This balancing of "consent and constraint"[4] has, of course, been the abiding concern of political philosophers, including but not limited to those who helped lay the intellectual foundation of the American system: Thomas Hobbes, John Locke, Montesquieu, and Jean-Jacques Rousseau.[5] It was no less a concern of our own country's founders. As Alexander Hamilton wrote, "Why has government been instituted at all? Because the passions of men will not conform to the dictates of reason and justice without constraint."[6] As James Madison wrote, "If men were angels, no government would be necessary."[7]

GUNS TO PREVENT TYRANNY?

In testimony before the U.S. Senate's Judiciary Committee in early 2013, National Rifle Association executive Wayne LaPierre was asked about the gun control measures then before Congress, including a proposed assault weapons ban. Democratic Senator Dick Durbin posed a question to LaPierre, in which he recounted meeting constituents in his home state of Illinois who had indicated to him that the Second Amendment was not just about hunting, sports, target shooting (actually, the Second Amendment is not about any of those things), or even just defending themselves from criminals. "We need the firepower," in Durbin's telling, "and the ability to protect ourselves from our government if they knock on our doors and we need to fight back." Durbin asked LaPierre if he agreed with this point of view. LaPierre responded: "I think without any doubt, if you look at why our founding fathers put it [the Second Amendment] there, they had lived under the tyranny of King George and they wanted to make sure that these free people in this new country would never be subjugated again and have to live under tyranny." With that, Durbin turned to a police chief also testifying and said, "Well, Chief Johnson, you've heard it. The belief of NRA is the Second Amendment has to give American citizens the firepower to fight back against you, against our government."[8]

Although LaPierre's comment might strike some as an aberration, the idea that the Second Amendment somehow protects or countenances a kind of reserved right of citizens to rise up against the government and apply violence using guns (the "arms" referenced in the amendment) should the American government somehow become tyrannical is a deeply entrenched belief held by some in the gun rights community. Obviously, it raises a host of questions, aside from whether the Second Amendment was designed to serve this purpose. Among them: How could civilians possess a "right" under our system of laws to use violence against our government? How would the imposition of "tyranny" be determined, and who would be entitled to make that determination? Against whom, exactly, would citizens use lethal force? Local police? State government leaders? Congress? The President? Judges? The Army? What would be the prospect that civilians might have any kind of success against a government with a large standing military force and against fifty state police forces? Would such a rebellion or insurrection have any chance of improving whatever political circumstances existed in the country at such a moment? Might it be a remedy that would prove worse than the ill it was designed to address? And even if citizens never actually used force against the government or some part of it, would the mere prospect that people might do such a thing somehow have a beneficial effect on the government's behavior, as some who support this idea claim? Stated differently, might the insurrection "remedy" actually be worse than the "disease" it claims to fight?

These claims are by no means limited to the margins of the national gun debate.[9] Aside from the likes of LaPierre[10] and media commentators like Glenn Beck,[11] elected officials,[12] and those seeking election, have embraced some version of this view. For example, the 2010 Republican nominee for the U.S. Senate from Nevada, Sharron Angle, said during the campaign, "Our Founding Fathers, they put that Second Amendment in there for a good reason and that was for the people to protect themselves against a tyrannical government. . . . [I]f this Congress keeps going the way it is, people are really looking toward those Second Amendment remedies. . . . "[13] While it might seem, to say the least, odd, that a candidate for Congress would refer approvingly of the use of violence against the very body to which she (unsuccessfully) sought membership, it is a telling revelation of how this idea has taken hold among some. A different indication of the tenacity of this idea among some in the public is a 2013 nationwide poll that found 29 percent of Americans agreeing with the proposition that "in the next few years, an armed revolution might be necessary in order to protect our liberties."[14] Even the Supreme Court, in its 2008 decision *U.S. v. Heller* (see Chapter 3), three times referenced in passing armed and organized men as possessing some kind of (unspecified) ability to resist, or serve as a safeguard against, tyranny.[15] (Some argue that civilian ownership of assault weapons is especially important to resist tyranny.[16])

Before getting to the question of whether gun-owning citizens possess such a right, there is a touchstone that is invoked by many to argue that the American system does indeed encompass a right of citizens to use violence against their government. It is found in the writings of the British political philosopher John Locke.

UNLOCKING LOCKE AND REBELLION

In his highly influential work *Two Treatises of Government,* Locke spurned absolute monarchies in favor of a constitutional monarchy—a system of government that retained limited monarchical rule, but a system where elected parliaments exercised "the supreme power of the commonwealth."[17] Locke wrote in the context of the late seventeenth century, and this work, formally published in 1690, is often seen as an apology and justification for Britain's Glorious Revolution of 1688–1689, when King James II was overthrown and replaced with a new monarch, while also establishing the supremacy of Parliament in British governance. The *Two Treatises* did indeed offer a justification for rebellion, but in fact Locke had completed an early draft of the work by 1681; in it argued broadly for the rejection of absolute monarchy as a form of governance. He also argued for the elevation of representative governance and for the recognition of the people as the ultimate or supreme source of power.[18]

Locke's writings exerted important influence on American thinkers and founders, most notably on the Declaration of Independence and Thomas Jefferson, who was its primary author. As is well known, the Declaration, issued in 1776, sought to explain and justify to the world the American rebellion from Britain. Drawing on Locke's "contract theory" of governance, whereby the government (to quote from the Declaration) derives its "just Powers from the consent of the governed," who are entitled to "alter or abolish" the government if it deprives people of their "unalienable rights": "Life, Liberty, and the pursuit of Happiness." Since the British monarch had established an "absolute Despotism" and "an absolute Tyranny over these States" by virtue of the monarch's failure to seek consent from the governed, the colonies were justified in declaring and establishing their independence, according to the document. Little wonder, given America's precarious experiment in autonomy, that it would seize on Locke's writings. But what was the nature of this right of rebellion about which Locke wrote?

First and foremost, according to Locke, ultimate sovereignty rests with the people. But the exercise of this sovereignty, when mobilized for rebellion against the government, was not to occur arbitrarily, lightly, casually, or in preference to democratic and lawful mechanisms of consent. And it was certainly not to be exercised over mere disagreements about policy.[19] Rather, "force is to be opposed to nothing but to unjust and unlawful force"[20] exercised by the government, meaning more specifically that the government attempts to "take away and destroy the property of the people," "reduce them to slavery under arbitrary power," and "put themselves into a state of war with the people."[21] Any effort at rebellion that fails to meet this stiff test "draws on himself a just condemnation both from God and man."[22]

Not only must the government have both violated the law and wreaked violence on its people, but a majority of the people must agree that such action is warranted.[23] To further qualify and hem in the act of rebellion and to underscore the preeminence of the rule of law and civil governance, Locke says that anyone who enters in to rebellion without adequate cause "is guilty of the greatest crime I think man is capable of. . . . [H]e who does it is justly to be esteemed the common enemy and pest of mankind, and is to be treated accordingly."[24] The abandonment of law by the government, its exercise of arbitrary or absolute power, and the government's application of extra-legal violence against the people—these are Locke's prerequisites for rebellion. Finally, the act of rebellion itself was based on an "appeal to heaven,"[25] not the laws of the state.

As mentioned, Locke's writings exercised important influence over many of the country's founders. But let us also note that the government Locke knew and wrote about was Britain's—a constitutional monarchy composed of two branches, only one of which was chosen by the people. He wrote a century before the writing of the modern American constitution, a document constructed after our establishment of a separate and independent nation and which rejected even a limited monarch, preferring an elected executive who served a fixed term. And the nation we formed was the United States of America, not the United States of John Locke. Then as now, the word of Locke did not equal the word of (American) law.

As for the Declaration of Independence, it was our clarion call to rebellion and unity. But its chief purpose was to persuade the rest of the world of the rightness of our rebellion.[26] It was a declaration, not a constitution. It did not establish or create a government or law, aside from proclaiming our right to form our own government based on the consent of our nation's people—the consent that had been lacking in Britain's decision making over America. Moreover, Jefferson's hand was not the only one that formulated the document, and writings from the Scottish Enlightenment played a great, perhaps even greater, role in Jefferson's early thinking than those of Locke and other English writers.[27]

Beyond that, the revolution proclaimed by the Declaration was against the British, but it was also *for* something else—our own governance and government, which at the time consisted of thirteen state governments and the Continental Congress. The following year, our leaders moved to create a more formal, powerful, and permanent national government. The American militias who were fighting British tyranny were the "quintessential expression of the idea of civic obligation and well regulated liberty," meaning that they were acting "to help secure the collective rights of all by sacrificing some measure of their liberty to participate in a well regulated militia."[28] The governing document that emerged in 1777, the country's first constitution, was the Articles of Confederation. In the late 1780s, it was cast aside because of the weakness of the one branch of government it established. The country's second constitution, the document completed in 1787, gave far more power, and powers, to the new three-branch national government.

The Constitution itself makes perfectly clear how rebellion is to be treated. It gives Congress the powers "[t]o provide for calling forth the Militia to execute the Laws of the Union, *suppress Insurrections* and repel Invasions (emphasis added)" in Article I, Section 8; to suspend habeas corpus "in Cases of Rebellion or Invasion" in Section 9; and to protect individual states "against domestic Violence" if requested to do so by a state legislature or governor in

Article IV, Section 4. Further, the Constitution defines treason in Article III, Section 3, this way: "Treason against the United States, shall consist only in levying War against them" (the United States was originally referred to in the plural). In other words, the Constitution specifically and explicitly gives the national government the power to suppress by force anything even vaguely resembling rebellion. Rebellion is by constitutional definition an act of treason against the United States. The militias mentioned in the document and in the Second Amendment (see Chapter 3) are thus to be used to suppress, not cause, rebellion or insurrection. These powers were further detailed and expanded in the Calling Forth Act of 1792,[29] which gives the president broad powers to use state militias to enforce both state and federal laws in instances where the law is ignored or in cases of open insurrection. This act was passed by the Second Congress shortly after the adoption of the Bill of Rights. In current law, these powers are detailed in the *U.S. Code* sections on insurrection.[30]

Alexander Hamilton addressed this very question of insurrection in one of the *Federalist Papers* (essays written mostly in 1788 by Hamilton, James Madison, and John Jay to explain and defend the new Constitution to the country). In Paper 28, Hamilton noted that "seditions and insurrections are, unhappily, maladies as inseparable from the body politic as tumors and eruptions from the natural body. . . . Should such emergencies at any time happen," he continued, "there could be no remedy but force." As long as an insurrection was relatively small-scale or limited, "the militia of the residue would be adequate to its suppression." If a larger-scale insurrection occurred, an armed national government would need to intervene. "Who would not prefer that possibility," Hamilton argued on behalf of a national military, "to the unceasing agitations and frequent revolutions which are the continual scourges of petty republics?"[31]

The "scourge" of rebellion is, of course, carried out against the government, which means against that government's constitution as well—including the Bill of Rights and the Second Amendment. One cannot carry out a "right" of rebellion against the government and at the same time claim protections within it. This fact was well understood by the country's founders (and by Locke). In 1794, for example, the government, through its militias and the leadership of President George Washington, moved to suppress the Whiskey Rebellion,[32] an uprising in western Pennsylvania that was denounced by Federalists and anti-Federalists alike. As the historian Saul Cornell noted, in the 1790s there was "widespread agreement that the example of the American Revolution did not support the rebels' actions" because Americans at the start of the Revolution "did not enjoy the benefits of representative government," whereas those who fomented the Whiskey Rebellion "were represented under the Constitution."[33] The following century, at the height of the Civil War (a conflict fought to defeat any notion of lawful or rightful rebellion against the government), Abraham Lincoln expressed a version of this sentiment this way: "Among free men, there can be no successful appeal from the ballot to the bullet; and that they who take such appeal are sure to lose their case, and pay the cost."[34]

Any who argue for a Lockean right of rebellion must, as Locke wrote, seek solace outside of the Constitution, the Bill of Rights (including the Second Amendment), and the laws of the country. This takes us to a related and central question: Who has the right to use force within this, or any, country? Not only can the government respond with force to rebellion, it must do so.

DOES AND SHOULD THE GOVERNMENT HAVE A MONOPOLY OVER THE USE OF FORCE?

Writing in the early 1900s, German sociologist and political theorist Max Weber famously argued: "The claim of the modern state to monopolize the use of force is as essential to it as its character of compulsory jurisdiction and of continuous organization." Yet this does not mean that citizens are stripped of any recourse to justifiable violence, as Weber also noted that "the use of force is regarded as legitimate only so far as it is either permitted by the state or prescribed by it."[35] Thus, for example, a citizen acting for personal self-defense acts as an individual but is nevertheless accountable to the state's judgment under the law (see the discussion of self-defense in Chapter 4).

Various gun rights activists have challenged Weber's idea about state power. Legal writer David C. Williams, for example, dismisses Weber and the militia-based view of the Second Amendment, saying that the latter "rests on a Weberian myth: with the sociologist Max Weber (although usually without referring to him) it holds that one of the defining characteristics of the state is its monopoly on the legitimate use of violence."[36] Another legal writer pegs Weber's analysis as "authoritarian" and "the core of the gun control movement,"[37] and yet another as "the product of a specifically German tradition of the (strong) state rather than of a strikingly different American political tradition that is fundamentally mistrustful of state power. . . ."[38]

Yet none of these assertions sustains scrutiny. Weber barely gets a mention in the vast writing on the militia-based analysis of the Second Amendment (see Chapter 3), and it is based on evidence that predates Weber. Weber was neither an authoritarian nor an apologist for

authoritarianism, any more than his analysis was a justification for it or for German authoritarianism whether under
the Kaiser or Hitler (Weber died in 1920). In fact, Weber's
analysis represents part of a long train of writing in political theory making this argument about the nature of state
power—it has nothing in particular to do with Germany—
and indeed Weber's analysis is correct. The argument about
the government's monopoly on the use of force is important enough to warrant more detailed attention.

Considered a founder of the modern field of sociology,
Weber clarifies the antecedents and consequences of the
state monopoly on the use of force in various writings. In
his writing, two features emerge: that Weber's analysis is
empirical (an analysis of what is true), and that it represents
his own formulation arising from past theorists. "Every state
is founded on force," Weber notes. "If no social institutions
existed which knew the use of violence, then the concept of
'state' would be eliminated, and a condition would emerge
that could be designated as 'anarchy'. . . . " Weber here is
referencing the Hobbesian state of nature and making the
empirical observation that the very existence of the modern
nation-state rests upon state-exercised force.

Referencing state authority to exercise violence or force,
under circumstances established by the laws of the state and
as the fountainhead of politics, Weber continues: "The
state is considered the sole source of the 'right' to use violence. Hence, 'politics' for us means striving to share power
or striving to influence the distribution of power, either
among states or among groups within a state."[39]

It is because of this state monopoly that nonviolent politics can occur in democratic nations. Obviously, in authoritarian nations, the government uses its monopoly of force
to suppress the liberties and freedoms of the people, beginning with those who would speak out or attempt to act

peacefully against the ruling regime. As one contemporary theorist has noted, "The essence of despotism is that there is no appeal, either in practice or in law, against the unchecked power of the master. . . . There is no parliament, no opposition, no free press, no independent judiciary, no private property protected by law from the rapacity of power. . . ."[40] Democratic nations, by definition, maintain constitutions, laws, and political practices that impose limits on governmental power to retain democratic processes, rights, and outcomes. Indeed, "democracy and the separation of powers are among the ways in which the sovereign power has been transformed so that it may not exploit the power of the state."[41] Thanks to this arrangement, democratic governments retain a monopoly over the use of force without degenerating into autocracy. Were it not for the state's monopoly, politics would quickly devolve into violence—precisely what occurs when regimes in the modern world are shaken or toppled by violence without stable regime replacement or succession and when weak regimes lack the ability to quell violence and mayhem within their countries.

For example, the New York Times' longtime bureau chief for East Africa, Jeffrey Gettleman, wrote in the aftermath of a deadly terrorist attack against a shopping mall in Nairobi, Kenya, in 2013 (over 100 people were killed) that the Kenyan government faced a major struggle in battling with al-Shabab, the Somalia-based terrorist group that staged the attack. Kenya, Gettleman wrote, faces a "profound disadvantage" in battling this well-organized terrorist group: "It has never invested in its public safety. Crime is rampant here, and police officers are badly paid . . . and often deeply corrupt. There is no 911 to call, and even if there were, it might not have mattered . . . because most officers do not have cars." Other African nations face even more dire straits because of their weak and ineffectual governments: "The Democratic Republic of Congo, Somalia, South Sudan, the Central African Republic—[are] places where the government is a ghost and civilians are stalked, raped and killed by men with guns."[42] None of the governments in these nations possesses a monopoly on the use of force.

A different contemporary example is found in this hemisphere, in El Salvador. Although that nation's civil war ended in 1992, it has been wracked by gang violence that has produced one of the highest murder rates of any nation in the world—70 homicides per 100,000 people. In 2011, 4371 Salvadorans were murdered, out of a population of about 6 million. That number peaked in early 2012, but then, remarkably, began to drop to about 40 murders per 100,000. The reason? The Salvadoran minister of security and justice, a retired military general, had secretly negotiated with the gang leaders to give them concessions in exchange for a truce between the two warring gangs—Barrio 18 and Mara Salvatrucha—to avoid murders at all costs that were the primary cause of the carnage. The past record made clear that the government's policy of military action and repression against the gangs was simply ineffective, because they were too powerful and the government was too weak. While widespread hatred of the gangs and gang violence among the general population prompted El Salvador's president to deny the existence of any negotiations, President Mauricio Funes was quick to claim credit for the drop in murders. Yet in May 2013, the security minister, General Munguia Payes, was removed from his position, whereupon the agreement unraveled; within three months, the murder rate spiked to prior high levels. The gangs applied "their greatest asset, their most valuable capital . . . death."[43] The Salvadoran government found itself able to confront that nation's awful death rate only by dealing with criminal gangs in the manner that one nation might negotiate with another, because the government lacks the monopoly over the use of force within its nation. Americans might argue that these examples represent instances of a different sort, where the power of force is taken from the government because of its weakness, not willingly shared with individuals. Yet this latter notion leads directly to the former, as theorists dating to ancient times understood.

Weber is hardly the first political thinker to argue that governments have a monopoly on the use of force. Not only does this notion span the contract theory writings of Hobbes and Locke,[44] it can be traced back to Aristotle[45] and even before. Indeed, one of the most ancient, pre-Aristotelian governing principles is that "every sovereign . . . has the right to punish anyone who pretends to a private revelation in order to oppose the laws."[46]

The writings of French political philosopher Jean Bodin (1530–1596) illustratively echo, and long predate, Weber's construct. In his *Six Books on the State*, Bodin offered a detailed formulation of modern state authority, including its monopoly on the use of force. "The state is a lawful government, with sovereign power. . . . [W]e speak of the state as 'lawful government' in order to distinguish it from bands of robbers and pirates, with whom it can have no part, commerce, or alliance." Bodin continues, "Sovereignty is the absolute and perpetual power of the state, that is, the greatest power to command." Bodin makes clear that the exercise of sovereignty is applicable in democratic as well as monarchical regimes: "While they are in authority they still cannot call themselves sovereign rulers, inasmuch as they are only custodians and keepers of sovereign power until it shall please the people or the prince to recall it . . . "

This power of the state, according to Bodin, encompasses power over the aristocracy and the people at large, as "power to dispose of their property and persons. . . ."[47]

The idea that the government in a democratic society does, and must, have a monopoly on the use of force is not limited to political philosophers or those outside of America. While serving as a college professor at Wesleyan University, future president Woodrow Wilson wrote in 1889 about this very subject. "The essential characteristic of all government, whatever its form, is authority. . . . [T]he authority of governors, [meaning those who govern] directly or indirectly, rests in all cases ultimately on *force*. Government, in its last analysis, is organized force." Wilson was careful to note that this principle applied to all governments, whether democratic or authoritarian, but that the "better governments of our day" are those that rest "upon the free consent of the governed" and that "are without open demonstration of force in their operations. . . . There is force behind the authority of the elected magistrate, no less than behind that of the usurping despot. . . . The difference lies in the *display* of coercive power. Physical force is the prop of both, though in the one it is the last, while in the other it is the first resort."[48] To be clear, none of this means that citizens may not have recourse to the legitimate use of violence under some circumstances, as is most clearly illustrated in a case of justifiable self-defense. As the discussion in Chapter 4 will make clear, such instances exist not in contravention of government authority or law but as granted by it.

As clear an expression of this view as any is found in a U.S. Supreme Court case from the nineteenth century, *Presser v. Illinois*. In 1879 Herman Presser was the leader of what today would be called a paramilitary group (meaning that they organized themselves in the manner of a military organization but functioned privately) called Lehr und Wehr Verein, which translates from the German roughly as "Education and Defense Association." On September 24 of that year, Presser and his group of 400 paraded through the streets of Chicago, outfitted and armed with rifles, but without having first obtained a license from the state governor. Under state law, it was illegal for organizations not recognized or licensed by the state to "associate themselves together as a military company or organization, or to drill or parade with arms in any city or town of this state."[49] Presser was found guilty and fined $10. He appealed his conviction, partly on Second Amendment grounds.

In the Supreme Court's 1886 ruling, it upheld his conviction, explaining that states had not only a right but also an obligation to maintain military forces and militias as a "rightful resource for maintaining the public security."[50] By the same token, the states (as well as the national government) had every right and power to regulate, or bar, private citizens from organizing as private military units. As the court explained:

> The right voluntarily to associate together as a military company or organization, or to drill or parade with arms, without, and independent of, an act of congress or law of the state authorizing the same, is not an attribute of national citizenship. Military organization and military drill and parade under arms are subjects especially under the control of the government of every country. They cannot be claimed as a right independent of law. Under our political system they are subject to the regulation and control of the state and federal governments, acting in due regard to their respective prerogatives and powers. The constitution and laws of the United States will be searched in vain for any support to the view that these rights are

privileges and immunities of citizens of the United States independent of some specific legislation on the subject.[51]

The court and state law were concerned not merely with the trappings of military behavior (uniforms, firearms, military-style rank and order) under the control of private citizens—after all, military surplus uniforms and guns were and are legally available to civilians. No, the root concern here is that, having adopted military accoutrements and organization, such private groups might then be emboldened *to behave with the authority of an actual military force* attached to the government. In other words, the government does and must possess a monopoly on the all-important ability to apply force of arms for public security and the public good. The court then explained exactly why such a power must be reserved solely to government, not left to private individuals (unless the government otherwise expressly granted such powers):

> It cannot be successfully questioned that the state governments, unless restrained by their own constitutions, have the power . . . to control and regulate the organization, drilling, and parading of military bodies and associations, except when such bodies or associations, are authorized by the militia laws of the United States. The exercise of this power by the states is necessary to the public peace, safety, and good order. To deny the power would be to deny the right of the state to disperse assemblages organized for sedition and treason, and the right to suppress armed mobs bent on riot and rapine [looting].[52]

In other words, a circumstance where the use of force is somehow shared with those not a part of the government to, say, countenance what some participants might consider a justifiable or necessary rebellion may be, to others, "sedition and treason," or "armed mobs bent on riot and rapine." Such a determination must belong to the government and its legal and democratic processes, not to private individuals for their sole or autonomous determination. A society can have no expectation of domestic peace when the state's monopoly on the use of force is no longer a monopoly. Again, this is no invitation to authoritarianism; dozens of democratic nations around the world, including our own, have managed to maintain their democracies by striking a judicious balance between state power, on the one hand, and individual rights and liberties, on the other (including a bounded individual right to take another life under certain limited circumstances; see Chapter 4).

Admittedly, America leans more to the side of individual rights than other, similar nations, and Americans maintain a long tradition of suspicion of government power, compared with citizens in other democratic nations. Yet it is easy to exaggerate American suspicion of government. In a 27-nation international survey conducted in 2013 of citizens' attitudes toward their own governments (both democratic and authoritarian), it turns out that Americans have less trust in their own government than citizens of Canada and Sweden, but they trust their government more than do citizens in the United Kingdom, Australia, Germany, and France.[53]

The answer to the question of whether citizens may use violence against the government begins with Locke (and not the selectively edited Locke that merely plucks a phrase or two from his writings), encompasses the Constitution's formulation of lawful peaceful expression of political opposition balanced with the responsibility of the government to suppress armed insurrections, and extends to the *Presser* Court's judgment that an armed assemblage cannot be countenanced in our system. The contemplation of rebellion against the American government cannot pretend to be based on any notion that our Constitution, or laws, countenance armed rebellion. They do not.

A prime example of an instance where America differs from other democratic nations in extending greater personal freedom is in its widespread lawful ownership and use of firearms by its citizens. The American gun-owning tradition, so much a puzzle to non-Americans, is nevertheless deeply embedded in American history, tradition, and culture. What modern Americans little appreciate, however, is that, while gun ownership is as old as the country itself, so is gun regulation—a lot of gun regulation, in fact. It is to that subject we now turn.

CHAPTER 2

Our Forefathers' Superior Gun Wisdom

The first formal legislative body created by European settlers in North America was convened in the Virginia colony on July 30, 1619, twelve years after the colony's establishment. The first General Assembly of Virginia met in Jamestown, where it deliberated for five days and enacted a series of measures to govern the fledgling colony. This itself was notable, because what later came to be known as the House of Burgesses inaugurated consent-based governance in America. Among its more than thirty enactments in those few days was a gun control law, which said this:

> That no man do sell or give any Indians any piece, shot, or powder, or any other arms offensive or defensive, upon pain of being held a traitor to the colony and of being hanged as soon as the fact is proved, without all redemption.[1]

If a death sentence for providing Native Americans with firearms and ammunition seems a little draconian even by the standards of the day, it punctuated the degree of tension, suspicion, and confrontation that existed between the settlers and the indigenous population.[2] Other colonies adopted similar measures, although they were of limited effectiveness—not only because of the difficulty of monitoring arms trading in early America but also because such trading was highly profitable, was fed by traders from other nations, including the French and the Dutch, and because many Native Americans allied themselves with settlers against various foes.[3]

Americans know that guns and gun possession are as old as America itself. Although important studies have established that gun regulations also existed from early times,[4] few appreciate the extent, variety, and breadth of such regulations. Drawing on newly available information, this chapter will establish that, if guns are as American as apple pie, so too are gun laws. The common notions that gun laws are largely a function of modern, industrial (or postindustrial) America, that gun laws are incompatible with American history and its practices or values, and that gun laws fundamentally collide with our legal traditions or individual rights are all patently false. Every imaginable gun regulatory scheme, from registration, licensing, and outright confiscation to restrictions on exotic or especially destructive types of weapons and accessories, was enacted among the states decades, even centuries, before the modern era. Viewed from the perspective of Chapter 1, we can say that guns in the hands of early Americans to a great degree represented the power *of* the state, once coherent indigenous governments appeared, not power *against* the state. This was clearly true as seen in the well-known American militia tradition but also in the extensive web of laws that are examined in this chapter. Before turning to early gun laws, however, we begin with a look at actual gun possession in early America.

HOW MANY GUNS?

Whether guns were rare or common in early America is an interesting but not necessarily important question for modern policy judgments about guns, gun control, and gun rights. The America of the modern era—an industrial and postindustrial giant that spans the oceans—is virtually nothing like the thirteen Atlantic Ocean–hugging agrarian states of the eighteenth century. Still, whether relatively rare or common at the outset, guns were undeniably here with the earliest European settlers; guns became more common and prolific around the middle of the nineteenth century, when manufacturing and materials resulted in an improved product that was more durable, more affordable, and more reliable, and when the nation became immersed in its most destructive conflict, the Civil War. Guns are of course common and prolific today, totaling roughly 300 million. Still, the frequency of guns in early America does contribute to the historical gun ethos that has too often combined fact and myth, which in turn has played an important role in the contemporary gun debate because of the extent to which contemporary political debates have been framed and judged by the extent to which modern policies are or are not compatible with the past. (More about that later.)

The contemporary debate over gun frequency in early America accelerated in the early 2000s when a historian, Michael Bellesiles, published a book that argued, contra prevailing impressions, that gun ownership was not just uncommon but rare in early America.[5] By his estimate, no

more than a tenth of the people owned guns from the colonial period through about 1850.[6] His findings were immediately challenged, and his critics vindicated, when various
researchers replicated his analysis and concluded that at least
some of his data were either fabricated or wrong.[7] Yet the
discrediting of Bellesiles's analysis did and does not answer
the question of the frequency of early gun ownership,
although it has spurred further (and welcome) analysis.

Reliable historical accounts have revealed variation as to
the frequency and distribution of gun ownership in colonial and early federal America. The very earliest colonial
settlements were apparently well armed. By one historical
account, a survey of the Jamestown, Virginia, colony in
1624 reported an equal number of colonists and firearms—
not a surprising conclusion, given the dangers of the time
and the small number of guns (in the hundreds) needed to
arm everyone. The same study also concluded that firearms
possession declined as the frontier receded and stable towns
were established.[8] Those impressionistic conclusions, published in the 1970s, have been borne out by more recent and
thorough analyses.

Historian Randolph Roth concluded in a 2002 article
that during this early period, "roughly half of all house-
holds owned at least one working gun."[9] A specialist on
historical homicide, Roth drew on a variety of sources to
note that firearms ownership rates varied by income, but
did not vary much by age. These numbers were more or
less consistent with surveys of militia members where, from
1803 to 1820, records showed firearms ownership rates of
over 40 percent.[10] Admittedly, this was a problematic number for national defense purposes, as government officials
noted at the time, since militia members were required
by law to obtain their own firearms instead of relying on
government military issue. A fighting force where more

than half of the men lacked proper (or any) firearms posed a considerable national security problem. To complicate matters, however, Roth notes that many of the personally owned firearms were of low quality, smaller caliber, and shorter range—suitable for hunting small game and vermin but unsuitable for military or battlefield use. And the transition to heavier military-grade weapons that fired large-caliber musket balls often found militia members facing "a very different enterprise" in learning how to operate these weapons.[11] This helps explain the frequent verdicts of America's military leaders early in the country's history that most military recruits were unprepared for service and unskilled in the handling of such weapons.[12]

A more recent, rigorous, and impressively thorough study of firearms in early America reaches very similar conclusions. In an article published in 2013, colonial historian Kevin Sweeney provides an exceptionally detailed and far-reaching analysis of early gun possession by examining probate records, militia information, census data, and much correspondence.[13] Sweeney's findings are generally consistent with the roughly 50 percent firearms ownership rate Roth reports, but Sweeney confirms five specific historical contours.

First, he, too, reports ample firearms in the early and mid-seventeenth century. According to two reports of the Virginia Company in 1620 and 1625, for example, the number of firearms equaled the 670 male inhabitants in 1620 and exceeded the number of male inhabitants (814) in 1625.[14] While Sweeney confirms that wealthy males were more likely to own firearms than those with little or no wealth, the cost of a gun was not beyond the reach of most. But second, as the colonies became safer and the frontier and Natives were pushed to the west, gun ownership began to decline. Noting a close historical correlation between the degree of military necessity and fluctuations in the rate of civilian arms possession as reported in probate records, for example, Sweeney finds that by the start of the eighteenth century, "efforts of colonies . . . to create an armed populace and an inclusive body of organized and trained militiamen had begun to fall by the wayside."[15] In New Jersey, for example, Sweeney reports gun ownership rates of 56 percent in the late 1600s but only about 31 percent by the 1740s.[16]

Third, Sweeney notes significant disparities in firearms ownership across the colonies/states. For example, Pennsylvania consistently had one of the lowest firearms ownership rates (34–38 percent, he estimates) partly because of the large Quaker population but also because of a long-standing antipathy among the state's population to the formation of a colonial militia. Pennsylvania's steadfast refusal to organize a militia (until shortly before the outbreak of the Revolution) meant that men could avoid two onerous obligations: the requirement to obtain firearms and military training obligations. Sweeney reports similar sentiments and patterns in New Jersey.[17] Colonies/states like Massachusetts and South Carolina, however, reflected far higher gun ownership rates and well-established militias. The latter state was highly motivated to maintain a high rate of gun ownership because it continued to face military threats, such as the Yamasee War (1715–1717), and the continuing need to maintain slave patrols to squelch slave uprisings.[18]

Fourth, by the time of the 1770s, the colonies found themselves mostly ill prepared, in weapons and organization, for large-scale armed conflict. Paralleling Roth's analysis, American gun owners mostly owned firearms unsuited for military use—lighter, small bore firearms useful for hunting small game rather than the heavier, larger-caliber muskets capable of receiving a bayonet that were needed for military service (contrary to what one might think, the absence of experience with military weapons proved to be a significant problem). Even in Massachusetts, county records found most militia units poorly or entirely ill equipped for service in the lead-up to the Revolution.[19] The weapons shortage problem was exacerbated by the high rate at which guns were reported to be broken, too old, or otherwise unserviceable (often 30–40 percent)—not so surprising given that they were made from iron, which deteriorates rapidly compared to steel, that replacement parts mostly had to be handmade, and that there was a high rate of misfires and accidents, underscoring the degree of skill needed to operate these weapons safely.[20] As the Revolution unfolded, proper and adequate arms continued to be in short supply, even in the face of aggressive efforts to obtain them. After the Revolution, the relative dearth of firearms continued to be a problem—both because the pressing need for such weapons ended with the Revolution (even though potential and actual threats to the young nation's security persisted) and because many weapons were either destroyed during the conflict or were confiscated by the British. As Sweeney observes about the post-Revolution period, "The states were in no position to supply the militias' lack of arms during the 1780s."[21]

Fifth, Sweeney notes that pistols were uncommon (generally 2–10 percent of all guns recorded), even rare, whether as reported in probate records or military records. The reasons are fairly obvious: they were simply less useful in terms of range and accuracy, whether hunting game or on the battlefield (the exceptions were some pistol-carrying by horsemen and officers and the "horseman's pistol," a hybrid weapon adapted for carrying and use on horseback). Civilian records undercut the commonly held contemporary notion that civilians routinely carried pistols for self-protection in the colonial or federal periods—although pistol ownership was reported to be somewhat higher in cities and significantly higher in places with active slave patrolling, like South Carolina.[22]

Military records and gun censuses continued to report a dearth of weaponry well into the nineteenth century. In 1793 Secretary of War Henry Knox estimated that the country had about 450,000 militiamen, of whom only about 20 percent had their own arms (as was required by the Uniform Militia Act, passed by Congress in 1792[23]), and that of the 44,000 muskets owned by the government, more than half were inoperable.[24] President Thomas Jefferson presented a comprehensive report of militia arms to Congress in 1804; the report noted that, as a whole, only half of the nation's militia forces had arms. In addition, their distribution varied widely from state to state. According to one rough estimate, Massachusetts and Connecticut militias were fully armed; New Hampshire reported eight out of ten men armed; for Rhode Island, it was seven of ten; New York was seven of ten; Pennsylvania and New Jersey were four of ten; Virginia was two of ten, with Georgia slightly less than that; North Carolina and South Carolina were about five of ten.[25] Later surveys by the government reported similar numbers.[26]

After the War of 1812, the country experienced a prolonged period of peace (aside from sporadic conflicts with Native Americans). The old militia system continued to deteriorate, and gun ownership also flagged. As one expert on the militias noted, "Evidence of the scarcity of arms [among the militias] is abundant." [27] (One significant source of information too rarely consulted in the analysis of early American gun ownership is the extensive writing on American military and militia history.) With the Civil War, however, millions of men were exposed to firearms, which the federal and Confederate governments now supplied to their vast armies. With greatly improved methods of gun manufacturing and aggressive marketing of firearms by companies like Colt, gun ownership—and especially handgun ownership—spread in the post–Civil War period.[28]

In sum, we can reasonably conclude that from the early eighteenth century on, civilian gun ownership probably fluctuated around or below the 50 percent number (bearing in mind variations by region, time period, degree of military threat, and other circumstances), with the vast majority of these firearms (over 90 percent) being long guns. But just as the claim that less than one adult male in ten owned a gun is false, the mythic and widespread image of a gun propped in the corner of every home or held in the hands of every adult white male is also false, as is the myth that handguns were common.

As this account suggests, private firearms ownership and government-organized arms acquisition were related. Most importantly, while state governments and, later, the national government aggressively acquired firearms and related supplies to distribute to soldiers in times of dire necessity (such as during the Revolution), for the most part the primary burden of arms acquisition was placed, by law, on militia-eligible men. Yet such laws were notoriously difficult to enforce; they often lacked specific penalties for noncompliance (as was the case of the 1792 Uniform Militia Act) and indeed were widely ignored.[29]

GUN CENSUSES

The fact that data about gun ownership from the colonial and federal periods exist is attributable, in part at least, to the fact that the government persistently expended efforts to count the number of guns in the colonies and later in the states. Everyone has heard of a census of population (required every ten years according to the Constitution), but few realize that gun censuses were also common in this period of the country's history. While accumulated by colonial governments from the 1600s on, after the adoption of the modern Constitution in 1789, such data were periodically accumulated by the secretary of war and in congressional reports. As historian Saul Cornell notes, the "government kept close tabs on the weapons citizens owned. . . . "[30] Gun censuses were typically conducted by militia officers or other local officials and occurred throughout the country. To take this routine practice from history and drop it into the modern context for a moment, imagine the firestorm of political reaction today if government representatives went door to door (or even administered a written questionnaire sent to homes through the mail, in the manner of the federal census of population), inquiring of the occupants' gun ownership, including the numbers, types, and functionality of weapons possessed.

Private arms fell into an unusual legal realm: firearms could be confiscated for public purposes or could be required to be kept in a central location for reasons of safety or ready access. Yet unlike other personal property, weapons suitable for militia use could be exempted from seizure from persons who owed debts, although other types of firearms were often treated in the same way as conventional personal property.[31]

In the Massachusetts colony in the 1640s, for example, colonial law created a position of "surveyor of arms," whose job encompassed not only surveying and chronicling arms in the colony but also to "gather into his hands . . . all the country's arms and ammunition within all the towns . . . that are within his jurisdiction, and to sue and recover the same from those that shall refuse to deliver them into his hands. . . ."[32] All this undergirds the larger notion that local and national defense needs rested primarily on government-organized militias that were subject to state and (later) federal regulation but where the primary costs were borne by the prospective militia members. For the typical militia-eligible man, it was, one might say, an early example of an unfunded government mandate. That arrangement ultimately changed as the old militia system decayed—its manifest limitations laid bare thanks to its abysmal performance in the War of 1812[33]—and declined in the pre–Civil War period and as the national government assumed the primary obligation for arming large-scale military forces in the Civil War.[34]

THE ARC OF AMERICAN GUN LAWS

Gun censuses and America's early governmental preoccupation with gun possession, storage, and regulation were clearly tied to the overarching concern for public safety, even as it intruded into citizens' private gun ownership and habits. Symptomatic of this is the fact that colonial and state governments enacted over 600 laws pertaining specifically to militia regulation and related militia activities.[35] Yet militia-related laws hardly constituted the extent of gun regulation in America.

A newly researched and compiled listing of state gun laws, spanning the period from America's founding up to 1934 (the year of the enactment of the first significant national gun law, the National Firearms Act), has recently become available.[36] It is by far the most comprehensive such compilation to date. This far-reaching compilation process, conducted by lawyer and researcher Mark Anthony Frassetto, has become possible thanks to the ever-growing digitization of state law archives and other electronic sources of historical information about law, including HeinOnline and the Yale Law School's Avalon Project. Aside from keyword electronic searches of these sources, Frassetto also consulted secondary sources to produce this prodigious list.

The result is a compilation of nearly a thousand gun laws of every variety (with some exceptions, this list does not include militia laws, hunting regulations, laws pertaining to gunpowder storage, and laws against weapons firing). Following Frassetto's method of organization, the laws discussed here are organized by law category. The laws themselves are listed in abbreviated form in an appendix to this book and are summarized by categories in Table 2.1. Within those categories, they are arrayed by state

Table 2.1 Numbers of Gun Laws in the States and Numbers of State Gun Laws, by Categories, 1607–1934[*]

Law Type	1607–1790	1791–1867	1868–1899	1900–1934
Ban guns laws	0	0	7	0
Number of states	0	0	5	0
Brandishing laws	2	4	14	7
Number of states	2	3	13	7
Carry laws	5	31	48	21
Number of states	4	19	28	18
Dangerous weapons laws	1	4	9	53
Number of states	1	4	8	35
Dueling laws	3	7	3	0
Number of states	2	7	3	0
Felons, foreigners, etc.	11	2	1	26
Number of states	5	2	1	19
Firing weapons	19	17	19	22
Number of states	9	14	17	20
Hunting laws	11	8	24	58
Number of states	8	5	21	43

(continued)

Table 2.1 (Continued)

Law Type	1607–1790	1791–1867	1868–1899	1900–1934
Manufacturing, inspection	2	11	11	22
Number of states	2	10	9	17
Militias laws	23	15	2	0
Number of states	11	15	2	0
Minors, etc. laws	0	2	15	21
Number of states	0	2	15	19
Registration, taxation laws	3	8	12	18
Number of states	2	6	11	15
Race/slavery**	5	18	0	0
Number of states	5	11	0	0
Sensitive areas, etc.	11	23	30	35
Number of states	7	17	20	26
Sentencing enhancement	3	3	5	12
Number of states	3	3	5	10
Storage laws	2	7	2	0
Number of states	1	6	2	0

Source: Mark Anthony Frassetto, "Firearms and Weapons Legislation up to 1934," Georgetown University Law Center, January 15, 2013. Available at http://papers.ssrn.com/sol3/papers.cfm?abstract_id=2200991.

*The full category titles of gun laws from Frassetto's paper are: Bans on Handguns/Total Bans on Firearms; Brandishing; Carrying Weapons; Dangerous or Unusual Weapons; Dueling; Felons, Foreigners, and Others Deemed Dangerous by the State; Firing Weapons; Hunting; Manufacturing, Inspection, and Sale of Gunpowder and Firearms; Militia Regulation; Possession by, Use of, and Sales to Minors and Others Deemed Irresponsible; Registration and Taxation; Race- and Slavery-Based Firearms Restrictions; Sensitive Areas and Sensitive Times; Sentence Enhancement for Use of Weapons; Storage.

**The small number of laws pertaining to slavery- or race-based restrictions pertaining to guns is not meant to suggest that the legal regime in the pre–Civil War South was somehow not uniformly harsh but rather reflects the fact that express statutory restrictions were not necessary in all places, given the South's uniformly oppressive system of slavery.

alphabetically within four historical periods: 1607–1789 (the colonial and pre–modern Constitution period); 1790–1867 (the pre–Fourteenth Amendment period); 1868–1899 (the post–Fourteenth Amendment period); and 1900–1934 (the twentieth century). Despite the admirable thoroughness of Frassetto's electronic database searches, he notes that his list cannot be considered definitive, owing to multiple spellings of common words and other glitches inherent in the nature of such searches. Thus, his total list of laws is an underestimate of the actual universe of gun statutes (indeed, I discovered a few early laws from Massachusetts in the 1600s that were not a part of Frassetto's list; they are discussed below).[37] While many of the laws examined here predate the inclusion of the Second Amendment in the Bill of Rights, adopted in 1791, our interest is in the arc of gun regulations throughout American history.

The types of gun laws span about every conceivable category. The two most common and prolific types of laws regulated hunting and the militias (as Frassetto noted in his compilation, he excluded from his list most hunting and militia laws, gunpowder storage laws, and laws against the firing of weapons, as there were simply too many of them, although those categories and laws are represented in the list). It is thus immediately clear that thousands of gun laws existed from the country's founding up to 1934. The data presented here represent a subset of these thousands of laws. Aside from Frassetto's exclusions, his full list includes over 800 laws. The version of his list I present here is somewhat shorter, as I have excluded state constitutional provisions, weapons laws that did not specifically mention firearms, and also British laws from the early colonial period that Frassetto included. Thus, the list presented here includes about 760 laws (see the Appendix for the full list of laws discussed below). Each category warrants detailed attention.

CATEGORIES OF EARLY GUN LAWS

A handful of laws established outright, categorical bans on firearms. All were enacted in the post–Civil War era. Six of the seven state bans (one each in Arkansas, Kansas, and Texas and three in Tennessee) were of pistols. The seventh, from Wyoming, banned all firearms (both handguns and long guns) from "any city, town, or village."[38] Arkansas also banned any sale or transfer of pistols, except for those in military use. Subsequent categories of gun laws also include specific bans on particular types of weapons, like automatic weapons, and on weapons accessories, like silencers.

States also enacted brandishing laws, designed to criminalize the threatening use of the weapons named in these laws (generally pistols along with specific, named knives used for interpersonal violence, such as dirks, sword canes, stilettos, and Bowie knives, and weapons like a "slung shot," which was a hand weapon made up of a piece of metal or other weight attached to a strap or flexible handle). The prohibited behaviors were typically described as to "exhibit any of the said deadly weapons in a rude, angry or threatening manner,"[39] or similar language. Some laws in the later 1800s also identified the prohibited behavior as to "draw or threaten to use"[40] such weapons. These laws also generally included exemptions for the use of such weapons in personal self-defense or for military purposes.

Carry restriction laws were widely enacted, spanning the entire historical period under examination, but proliferated in the early 1800s, and then exploded in numbers during the post–Civil War period (coinciding with the settling of the West). Laws in the eighteenth century did not typically identify weapons concealment, per se, as criminal but did restrict more general carrying of firearms, usually if done in crowded places or by groups of armed people. Among the earliest laws criminalizing the carrying of concealed weapons was that of Kentucky in 1813[41] (as with the brandishing laws, concealed carry laws normally targeted pistols as well as various knives, the chief feature of which was that they had long, thin blades, and which were favorites in interpersonal fights). Louisiana enacted a similar law that same year. A particularly sharp comment on the intent behind such laws was expressed in Tennessee's 1837 law, which referred to "Each and every person so degrading himself"[42] by carrying pistols or other named weapons. The preamble of Georgia's 1837 law began this way: "AN ACT to guard and protect the citizens of this State, against the unwarrantable and too prevalent use of deadly weapons."[43] Alabama's 1839 concealed carry law reflected similar antipathy to the practice it was prohibiting: "AN ACT To suppress the evil practice of carrying weapons secretly."[44] Concealed carry laws generally made exceptions for travelers passing through an area while armed. As the Appendix shows, these laws were enacted in most states of the union and all across the country, including territories. In the nineteenth-century laws, the main emphasis was on prohibiting concealed carry, whereas early-twentieth-century laws generally applied to all carrying, whether concealed or open. Aside from hunting and militia laws, they were among the most common and widely accepted gun regulations to be found in our post-1789 history. These laws therefore pose an especially stark contrast with the contemporary American political movement (dating to the early 1980s) to spread the legality of concealed carry (more about that later).

The appearance of many southern states among those seeking to curtail gun carrying, as well as other laws pertaining to criminal uses of guns, is generally attributable to the fact that "the Antebellum South was the most violent region in the new nation."[45] After the Civil War, the ravaged South, facing a new, postslavery racial order, again witnessed violence at rates greater than the rest of the country.[46] Thus, states with greater violence, and greater gun violence, turned in part to stronger gun laws as a remedy.

Before proceeding with consideration of other types of gun laws, it is important to note that concealed and open carry restrictions were common on the American frontier during the nineteenth century in the so-called Wild West. The truth of life in the Old West, and the actual role of guns in it, is known but not well known. Axiomatic expressions such as "the guns that won the West" and "arm[s] that opened the West and tamed the wild land" still too often typify what in actuality is a romanticized and wildly exaggerated assessment of the importance of guns in the settling of the West. Indeed, some have gone so far as to claim that "the American experiment was made possible by the gun."[47] These characterizations can be faulted for ignoring the central role of homesteaders, ranchers, miners, tradesmen, businessmen, and other settlers across the western plains. The "taming" of the West was, in fact, an agricultural and commercial movement, attributable primarily to ranchers and farmers, not gun-slinging cowboys.[48] In fact, the six-shooter and rifle played relatively minor roles in the activities of all these groups—even the cowboys. According to historian Richard Shenkman:

> The truth is many more people have died in Hollywood westerns than ever died on the real frontier. . . . In the real Dodge City, for instance, there were just five killings in 1878, the most homicidal year. . . . In the most violent year in Deadwood, South Dakota, only four people were killed. In the worst year in Tombstone, home of the shoot-out at the OK Corral, only five people were killed. The only reason the OK Corral shoot-out even became famous was that town boosters deliberately overplayed the drama to attract new settlers.[49]

Even in the most violence-prone towns, the western cattle towns, vigilantism and lawlessness were only briefly tolerated. In his sweeping history of the West, the historian Ray Allen Billington noted that local businesspeople and other leaders quickly pushed for town incorporation in order to establish local police forces, which were supported by taxes levied against local bars, gambling establishments, and houses of prostitution. The prohibitions against carrying guns analyzed here were strictly enforced, and there were few homicides. The gun "disarmament" that was routinely practiced in newly formed western towns was well understood as a signpost of stability, improved public safety, and civilization. The western-style shoot-outs glorified in countless books and movies were literally "unheard of."[50] In the most violent cow towns of the old West—Abilene, Caldwell, Dodge City, Ellsworth, and Wichita—a total of forty-five killings were recorded between 1870 and 1885, and only six of these killings were from six-shooters; sixteen killings were by police. Outside populated areas, cowboys and other range riders who carried six-guns almost never used them in Hollywood-style gunfights or to enforce some brand of western justice. As cowboy experts Joe B. Frantz and Julian E. Choate observed, "The six-shooter has been credited with use entirely disproportionate with the facts."[51] Even western outlaws illustrate the extent to which myth replaced fact with respect to guns and lawlessness. Many studies of the famed western outlaws demonstrate that "they were few, inconspicuous, and largely the invention of newspaper correspondents and fiction writers." Moreover, "the western marshal [was] an unglamorous character who spent his time arresting drunks or rounding up stray dogs and almost never engaging in gun battles."[52] Most of the killing that took place on the frontier involved the wars between the U.S. Cavalry and those Native Americans who rebelled against harsh and duplicitous treatment at the hands of whites.[53] States moved to enact laws restricting or barring certain dangerous or unusual weapons—also a subject that has contemporary reverberations. Such laws in the country's early decades were aimed, in part, at pistols and offensive knives (as was the focus of most concealed carry laws), but also at the practice of rigging firearms to be fired with a string or similar method to discharge a weapon without an actual finger on the firearm trigger. Referred to as "gun traps," the earliest of such laws was enacted by New Jersey in 1771. Some laws later referred to such weapons as "spring guns,"[54] "trap guns,"[55] and "infernal machines."[56]

The bulk of the laws identifying certain weapons as dangerous or unusual, however, appeared in the early 1900s, when most states moved aggressively to outlaw machine guns (usually meaning fully automatic weapons), sawed-off shotguns, pistols, weapons and mechanisms that allowed firearms to be fired a certain number of times rapidly without reloading, silencers, and air guns (whereby projectiles are propelled by compressed air rather than gunpowder). The first state to enact an anti–machine gun law was West Virginia in 1925. Nine states enacted anti–machine gun laws in 1927 alone (a year in which a concerted national push unfolded to regulate these and other gangster-type weapons). In all, at least twenty-eight states enacted anti–machine gun laws during this period. Texas, for example, defined machine guns in 1933 as those from which more than five bullets were automatically discharged "from a magazine by a single functioning of the firing device."[57]

Of particular relevance to the modern gun debate is the fact that at least seven and as many as ten state laws specifically restricted semi-automatic weapons (those that fire a round with each pull of the trigger without manual reloading), anticipating by seven decades the semi-automatic assault weapons ban debates and related efforts to restrict large-capacity bullet magazines from the 1990s to the present. States in this category typically combined fully automatic and semi-automatic weapons under a single definitional category. A 1927 Rhode Island measure defined the prohibited "machine gun" to include "any weapon which shoots automatically and any weapon which shoots more than twelve shots semi-automatically without reloading."[58] A 1927 Massachusetts law said this: "Any gun or small arm caliber designed for rapid fire and operated by a mechanism, or any gun which operates automatically after the first shot has been fired . . . shall be deemed a machine gun."[59] Michigan's 1927 law prohibited machine guns or any other firearm if they fired more than sixteen times without reloading. Minnesota's 1933 law outlawed "any firearm capable of automatically reloading after each shot is fired, whether firing singly by separate trigger pressure or firing continuously by continuous trigger pressure."[60] It went on to penalize the modification of weapons that were altered to accommodate such extra firing capacity. Fully automatic .22 caliber "light sporting rifles" were also considered machine guns under the law, but .22 caliber semi-automatic weapons, called "light sporting rifles" in the law, were exempted. Ohio also barred both fully automatic and semi-automatic weapons in a 1933 law, incorporating under the banned category any gun that "shoots automatically, or any firearm which shoots more than eighteen shots semi-automatically without reloading."[61] The law specifically defined semi-automatic weapons as those that fired one shot with each pull of the trigger. South Dakota barred machine guns by defining them as weapons "from which more than five shots or bullets may be rapidly or automatically, or semi-automatically discharged from a magazine."[62] Like several other states, Virginia outlawed weapons "of any description . . . from which more than seven shots or bullets may be rapidly, or automatically, or semi-automatically discharged from a magazine, by a single function of the firing device, and also applies to and includes weapons, loaded or unloaded, from which more than sixteen shots or bullets may be rapidly, automatically, semi-automatically, or otherwise discharged without reloading."[63]

Aside from these seven states, another three included language that was somewhat ambiguous as to whether they extended prohibitions to semi-automatic as well as fully automatic weapons. Illinois enacted a 1931 law that prohibited "machine guns and sub-machine guns of any caliber whatsoever, capable of automatically discharging more than eight cartridges successively without reloading, in which ammunition is fed to such gun from or by means of clips, disks, belts, or other separable mechanical devices."[64] Louisiana's 1932 anti–machine gun law and South Carolina's 1934 law both defined machine guns in the same way using the identical language, also including the eight-cartridge standard. In the case of these three laws, the word "automatically" would seem to refer to fully automatic firing, but when that wording is married with "discharging more than eight cartridges successively without reloading," it would seem to encompass semi-automatic firing as well. Table 2.2 summarizes the key portions of the laws from these ten states.

A well-known category of gun laws, tied to American history, is the prohibition of dueling. Prominent public figures from early in our history, from Alexander Hamilton to Andrew Jackson, found themselves in highly publicized duels. Hamilton's long-standing political feud with fellow

Table 2.2 State Laws Barring Semi-Automatic Weapons, 1927–1934*

State and Year	Provision of Law
Massachusetts 1927	"rapid fire operated by a mechanism"
Michigan 1927	"any machine gun or firearm which can be fired more than sixteen times without reloading"
Minnesota 1933	"any firearm capable of automatically reloading after each shot is fired, whether firing singly by separate trigger pressure or firing continuously by continuous trigger pressure"
Ohio 1933	"any firearm which shoots automatically, or any firearm which shoots more than eighteen shots semi-automatically without reloading"
Rhode Island 1927	"any weapon which shoots automatically and any weapon which shoots more than twelve shots semi-automatically without reloading"
South Dakota 1933	"a weapon of any description . . . from which more than five shots or bullets may be rapidly or automatically, or semi-automatically discharged from a magazine"
Virginia 1933	"a weapon of any description . . . from which more than seven shots or bullets may be rapidly, or automatically, or semi-automatically discharged from a magazine, by a single function of the firing device, and also applies to and includes weapons, loaded or unloaded, from which more than sixteen shots or bullets may be rapidly, automatically, semi-automatically, or otherwise discharged without reloading"

Ambiguous State Laws

Illinois 1931	"machine guns and sub-machine guns of any caliber whatsoever, capable of automatically discharging more than eight cartridges successively without reloading, in which ammunition is fed to such gun from or by means of clips, disks, belts, or other separable mechanical devices"

(continued)

Table 2.2 (Continued)

State and Year	Provision of Law
Louisiana 1932	"machine rifles, machine guns and sub machine guns of any caliber whatsoever, capable of automatically discharging more than eight cartridges successively without reloading, in which ammunition is fed to such gun from or by means of clips, disks, belts, or other separable mechanical device"
South Carolina 1934	"machine rifles, machine guns and sub-machine guns of any caliber whatsoever, capable of automatically discharging more than eight cartridges successively without reloading, in which ammunition is fed to such gun from or by means of clips, disks, belts or other separable mechanical device"

*Source: State laws: 1927 Massachusetts Acts 413, chap. 326; 1927 Michigan Public Acts 888, no. 372; 1933 Minnesota Laws 231, chap. 189; 1933 Ohio Laws 189, sec. 12819–3; 1927 Rhode Island Public Laws 256, sec. 1; 1933 South Dakota Session Laws 245, sec. 1; 1933–1934 Virginia Acts 37, sec. 1; 1931 Illinois Laws 452, sec. 1; 1932 Louisiana Acts 336–37, sec. 1; 1934 South Carolina Acts 1288, sec. 1.

New York politician Aaron Burr ended when the two men dueled in New Jersey in 1804 (Burr was vice president at the time; New York barred dueling, so they traveled to the neighboring state). Hamilton died from his wounds, and Burr's political career never recovered. Jackson engaged in numerous duels and was wounded in one in 1806. Though not barred in every state, the practice declined in the North after the Hamilton–Burr duel[65] but persisted in the South until the mid-nineteenth century.

Gun laws aimed at barring felons, foreigners, or others deemed dangerous from possessing firearms focused early in the country's history on Native Americans, with at least five colonies enacting such laws (including the 1619 Virginia law cited at the start of the chapter). In the 1770s, Pennsylvania enacted laws to bar or strip guns from those who refused to swear loyalty to the new American government. In fact, ten of the thirteen states had laws allowing the impressment (taking) of privately held firearms during the Revolutionary War.[66] Massachusetts also enacted such a law in 1776[67] (although it does not appear in Frassetto's list). By the early 1900s, as anti-immigrant sentiment spread, many states enacted laws aimed at keeping guns from noncitizens, as well as the young, those who were inebriated, felons or other criminals, and out-of-state residents.

Concerns over the inherent harm and risk attendant to the firing of weapons near others spawned a steady stream of such laws from the 1600s through the early 1900s. Early such laws prohibited not only the firing of firearms in or near towns but also firing after dark, on Sundays, or near roads. Early laws also punished firing that wasted gunpowder or that occurred while under the influence of alcohol (a 1655 Virginia law specifically exempted drunken firing at weddings and funerals!). A North Carolina law from 1774 barred hunting by firelight at night, citing this concern in its preamble: "WHEREAS many Persons under Pretence of Hunting for Deer in the Night, by Fire Light, kill Horses and Cattle, to the Prejudice of the Owners thereof."[68] In the 1800s and 1900s, such laws were focused almost exclusively on firing in, around, or near towns or other populated areas or events.

The hunting laws represented here are significant for the extent to which early ones reflect contemporary concerns. While one imagines the America of the seventeenth to the nineteenth centuries as a nation little concerned (or need-ing to be concerned) about matters related to wildlife man-agement, safe hunting practices, or the like, these concerns are expressed early, as in the North Carolina nighttime hunting law just quoted. Early hunting laws were aimed at those who hunted on private lands or in preserves, those who hunted certain types of game, most notably water-fowl—often tied to prohibitions against hunting of such game from canoes, skiffs, or other water craft—and even the common deer. For example, it comes as something of a revelation to note that Pennsylvania established a deer hunting season, penalizing out-of-season hunting, as early as 1721, and North Carolina as early as 1768 (New Jersey also had such a law in the early 1700s). The penalty for violation of the North Carolina law was a fine of 5 pounds and "forfeiture of his gun."[69] Hunting even in this early period also sometimes required a license. Similarly, laws in the 1800s also restricted what was by then termed "fire-hunting" (hunting by firelight at night), poaching on pri-vate lands, and the use of certain restricted weapons, such as a "punt gun" or "swivel gun" (defined as a smooth bored gun that fires a charge of shot mounted on a swivel to bring down waterfowl) or any weapon not fired from the shoul-der. Measures were also enacted to protect certain game, require licensing, and bar fishing "with any kind of gun."[70] In the twentieth century, in addition to the types of laws already mentioned, states barred hunting with silencers, from aircraft, by underage persons, or with certain kinds of weapons (still including swivel guns, but now including automatic weapons).

Gun laws also dealt broadly with manufacturing, inspec-tion, and sale of weapons. Many of the laws in this category pertained to the manufacture, sale, transport, and storage of gunpowder. Gunpowder matters were of great concern because early firearms operated with the addition of loose gunpowder to serve as the igniting or explosive force to propel a projectile; the two were inextricably linked. But beyond the safety concerns about explosions or fires resulting from the mishandling of gunpowder, safety issues also led to other early regulations. In 1814, for example, Massachusetts required that all musket and pistol barrels manufactured in the state be first tested or "proved" to ensure that they could withstand the firing process without rupturing. Moreover, the law provided for a "person appointed according to the provisions of this act"[71]—that is, a state inspector—to oversee or conduct the testing. New Hampshire created and appointed state gunpowder inspectors to examine every storage and manufacturing site. Twentieth-century laws extended safety regulations pertaining to gunpowder and other explosives; one state, South Carolina, prohibited the use of explosives to kill fish (hardly a sporting enterprise).

At least eight states regulated, barred, or licensed firearms sales. For example, Florida (1927), Georgia (1902), and North Carolina (1905) gave localities the power to license, regulate, or even bar the commercial sale of firearms. In a 1917 law, New Hampshire required the licensing of gun dealers, requiring them to record the name, address, date of sale, amount paid, and date of the purchaser's permit for all who made gun purchases. In turn, this information was to be passed to the local city or town clerk or county office, and "the records thus filed shall at all times be open to the inspection of the police departments, or other public authorities."[72] New Jersey prohibited pawnbrokers from selling or in any manner transferring any firearms. New York established a system of registration for all handgun sales (part of what was known as the Sullivan Law; see Chapter 5), including the requirement that the gun owners had to obtain a permit for ownership. In a 1925 law,

West Virginia barred the "public display" of any firearms, whether for sale or rent, or ammunition. Gun dealers were also to be licensed and were required to record the name, address, age "and general appearance of the purchaser,"[73] as well as all identifying information about the gun, which was then to be immediately reported to the superintendent of the local department of public safety.

The militia laws that appear on this list represent one category of early gun laws that have been carefully studied elsewhere.[74] Not surprisingly, the laws here replicate what is now well known about the American militia system. Early laws confirmed the power of state governments to impress or take the firearms of citizens if needed. Militia-eligible men were typically required to obtain and maintain in working order the necessary combat-worthy firearm (at their own expense), along with the necessary accoutrements of powder, shot, and the like. In Virginia in the early 1600s, men were required to bring their firearms to church for fear of Indian attacks. In some states, laws stipulated when, where, and under what circumstances guns were to be loaded or unloaded. In Maryland, privates or noncommissioned officers who used their muskets for hunting were fined, according to a 1799 law. These laws disappeared with the end of the old militia system in the mid-1800s.

Numerous laws restricting gun access by minors (minimum ages ranged from 12 to 21) or others deemed irresponsible arose in the late 1800s, becoming more common in the early 1900s. Some states added other barred categories, including convicts or those of poor moral character, those inebriated, and people of unsound mind. In 1907 the then-territory of Arizona barred "any constable or other peace officer . . . while under the influence of intoxicating liquor of any kind, to carry or have on his person a pistol, gun, or other firearm, or while so intoxicated to strike any person, or to strike any person with a pistol, gun or other firearm."[75]

As is the case with virtually every sort of contemporary gun law, arms and ammunition trafficking was a concern as early as the seventeenth century, just as it is today. Various registration or taxation schemes sought to address this concern. For example, a 1652 New York law outlawed illegal trading of guns, gunpowder, and lead by private individuals. A 1631 Virginia law required the recording not only of all new arrivals to the colony but also "of arms and munitions."[76] Twenty years later, Virginia required that "all ammunition, powder and arms, other than for private use shall be delivered up" to the government.[77] In the 1800s, three southern states imposed taxes on personally held firearms. Georgia in 1866 levied a tax of "one dollar a piece on every gun or pistol, musket or rifle over the number of three kept or owned on any plantation."[78] In 1867 Mississippi levied a tax of between $5 and $15 "upon every gun and pistol which may be in the possession of any person . . . which tax shall be payable at any time on demand by the sheriff, and if not so paid, it shall be the duty of the sheriff to forthwith distrain [to seize property for money owed] and seize such gun or pistol, and sell the same for cash."[79] In 1856 and 1858, North Carolina taxed pistols and other weapons "used or worn about the person."[80] An 1851 Rhode Island law taxed anyone who owned or kept a pistol or rifle shooting gallery in certain locations (Louisiana did the same in 1870, and Mississippi in 1886). Alabama imposed a tax on firearms dealers in 1898. That same year, Florida required a license for anyone owning "a Winchester or repeating rifle," and further required the licensee to "give a bond running to the Governor of the State in the sum of one hundred dollars, conditioned on the proper and legitimate use of the gun with sureties to be approved by the county commissioners."[81] Hawaii licensed firearms for sporting purposes

in 1870, as did Wyoming in 1899, and Georgia imposed a pistol dealers' tax in 1894. Nebraska granted to city mayors the power to issue licenses to carry concealed weapons, adding mayoral discretion to "revoke any and all such licenses at his pleasure."[82]
Registration and taxation laws were enacted with greater frequency in the twentieth century. At least six states imposed various gun sales/dealer registration, regulation, or taxation, and six imposed gun registration for gun owners (the earliest of which, applicable to purchasers of all firearms, was Michigan in 1913; New York's 1911 law applied to handguns only). Michigan also mandated in 1927 that all pistols be presented by their owners "for safety inspection"[83] to local officials if they lived in an incorporated city or village. Perhaps most remarkable was this sweeping law, enacted by Montana in 1918, titled "An Act providing for the registration of all fire arms and weapons and regulating the sale thereof":

> Within thirty days from the passage and approval of this act, every person within the state of Montana, who owns or has in his possession any fire arms or weapons shall make a full, true and complete verified report upon the form hereinafter provided to the sheriff of the county in which such person lives, of all fire arms and weapons which are owned or possessed by him or her or are in his or her control, and on sale or transfer into the possession of any other person such person shall immediately forward to the sheriff of the County in which such person lives the name and address of that purchaser and person into whose possession or control such fire arm or weapon was delivered. . . . For the purpose of this Act a fire arm or weapon shall be deemed to be any revolver, pistol, shot gun, rifle, dirk, dagger, or sword.[84]

The sweep of this statewide scheme of gun registration is exceeded only by its early provenance.

Finally, in all the nearly 1,000 statutes examined in this analysis, only one referenced, in either general or specific terms, the right to bear arms (although it managed to misquote the Second Amendment—it is "the right *of* the people" not "the right *to* the people"). In 1868 Oregon enacted "An Act To Protect The Owners Of Firearms":

> Whereas, the constitution of the United States, in article second of amendments to the constitution, declares that "the right to the people to keep and bear arms shall not be infringed"; and the constitution for the state of Oregon, in article first, section twenty-seven, declares that "the people shall have the right to bear arms for the defense of themselves and the state"; therefore, sec. 1. Every white male citizen of this state above the age of sixteen years, shall be entitled to have, hold, and keep, for his own use and defense, the following firearms, to wit; either or any one of the following named guns and one revolving pistol: a rifle, shot-gun (double or single barrel), yager [a heavy, muzzle-loading hunting rifle], or musket. . . . No officer, civil or military, or other person, shall take from or demand of the owner any fire-arms mentioned in this act, except where the services of the owner are also required to keep the peace or defend the state.[85]

Note that even in this articulation of a specified right to guns, the law extends that right to "any one of the following," limiting citizens' gun rights both as to numbers of guns to be owned and to the specified types. Here, indeed, is a "well-regulated right."

The history of firearms regulations pertaining to race and slavery is surprising only in the relatively small number

of state restrictions. Yet that is not to suggest that the antebellum slavery regime was somehow less than uniformly
oppressive. Two competing values shaped the relationship
between slavery and guns. First, many sought to maintain
some discretion regarding the arming of slaves. Early in the
country's history, slave owners found it not only useful but
also necessary to arm slaves in early conflicts with Native
Americans. For example, during the bloody Yamasee War
(1715–1717) in South Carolina, nearly half of the colonist
militia forces deployed were slaves.[86] Later on, the practice
of enrolling slaves or indentured servants in local militias
was largely abandoned. In addition, individual slave owners
also often wished to arm their slaves when hunting or trav-
eling. The second, opposing value was the overriding fear
of slave rebellions. With so much of the population of the
South composed of people in bondage, whites lived in constant fear of violent uprisings. Part of the pathology of control extended to deterring and catching runaway slaves.[87]
With or without laws, southern whites well understood the
racial hierarchy in their region. Finally, gun prohibitions
often extended to free blacks as well, although some laws
distinguished between those in bondage versus those who
were free. For example, Virginia enacted a law in 1806 that
permitted "every negro or mulatto" to own guns, as long
as they were not slaves.[88] Most of the laws listed here either
penalize slaves for gun hunting or gun carrying without
their owners' authorization or presence. Others barred
slave gun carrying entirely or barred guns to free blacks or
those of mixed race.

Probably the most common type of gun law in America
today is that which restricts the use of firearms in sensitive areas and times. One would be hard pressed to find a
city, town, or village in the contemporary United States
that does not have a law against the discharge of firearms

within its jurisdiction. Indeed, such laws existed early in our history (some of which fell into categories previously examined in this chapter). Early such laws barred firearms carrying and discharges in named or generic public places, communal gatherings, schools, entertainments, on Sundays, or on election day. A spate of laws were enacted in the late 1700s and 1800s to bar firearms discharges in cemeteries (clearly a source of significant mischief), on or at trains or other public conveyances, near roads, churches, bridges, homes or other buildings, or state parks.

The idea that those who commit crimes with guns should suffer a greater punishment is an old idea but not one widely found during the period under study here. In 1783 Connecticut enacted a law that called for the death penalty for those who committed a burglary or robbery with a gun because it was seen to "clearly indicate their violent intentions."[89] By comparison, commission of the same crimes without a gun resulted in a whipping and jail time. A 1788 Ohio law increased the penalty and jail time for anyone convicted of breaking and entering with a dangerous weapon, including firearms. Several states provided for enhanced sentences for crimes committed with firearms in the 1800s. In the 1900s, extended sentences were meted out to those who used explosives or guns while committing crimes (sometimes machine guns or pistols were stipulated).

The final category of gun regulation pertains to storage regulations. Many early laws imposed storage restrictions on gunpowder, but similar rules sometimes extended to firearms as well. For example, Massachusetts enacted a 1782 law specifying that any loaded firearms "found in any Dwelling House, Out House, Stable, Barn, Store, Ware House, Shop, or other Building . . . shall be liable to be seized" by the "Firewards" of the town. If the storage was found to be improper by a court, the firearms were to "be adjudged forfeit, and be sold at public Auction."[90] Armories and gun houses were subject to regular inspection by the terms of an 1859 Connecticut law. In 1919 Massachusetts passed a law to authorize the issuance of warrants for any complaint alleging that someone was keeping "an unreasonable number of rifles, shot guns, pistols, revolvers or other dangerous weapons, or that an unnecessary quantity of ammunition, is kept or concealed for any unlawful purpose in a particular house or place."[91] If a court concluded that the possession was not justified, it could order the weapons and ammunition forfeited.

CONCLUSION: FIREARMS LAWS ARE AS AMERICAN AS GUN OWNERSHIP

Early gun laws were comprehensive, ubiquitous, and extensive. Taken together, they covered every conceivable dimension of gun acquisition, sale, possession, transport, and use, including deprivation of use through outright confiscation. Given that the dark fear of contemporary gun rights enthusiasts is government confiscation of firearms, it bears noting that this survey of early gun laws included measures that invoked gun confiscation for this wide range of reasons or offenses: military/defense necessity; failure to swear a loyalty oath to the government; improper storage of firearms; improper firearms possession of weapons legal to own under certain circumstances, including, but not limited to, possession of specific, named types of prohibited firearms (especially handguns and machine guns); violations of certain hunting laws; and failure to pay a gun tax.

Another category of gun regulation, remarkable in its own right, is the existence of laws in up to ten states that prohibited semi-automatic weapons. This important statutory prohibition, unknown until now, also has contemporary reverberation as a precedent for the assault weapons ban debates in the 1990s and 2000s (see Chapter 3).

In all this law making, there is no hint that these laws infringed on anything related to any "right to bear arms" (remembering that the Second Amendment did not apply to the states until the Supreme Court did so in 2010), whether referencing the U.S. Constitution's Second Amendment or the various state constitutions' right-to-bear-arms-type provisions. Many state laws predated the modern state and federal constitutions, but there is no indication that subsequent state laws were somehow inhibited or stymied after the adoption of right-to-bear-arms provisions, aside from occasional court challenges.[92] Many of these laws did, however, include two types of exemptions: those related to militia or military activities, and instances when individuals used firearms for justifiable personal self-defense. As Saul Cornell has noted, "The common-law right of individual self-defense"[93] was not only well established long before codification of the right to bear arms in American constitutions but existed independent of that right.[94] (This subject receives closer scrutiny in Chapter 4's treatment of modern stand your ground laws.)

Taken together, these sixteen categories of gun laws (bearing in mind that some laws contained multiple provisions that overlapped two or more categories) span a wide range. Some encompass anachronistic practices—slavery, dueling, the old-style militias—that nevertheless reflected the scope of government power over the kinds of persons who could carry guns, the circumstances of gun carrying, criminal gun behavior, and military/defense exigencies. Others reflect the most basic efforts to extend safety, including laws that criminalized menacing behavior with guns (brandishing), the firing of weapons in populated areas, hunting laws, some of the laws related to manufacturing and inspection pertaining to firearms, laws restricting firearms access to minors, criminals, and those mentally incompetent, laws restricting firearms in sensitive areas or places, sentence enhancement laws, and storage laws. Finally, some of the gun law categories represented more sophisticated, ambitious, or seemingly modern approaches to gun regulation. Dangerous weapons barred outright by law focused primarily on machine guns and similar automatic weapons that were banned before Congress moved against such weapons in 1934. Yet laws also barred silencers, air guns, and, as noted, even semi-automatic weapons in some states, as well as the early equivalent of large-capacity bullet magazines. While standards varied, some states barred weapons or mechanisms that could fire more than five, seven, eight, sixteen, or eighteen bullets without reloading. The concerns then were akin to those that motivated Congress to enact the Assault Weapons Ban of 1994[95] (which also included a provision that limited bullet magazines holding more than ten rounds): excessive firepower in the hands of civilians and the related question of public safety. Beyond these laws are those that are essentially off the agenda in the contemporary political environment: registration and licensing laws and, significantly, categorical gun bans.

Taking most of these gun law categories together, one overarching concern straddles them: the conviction that handguns represented a uniquely dangerous threat to society. Even though these laws were enacted long before the government or private researchers began to collect systematic data on gun violence, there is no doubt that the carrying of pistols was seen as an activity largely confined to those who contemplated or committed crimes or other forms of interpersonal violence and that therefore they should be subject to stricter rules and standards, including in many instances their prohibition. While gun control proponents continue to make the same arguments in modern America, it is abundantly clear that those arguments carried far more weight in the America of the 1600s through the early 1900s than they do today. The relationship between citizens and their governments with respect to guns discussed in the first chapter contemplates a regulatory regime that bears little resemblance to the modern gun rights narrative of the past. Yes, there was lawlessness, rebellion, and rugged individualism. But the context was that of a governing framework where the state confined and defined lawful use of force by individuals.

Gun laws are as old as the country; more to the point, the *idea* of gun laws and regulation is as old as the country. The prevailing gun law movement in America in the last three decades toward the relaxing of gun restrictions (e.g., the reduction of gun sale inspections, the shielding of manufacturers and dealers from criminal and civil liability, the rise of unregulated Internet gun and ammunition sales), as well as the spread of concealed carry laws, the open carry movement, and most recently stand your ground laws (see Chapter 4), are not a return to the past. They are a refutation of America's past, a determined march away from America's gun regulation tradition. And these changes have nothing to do with improving safety or security in society, but they have everything to do with politics. In the next chapter, we turn expressly to the Second Amendment's right to bear arms, which frames this larger debate.

CHAPTER 3

What about the Second Amendment?

In a press conference with reporters on July 19, 2013, President Barack Obama spoke extemporaneously for over fifteen minutes about his feelings concerning the verdict in the trial of George Zimmerman. In a trial that riveted the nation, the Florida man and neighborhood watch volunteer had just been acquitted on the charge of second-degree murder for killing unarmed 17-year-old African American teenager, Trayvon Martin, on a dark, rainy night in February 2012. Martin had been visiting his father in a neighborhood unfamiliar to the teenager and was returning from the store. Many believed that the man's acquittal was an unjust verdict and that race had played a role in the killing and perhaps the verdict (Zimmerman, armed with a handgun, claimed that he had killed Martin in self-defense because the teenager had attacked him). During his wide-ranging remarks, Obama included comment on Florida's "stand your ground law," a measure enacted in 2005 that made it far more difficult to investigate and prosecute killings in public places when the shooter claimed that he or she feared for his or her life (see Chapter 4). Obama said this:

> . . . If we're sending a message as a society in our communities that someone who is armed potentially has the right to use those firearms even if there's a way for them to exit from a situation, is that really going to be contributing to the kind of peace and security and order that we'd like to see? And for those who resist that idea that we should think about something like these "stand your ground" laws, I just ask people to consider if Trayvon Martin was of age and armed, could he have stood his ground on that sidewalk? And do we actually think that he would have been justified in shooting Mr. Zimmerman, who had followed him in a car, because he felt threatened? And if the answer to that question is at least ambiguous, it seems to me that we might want to examine those kinds of laws.[1]

Obama critics responded immediately. Among them was Texas Republican Senator Ted Cruz, who criticized Obama's remarks by saying: "It is not surprising that the president uses it seems every opportunity he can to try to go after our Second Amendment right to keep and bear arms. I think it is unfortunate that this president and this administration has a consistent disregard for the Bill of Rights."[2] Cruz, a graduate of Harvard Law School, was inferring that Florida's law protecting the right of citizens to carry and use lethal force in a confrontation in a public place where they reported feeling threatened was somehow within the umbrella of a Second Amendment–based right or that Obama's questioning of the law somehow assailed a constitutional right. To date, no one has argued that stand your ground laws are unconstitutional, but not everything that is legal comes under the umbrella of the federal Constitution—far from it, in fact. Under the principle of federalism, states exercise primary control over their own criminal laws, including stand your ground laws. Obama's suggestion that these laws might not be good public policy bears no relationship to any attack on the Second Amendment, nor is it anything resembling "disregard for the Bill of Rights," Senator Cruz's protestations notwithstanding.

That a Harvard Law School–trained lawyer would make such an elementary mistake may be a commentary on his own inapt legal acumen, but more likely it reflects the contemporary state of the gun debate in America, where, in the minds of many, any instance where a person's hand comes into contact with a firearm is, perforce, somehow protected under the Second Amendment (a supposition contradicted by the gun laws examined in the last chapter). The gun debate is a clear instance where political hyperbole is taken by many as literal fact and also as a way to establish or fortify (in this case conservative) political credentials—a fact that Senator Cruz undoubtedly knows.

As Chapter 2 made clear, gun laws and regulations are not only as old as the country, they were incredibly prolific and wide-ranging, covering about every aspect of humans' interactions with firearms. As also noted in the last chapter, while very few of these laws have been subject to Second Amendment–based challenges, the laws have invariably prevailed. Ironically, it is now in the contemporary political era that many have come to believe that gun laws somehow inherently tread on Second Amendment quicksand—that the right to bear arms is somehow absolute.[3] Once again, we see an instance where the contemporary gun debate, purported to be rooted in the past, has virtually no connection to the actual past. So what rights, then, does the Second Amendment protect?

The answer to this question is quite straightforward, although not entirely complete. Since the Supreme Court handed down its landmark (and controversial) ruling in 2008 on the Second Amendment, *D.C. v. Heller*, the answer has been this: American citizens have a Second Amendment right to own a handgun for personal self-protection in the home. Further, that right is generally subject to reasonable regulation by the government, especially if such laws have historical provenance. That conclusion by the High Court is notable because it was a decision deeply grounded in history; in fact, it was one of the most history-driven decisions in modern Court history. This again underscores and punctuates the fact that history and perceptions of history play an overweening role in how the modern gun issue is framed.

ORIGINALISM VERSUS LIVING CONSTITUTION VIEWS

The legal and political battle over the meaning of the Second Amendment has been fought in the midst of a great political and legal war over competing perspectives regarding how the Constitution is or should be interpreted. One view, "Constitutional originalism," says that judges should interpret the Constitution based on the document's original intent or "fixed" meaning, filtering out contemporary values and preferences. As Supreme Court Justice Antonin Scalia has said, judges should "begin with the text, and to give that text the meaning that it bore when it was adopted by the people."[4] Constitutional interpretation should avoid anything like contemporary societal values or other similar considerations.

The "living Constitution" view does not abandon the constitutional text but notes that the Constitution was the product of many hands, that it is often vague as to meaning, that it often raises more questions than it answers, that the framers themselves disagreed about not only the meaning of the document but how strictly to adhere to its provisions, and that for the document to survive, it must be adapted to modern society and conditions that could not have been anticipated in the eighteenth century.[5] As one analyst has noted, "Scholars disagree on the original meaning of almost every important constitutional provision."[6]

The originalist movement (the antecedent of which was dubbed constitutional "strict construction") is largely the product of the last few decades, arising in reaction to what were seen as the excesses of liberal judicial activism of the 1950s to the 1970s. This reaction to judicial activism was an integral intellectual component of the New Right political movement that arose in the late 1970s and early 1980s. Among its champions were former federal judge Robert Bork and Justice Scalia.[7]

The driving theory behind the Supreme Court's 2008 *Heller* ruling was original intent, predicated on a heavy reliance on historical analysis as a basis for justifying its expansive view of Second Amendment gun rights. As mentioned, the *Heller* case is considered one of the most history-driven and history-based (as opposed to law-based) rulings in modern times.[8]

UNDERSTANDING THE SECOND AMENDMENT

Before examining the individual or personal right to have guns established in this 2008 case, we confront a prior question: How was the amendment interpreted before that?

The answer is found in the plain wording of the amendment itself: "A well regulated Militia, being necessary to the security of a free State, the right of the people to keep and bear Arms, shall not be infringed." That is, as former Supreme Court Chief Justice Warren Burger noted, the Second Amendment "must be read as though it began with the word 'because,'" meaning that "the need for a state militia was the predicate of the right guaranteed [i.e., the right to bear arms]; in short, it was declared 'necessary' in order to have a state military force to protect the security of the state." [9]

Aside from the text itself, supporting the militia-based view is the fact that all the direct evidence, including most importantly the debate during the First Congress in 1789 (when the amendment was proposed, debated, revised, and passed), pertained to military/militia/national defense matters.[10] At no time was there any debate or discussion saying or suggesting that the amendment had anything to do with a personal right to guns aside from militia service. As the Pulitzer Prize–winning historian Jack Rakove wrote, the contemporaneous debate about what became the Second Amendment "was about the militia as an institution, not an individual right that no one in 1789 understood to be on the table."[11] This, however, did not mean that people had no legal right to defend themselves. Indeed, the common-law principle of individual or personal self-defense was well established, long predated (and postdated) the enactment of the Second Amendment, and existed in law independent of that amendment until the two were brought together by the Court in 2008.[12] And as the previous chapter showed, gun ownership was as old as the European founding of the country.

More to the point, from the time of its writing in 1789 through the end of the twentieth century, the Second

Amendment was interpreted as protecting a right to bear arms only in connection with the militia service referenced in the first half of the sentence—that is, only in connection with citizen service in a government-organized and regulated militia. This militia-based understanding was confirmed by the Supreme Court most notably in an 1886 case (*Presser v. Illinois*[13]) and a 1939 case (*U.S. v. Miller*[14]) and in nearly fifty lower federal court cases handed down from the 1940s through the beginning of the twenty-first century.[15] In fact, no gun law had been declared unconstitutional as a violation of the Second Amendment until what became the *Heller* case came along.

Given this, one may wonder how the Court managed this significant change in law in the face of past history. The answer is twofold: that the Court played fast and loose with the history, and that the decision was actually an exercise in a living Constitution approach, not originalism.

In *Heller's* aftermath, many observed that the Court's account of the history of the Second Amendment was, at the least, flawed, as most historians and legal historians of the period observed.[16] As many critics have noted, Scalia's opinion derides and dismisses the pertinence of Congress's debates on the Second Amendment, instead relying on a dissenting opinion expressed at the Pennsylvania State ratifying convention of 1788 and similar lone dissenting opinions from the New Hampshire and Massachusetts conventions,[17] all of which were ignored by those who framed and wrote the Second Amendment (the point about Scalia's reliance on these orphan dissenting opinions is that they were minority voices that did not prevail and were ignored). Worse, Scalia relied on sources that were not even from the founding period: two legal treatises written in the nineteenth century and an early-eighteenth-century British case.[18]

The noted conservative federal judge Richard A. Posner wrote about the decision by saying that "professional historians were on Stevens's side" (Stevens authored the *Heller* dissent, which also was a deeply historical account but one that contradicted the majority's historical narrative), and that it was a case of "faux originalism." Scalia's distortion of history, according to Posner, is an example of "law office history,"[19] meaning that it is the product of lawyers "tendentiously dabbling in history, rather than by disinterested historians." Posner archly concluded that Scalia's decision "is evidence of the ability of well-staffed courts to produce snow jobs."[20] Other commentators, notably prominent conservatives, accused Scalia of unwarranted judicial activism (a criticism usually reserved for liberals) and distortion of history, arguing that an accurate "originalist" reading of the Second Amendment leads to the militia-based understanding of the amendment, not the individualist view.[21]

Scalia's reason for taking this route, and that of his fellow justices who sided with him, is not hard to discern. Given his conservative bona fides, lifelong fealty to originalism, and disdain for a living Constitution approach, he could never abandon that constitutional methodology, even in the face of his reinterpretation of the Second Amendment that, in effect, wrote the first half of the sentence composing the Second Amendment out of existence. For Scalia to admit to embracing a living Constitution approach would be the equivalent of the good Justice delivering a full, man-to-man, open-mouthed kiss to the Devil himself.

Scalia could maintain the semblance of originalism, thanks to what legal analyst Jeffrey Toobin described as the work and writing of a "small group of activists" who "took a fringe and discredited constitutional interpretation, injected their considerable passion, intelligence, and financial resources"[22] to produce the individualist counternarrative that eventually won five votes on the Supreme Court. In fact, the individualist view of the Second Amendment as a coherent legal theory has a recent provenance. It first appeared in a law review article in 1960.[23] Prior to that time, the militia view was the sole basis for understanding and analyzing the Second Amendment in the thirteen law journal articles published from 1874 to 1959 that examined the Second Amendment.[24] Toobin concludes that "Scalia's decision had little to do with the original meaning of the Second Amendment. It was an improvisation designed to reach a policy goal [i.e., to expand gun rights], which was, not coincidentally, one of the top priorities of the modern Republican Party."[25] Legal commentator Adam Winkler stated the matter this way: "The irony of Scalia's opinion was that the heralded 'triumph of originalism' in fact reflected a thoroughly modern understanding of gun rights."[26] Historian Saul Cornell wrote that this decision "ultimately has nothing to do with history; it is a modern ideology dressed up in historical clothing."[27]

Still, one may argue that while this past is interesting, it is in equal measure irrelevant given that *Heller* now defines the Second Amendment as an individual or personal right unrelated to a citizen's militia service and given further that in a 2010 case, *McDonald v. Chicago*,[28] the Court affirmed *Heller* and applied it to the states.[29] Fair enough. (And after all, while the Court cannot change history, it can certainly change law.) In this light, it is important to understand the nature of the right the Court established.

The individual right laid out in *Heller* was carefully, if perhaps incompletely, defined. Asserting that "the inherent right of self-defense has been central to the Second Amendment right,"[30] Justice Scalia noted that the right "is not unlimited," and that "the right was not a right to keep and carry any weapon whatsoever in any manner and for whatever purpose," citing as an example long-standing laws against the carrying of concealed weapons (as the last chapter made clear).[31] In addition, the Court said that "weapons that are most useful in military service—M-16 rifles and the like"[32] are also subject to regulation. Emphasizing the historical nature of the decision, Scalia wrote that, while "we do not undertake an exhaustive historical analysis today of the full scope of the Second Amendment, nothing in our opinion should be taken to cast doubt on long-standing prohibitions on the possession of firearms by felons or the mentally ill, or laws forbidding the carrying of firearms in sensitive places such as schools and government buildings, or laws imposing conditions and qualifications on the commercial sale of arms." The Court also noted that the historical record supported "prohibiting the carrying of 'dangerous and unusual weapons'" [33] and countenanced "laws regulating the storage of firearms to prevent accidents."[34] The opinion also quoted with approval an earlier Court decision to say that the amendment "does not protect those weapons not typically possessed by law-abiding citizens for lawful purposes, such as short-barreled shotguns," which "accords with the historical understanding of the scope of the right. . . ."[35] On the other hand, the Court also said that the "Second Amendment extends" to weapons "that were not in existence at the time of the founding."[36] As Supreme Court Justice Stephen Breyer noted in an article he authored after the *McDonald* case (Breyer also wrote a separate dissenting opinion in *Heller*), the majority opinion in *Heller* "looked primarily to history, not only to determine that the Second Amendment protected a right to armed self-defense but also to define the scope of that right. . . ."[37]

Within the context of these parameters, in the first five years since *Heller*, over 700 Second Amendment–based challenges (although these challenges often rely on other bases as well) to gun laws have been filed in federal and state courts. To date, nearly all these challenges have failed. In addition, over 60 of these cases have been appealed to the Supreme Court, but it has declined to hear any of them to date (one may reasonably assume, though, that new cases will eventually be accepted for review by the High Court).[38]

Among the gun laws left standing in the wake of legal challenges are laws that require concealed carry gun permit applicants to show "good cause" as the basis for the permit to be granted; firearm storage requirements; laws barring guns from felons, those convicted of certain misdemeanors, and those adjudged mentally incompetent; firearms registration requirements; the regulation of gun shows on public property; barring guns to those under the age of 21; substantial handgun permit fees; and laws limiting concealed carry permits to state residents. Unresolved questions as of this writing include the extent to which the amendment's protections apply outside of a home, which types of weapons might be beyond the pale of protected citizen possession, and the degree of "scrutiny" to apply when considering challenges to gun laws (i.e., how high a legal standard should be applied by the courts when considering whether a gun law is constitutional).[39]

One notable ruling that adopted a gun rights argument is a 2012 case from the Seventh Circuit, U.S. Court of Appeals, *Moore v. Madigan*,[40] in which two members of a three-judge panel ruled that, under the Second Amendment, Illinois had to adopt some kind of law to allow citizens to carry concealed weapons[41] (until 2013, Illinois was the only state of the fifty that barred concealed carrying of weapons entirely; other states have either stricter "may issue" or less strict "shall issue" concealed carry laws). Other appeals courts have upheld strict concealed carry laws.[42] Interestingly, the *Moore* decision was authored by the very same Judge Posner who was so critical of *Heller*. In *Moore*, Posner wrote as a judge in a lower court bound by a higher court ruling, writing that "we are bound by the Supreme Court's historical analysis because it was central to the Court's holding in *Heller*."[43] The decision later referenced Posner's dispute over *Heller*'s version of history in a parenthetical aside: "(apart from disagreement, unnecessary to bore the reader with, with some of the historical analysis in the opinion—we regard the historical issues as settled by *Heller*). . . ."[44]

THE CASE OF THE ASSAULT WEAPONS BAN

A useful way to get a handle on post-*Heller* gun regulation is to examine what, in the current political environment, represents the most strict proposed national gun law that has been subject to serious scrutiny in recent years: a ban, or restrictions, on assault-style weapons. A limited nationwide ban was enacted in 1994 and was in effect for ten years, when it lapsed by its own terms in 2004. Congress failed to reenact the ban then, and while periodic efforts to revive the law were subsequently proposed in Congress, little momentum existed behind such efforts until 2012, when in the aftermath of mass shootings (where assault weapons were used) in a movie theater in Aurora, Colorado, and an elementary school in Newtown, Connecticut, a major push was undertaken to revive the ban.

By way of background, the 1994 law imposed a ten-year ban on the manufacture, sale, transfer, or possession of nineteen named types of semi-automatic assault weapons, along with several dozen copycat models. Such weapons were defined as military-style weapons in the category of those "capable of providing by a selector switch either semiautomatic . . . or fully automatic"[45] fire, except that the weapons available to civilians did not include such switches. (Fully automatic weapons fire a continuous stream of bullets when the trigger is depressed; semi-automatic weapons fire one bullet or round with each pull of the trigger.) Beyond this, the barred weapons also possessed the ability to accept a detachable bullet magazine and at least two other features, including a folding or telescoping stock, a pistol grip, a bayonet mount, a flash suppressor or threaded barrel to receive one, or a grenade launcher. Some of these features were designed to facilitate "spray fire." The law also specifically exempted 661 named types of firearms and outlawed the sale, transfer, or possession of ammunition-feeding devices (commonly called "magazines") that held more than ten rounds. In the case of both the weapons and magazine ban, the law grandfathered in (i.e., exempted from these restrictions) those items manufactured before the date of the passage of the law. During this period, seven states—California, Connecticut, Hawaii, Maryland, Massachusetts, New Jersey, and New York, plus the District of Columbia—also adopted versions of assault weapons bans (Cook County, Illinois, also enacted a ban; in 2013 New York strengthened its law; see Chapter 5).[46]

These exemptions, plus the limited number of weapons covered, plus the law's ten-year time limit, prompted gun control supporters to criticize the law for being too weak. Gun manufacturers readily exploited loopholes in the law by making minor design alterations in weapons that would have wound up on the prohibited list to then market legal versions. Opponents of the law objected to its very attempt to restrict civilian access to such weapons, variously arguing that the law would be ineffective, that it involved weapons rarely used in crimes, and that the law fixated on cosmetic features unrelated to the weapons' actual firing capabilities. In addition, critics noted that many mistakenly think that the weapons subject to regulation are fully automatic (i.e., popularly referred to as "machine guns"), when they are in fact semi-automatic weapons that fire with the same mechanism as many traditional hunting weapons. Finally, many believe that such restrictions infringe on citizens' rights.

Like other gun laws, this one was subject to several legal challenges, but these were based on alleged violations of the U.S. Constitution's Commerce Clause and Equal Protection Clause, not the Second Amendment.[47] These challenges failed.

At the start of 2013, California Democratic Senator Dianne Feinstein introduced the Assault Weapons Ban of 2013; a companion bill was also introduced in the House of Representatives. That bill sought to reenact a law similar to that of 1994. It specified a list of over 150 named weapons to be barred but expanded the definition by defining them as having the ability to accept a detachable magazine (as well as those that had a fixed magazine that could accept more than ten rounds) but also possessing one (as opposed to two in the 1994 law) of the listed characteristics, including a pistol grip, a forward grip, a folding, telescoping, or detachable scope, a grenade or rocket launcher, a barrel shroud, or a threaded barrel. The bill also exempted 2258 named weapons and allowed the transfer of older assault weapons only if a background check was completed by a federal firearms licensed dealer. The bill included no sunset date.[48]

Feinstein's bill was introduced along with several other new gun measures in the wake of the Sandy Hook Elementary School shooting in December 2012, when twenty children and six school personnel were shot and killed by 20-year-old Adam Lanza. While Lanza had three weapons with him, plus a shotgun in his car, he used a military-style Bushmaster XM-15 .223 caliber M4 carbine (a variant of the popular AR-15, a civilian version of the military M-16 and M-4) to kill his victims, firing 152 shots in the space of less than five minutes, with the assistance of multiple thirty-round magazines. He then used a handgun to kill himself.[49]

The nation's shock at this shooting and the decision by President Obama to launch an effort to win enactment of new federal gun measures resulted in several measures introduced in the Democratic-controlled Senate and Republican-controlled House (although no House action occurred). In April the full Senate voted on the Feinstein bill, defeating it by a 40 to 60 vote. Other gun measures garnered greater support, including a bipartisan proposal to establish universal background checks for all gun purchases, yet that measure fell short by a vote of 54 to 46 (60 votes were needed to advance the bill because it was under filibuster threat), as did the others. Supporters vowed to bring that measure back; the assault weapons ban, however, was clearly dead.[50]

WHAT IS AN ASSAULT WEAPON?

The debate over the assault weapons ban raises a series of issues related to the scope of gun rights under *Heller*, as related not only to the law but also to the politics of the law and the symbolism of the law. As noted earlier, the 1994 law withstood constitutional challenges, but those challenges occurred before the *Heller* ruling, so a new such federal law would obviously invite a Second Amendment–based challenge. More on that in a bit. First, however, it is useful to examine the core arguments for and against such a ban. While it is a mistake to slip into facile false equivalence by simply saying that both sides are in some respects right or wrong, this is one instance where that observation has some merit.

First, it is true that the weapons targeted for regulation by Congress in 1994 and again in 2013 are semi-automatic, not fully automatic in the method by which they fire, as is true of many traditional hunting weapons (and handguns). Many did and do continue to misunderstand this difference in firing feature[51] and the fact that fully automatic weapons have been strictly (and effectively) regulated by the federal government since the National Firearms Act of 1934 and by the Firearms Owners Protection Act of 1986.[52] This confusion has been repeatedly reported and decried by guns rights organizations,[53] but it has been noted by gun control organizations as well, such as the Violence Policy Center, which referred in a report to the "weapons' menacing looks, coupled with the public's confusion over fully automatic machine guns versus semi-automatic assault weapons. . . ."[54] That, however, does not mean that they are indistinguishable from or the same as traditional hunting weapons. This part of the story is less well known.

The term "assault weapon" is neither a "public relations stunt"[55] nor a ginned-up label invented by gun control organizations—although they are certainly content to stick with the term in the ongoing public debate. In fact, it was the very term used by the companies that first produced, marketed, and sold such weapons to the public. Tom Diaz, a specialist on and critic of the gun industry, has chronicled the marketing strategies employed by gun manufacturers and gun publications from the time that such weapons were first introduced to the American civilian market in a significant way in the 1980s. He reports on and quotes directly from gun company advertisements and gun magazines, like Heckler and Koch selling its "HK 91 Semi-Automatic Assault Rifle," the "Bushmaster assault rifle," the AKM "imported assault rifle," the Beretta M-70 that "resembles many other assault rifles," the AR 10 (made by Paragon

S&S Inc.) advertised as a "famous assault rifle [that] is now available in a semi-auto form!," the "AMT 25/.22 Lightning Carbine" that was advertised as an "assault-type semi-auto," among many other examples.[56] As a standard buyer's guide on assault weapons noted, the "popularly-held idea that the term 'assault weapon' originated with anti-gun activists, media or politicians is wrong. The term was first adopted by the manufacturers, wholesalers, importers and dealers in the American firearms industry. . . ."[57] The more expansive phrase "assault weapon" is generally used over "assault rifle" because "weapon" includes not only rifles but also some shotguns and handguns that were additionally subject to regulation in the 1994 and subsequent laws.

By the early 1990s, both the gun industry and National Rifle Association abruptly changed course in their reference to such weapons as pressure built on Congress and in some states to enact curbs (California enacted the first assault weapons ban in 1989 in the aftermath of a school shooting in Stockton, California, committed with an AK-47), and that led to the remarketing and rebranding of such weapons as no different from typical, traditional hunting weapons that also fired in semi-automatic fashion. That effort has persisted to the present, with terms like "tactical rifles" and "modern sporting rifles" typically offered by gun organizations, including the National Rifle Association (NRA) and National Shooting Sports Foundation (NSSF), as preferred terms for such weapons.[58]

Persistent efforts at rebranding—and parallel denials of the past just described—accelerated through the 2012 and 2013 national debate over assault weapons, as seen, for example, in the NSSF website and literature. A widely circulated "Modern Sporting Rifle Pocket Fact Card"[59] says that such weapons are "widely misunderstood" because of their cosmetic resemblance to military weapons (obviously, an intentional design feature). It urges gun owners to use the information on the card and website "to correct misconceptions about these rifles." Among the "corrections" it offers: "AR-15-style rifles are NOT 'assault weapons' or 'assault rifles.' An assault rifle is fully automatic—a machine gun." It adds, "Please correct them" if they use the term "assault weapon," claiming further that it "is a political term" created in the 1980s.

Yet a similarly recent article in *Outdoor Life* on this subject belies the claim that assault weapons are limited only to those that fire fully automatically. That article, too, urges its readers to share its information with nonshooting friends to dispel "myths" about "assault weapons." In its account, it notes correctly that "the term 'assault weapon' did not have a precise meaning, but it generally referred to a type of light infantry firearm initially developed in World War II; a magazine-fed rifle and carbine suitable for combat, such as the AK-47 and the M16/M4. These are selective-fire weapons that can shoot semi-auto, full-auto, or in three-round bursts. . . ."[60]

This all makes clear that contemporary assault weapons available to civilians are a subcategory of the military-style weapons, with the modification that civilian weapons do not have a "selective fire" option but can only fire in semi-automatic mode. Ironically, the fully automatic mode is often less useful on the battlefield because the weapon can "ride up" as it fires, whereas semi-auto firing facilitates keeping the weapon on target.[61] The same lesson has applied to those who have used such weapons to commit mass murders in recent decades.

The modern assault weapon arose during World War II, when the Germans developed the STG44, or *Sturmgewehr*. That soldier-carried weapon was studied and copied by the Soviets, who produced the well-known Soviet AK-47 in 1947, which has been the most successful and prolific soldier-held battlefield weapon in modern times.[62] The AK-47 gave rise to the American M16, which was the basis for what is now the most popular civilian version of this weapon, the AR-15 (see Chapter 5), as well as many copycat models. These weapons did not catch on in the American market in a significant way until the late 1980s,[63] when the Chinese flooded the market with cheap weapons, including their own semi-automatic version of the AK-47[64] (in 1987 Chinese rifle imports jumped to 22 percent of all such imports, peaking at 64 percent of the total rifle import market by 1994). The Chinese dumping was curtailed by President Bill Clinton in 1994.[65] Popular culture in the 1980s also dramatized and glorified such weapons in movies and television programs, including *Scarface, Rambo, Commando, Miami Vice,* and *The A-Team.*[66]

The ongoing effort to rebrand "assault weapons" as something more benign and severed from its military origins was seen in the publication struggles of Phillip Peterson, whose book, titled as recently as 2008 *Gun Digest Buyer's Guide to Assault Weapons,*[67] is a well-known reference work on the subject. As Peterson explained, the gun industry "moved to shame or ridicule" those who used the phrase "assault weapons," insisting that the term should now only apply to fully automatic weapons. Peterson noted that the origin of the term "assault weapon" was the industry itself.[68] He found that the NRA refused to sell his book until he changed the title, which in 2010 he renamed *Gun Digest Buyer's Guide to Tactical Rifles.*[69]

But what about the other features of these weapons, aside from their basic semi-automatic firing mode, that attracts so much attention—what many call these weapons' "cosmetic" features? It is certainly fair to say that features like barrel shrouds, pistol grips, and large-capacity bullet magazines do give these weapons (especially to those unfamiliar with their use) a more fearsome, intimidating look, and that some of the listed features, such as a bayonet mount and grenade launcher, are indeed cosmetic to the extent that they are unrelated to the weapons' firing properties and are unlikely to be actually used either by sports people or criminals (grenades are not available to civilians). So why bother with them?

The answer, again, is their military derivation and the very appeal of such weapons' stylistic features to American gun purchasers (and, unfortunately, to some criminals),[70] which helps explain the marketing schizophrenia to extol the weapons' similarity to battlefield weapons yet deny the very same lineage. Gun owners become understandably frustrated at the notion that traits like grenade launchers are included as part of what defines these weapons as a type that should be more regulated. This underscores the fact that all these features have been often treated in the law as equivalent, when, in fact, only some of these features are important because they do bear directly on how the weapon is fired, like these weapons' more compact design, ability to receive large-capacity bullet magazines, thumb-hole grips, forward handgrips, collapsible or telescoping stocks, and extensive use of plastic stampings. These features make them more lightweight and concealable and also facilitate a key trait for battlefield use: their ability to fire large numbers of rounds without reloading to lay down "spray fire," also referred to as "hosing down" an area.[71] No sane person goes hunting by laying down a field of fire, but such a firing process is a source of entertainment—of fun—for some shooting enthusiasts (more about that later). It is also central to the appeal to mass shooters.

One other argument offered by some AR enthusiasts is that assault weapons are, in their view, "the firearm *most* protected by the Second Amendment."[72] According to this view, the modern AR is the descendant of eighteenth-century muskets—the weapons carried by militias to defend the country. Ironically, this view accepts that the ARs are, in fact, the closest approximations to military weapons available to civilians. Here again, part of the appeal of assault weapons is their military provenance. This argument, however, fails regardless of how one conceives of the Second Amendment right. As defined by the Court in 2008, the Second Amendment is not connected with militia or military service. As defined historically, citizen acquisition of military-style weapons would only come into play for (1) militia members who (2) would be called up to serve in a government-organized militia and (3) if those individuals had to obtain their own weapons instead of relying on government issue.

ASSAULT WEAPONS AND CRIME?

A key element of the debate over assault weapons is whether they pose any actual threat or use in crime. Here, too, the picture is mixed. As critics of assault gun regulation correctly note, the vast majority of gun crimes—about 80 percent—are committed with handguns, not long guns (although some handguns fall into the assault weapon category), even though, of the nation's roughly 300 million firearms in civilian hands, two-thirds of them are long guns, and long guns are generally easier to obtain.[73] In 1994 only about 1.5 million assault weapons were estimated to be in private hands; before the federal ban, between 2 and 8 percent of gun crimes were committed with assault weapons—a larger-than-proportionate percentage but still a fairly small number. Large-capacity bullet magazines (also restricted by the law to those holding ten bullets or less), however, were often used in gun crimes—about 20 percent.[74]

The federal assault weapons ban provides the closest approximation to a real-world experiment on such a measure, and here again, critics note correctly that the ban was not correlated with any overall decline in crime or in gun crime. But critics overstated the case when they claimed during congressional testimony in 2013, for example, that studies "proved" the law to be ineffective or a failure.[75] The three studies of the effects of the law referenced by both critics and supporters were conducted by independent researchers from the University of Pennsylvania, headed by Christopher Koper. While the final report said that "we cannot clearly credit the ban with any of the nation's recent drop in gun violence," the report also noted that such weapons "account for a higher share of guns used in murders of police and mass public shootings." It noted the express purpose of the assault weapons ban: to "reduce gunshot victimizations" by limiting the availability of weapons and features that "enable shooters to discharge many shots rapidly" and other features "conducive to criminal use."[76] It also found that in a study of crime in selected cities, the proportion of gun crimes using assault weapons declined an average of 45 percent during the period of the ban.[77] The researchers concluded that the effects of the law lagged behind its enactment (partly because of the law's limitations), meaning that its effects took several years to yield results, and that while the ban apparently did have some effect, the "most important part of the semiautomatic assault weapons ban . . . is probably the restriction on large ammunition magazines. . . ."[78]

After the expiration of the ban in 2004, police organizations (which have largely supported the law and its renewal) reported an increase in the use of assault weapons in crime and by drug gangs[79] and in an escalation in what has become increasingly prolific weapons trafficking between the United States and Mexico. In fact, a recent empirical study has found that such weapons trafficking was significantly greater in border states that imposed no restrictions on assault weapons (Arizona, New Mexico, Texas) than in California, which has had a ban in place since 1989. The researchers estimate that the expiration of the federal assault weapons ban resulted in an average of 239 additional deaths annually in Mexican communities located near the U.S. border after 2004.[80]

The other area where assault weapons have played a greater role is in police shootings. Using FBI data, the Violence Policy Center reported that from 1998 to 2001, 41 of 211 police officers (20 percent) killed in the line of duty with firearms were shot with assault weapons (in all, 224 police officers during this period were killed in the line of duty from all causes).[81] Data from 2009 found that of 45 officers killed by firearms nationwide, 8 (18 percent) were shot with assault weapons.[82] While this represents a minority of all police gun deaths, it is a far higher proportion than that of assault weapons in society. These results are also consistent with anecdotal information from police organizations and the widely noted popularity of assault weapons with gangs.

WHAT ABOUT MASS SHOOTINGS?

Much of the debate over assault weapons has been driven by high-profile, horrific mass shootings. While small in number, they have shocked the nation's sensibilities for their seemingly random nature and degree of destruction. And not without reason: even though such shootings in the last fifty years represent a small fraction of 1 percent of all murders, according to several studies of mass shootings, they have increased since the 1990s[83] (some argue that they have not declined, based on how these events are counted[84])—at the very time when crime in virtually every category, including murder, has been declining.[85] A 2014 study by the FBI reported that mass shootings rose sharply from 2007 to 2013, with an average of 16.4 such shootings per year during this period, compared with an average of 6.4 mass shootings from 2000 to 2006.[86]

Indeed, among those that have garnered the greatest national attention—such as the Stockton, California, elementary school shooting in 1989; the Columbine High School shooting in 1999; the Aurora, Colorado, movie theater shooting in 2012; and the Sandy Hook Elementary School shooting also in 2012—all involved the use of assault weapons. Yet the firearms used most frequently in mass shootings were handguns (some of which could be counted in the assault weapons category). An intensive study of all mass shootings (defined as those where four or more persons were killed) from 1982 to 2012 identified 62 such events. Of the 143 firearms used in these events, 50 percent were semi-automatic handguns (another 14 percent were revolvers); 34 percent of them were assault weapons that would have been banned under the 2013 assault weapons ban proposed by Senator Feinstein.

In terms of the number of shooting incidents rather than number of guns, 75 percent of the sixty-two mass shootings involved semi-automatic handguns, 87 percent had handguns of some type, and over a third of them had assault weapons.[87] By either measure, handguns play a major role[88] (about comparable to their use in all gun crimes), but assault weapons play a disproportionately large role, as compared with all gun crimes or as compared with all guns in society (assault weapons represent a little over 1 percent of all guns; see the discussion that follows). Thus, the connection between mass shootings and assault weapons—and the use of high-capacity bullet magazines, which were employed in half of all mass shootings[89]—is significant. Aside from the weapons used, it is also important to point out that while such mass shootings are rare, they possess other very distinctive traits that distinguish them from other violent crime—traits that suggest that more could be done to identify and therefore thwart at least some of them. Both the thirty-year and fifty-year studies of mass shooters found that more than half of the perpetrators had histories of significant serious diagnosed mental illness (such as schizophrenia, paranoia, or delusions) and that these problems were known to family and friends of the killers; they were more likely to have a military background; they were overwhelmingly white males; they had recently undergone a stressful event like a job loss or relationship breakup; the events they committed were planned, not impulsive (most murders are relatively impulsive acts); nearly two-thirds gave clear warnings to others that they were contemplating serious violence; they were most likely to kill strangers (also a departure from most murders); and the fifty-year study reported that at least 55 percent of the perpetrators either killed themselves, tried to do so, or were killed by police, while the thirty-year study reported a combined suicide plus likely "suicide by cop" rate of 70 percent.[90]

CONCLUSION: BACK TO THE CONSTITUTION

This extended look at the assault weapons ban seems to have taken us away from the Constitution / Second Amendment question, but it, in fact, returns us to that very matter. Drawing on the *Heller* standards described earlier, four related regulatory criteria from the ruling could apply to the regulation of assault weapons: long-standing gun regulations with historical provenance, the regulation of commercial sales, firearms deemed dangerous or unusual, and those not typically possessed by civilians (i.e., militarily useful weapons).

Before getting to these criteria, some post-*Heller* challenges have been mounted against assault weapons bans in the states. To date, these laws have withstood constitutional challenges. The California court of appeals upheld that state's assault weapons ban in 2009, citing the *Heller* "dangerous or unusual" standard, concluding that the California ban did not obstruct the Second Amendment right.[91] The ruling was upheld on appeal. After the District of Columbia lost in *Heller*, it changed its regulations, which included an assault weapons ban. In the second *Heller* case (called *Heller II*), the federal D.C. Circuit upheld the city assault weapons ban, concluding that it was consistent with D.C.'s efforts at crime control and did not limit citizens' ability to exercise their right to bear arms for personal self-protection.[92] An assault weapons ban in Cook County, Illinois (the county encompassing Chicago), faced a Second Amendment–based challenge in state court. In 2012 that state's supreme court rejected other bases for challenging the law but was inconclusive on the right-to-bear-arms challenge, as the court did not feel that it had enough information about whether assault weapons were sufficiently distinct to warrant the regulation in question, based on the criteria found in *Heller* and *Heller II*. It sent the case back to the lower court for further proceedings.[93]

As these cases suggest, the fierce debate over the military provenance of modern assault weapons addresses at least two of these criteria. Without question, contemporary assault weapons derive from military weapons dating to World War II. Efforts by organizations like the NRA and the NSSF to deny this provenance amount to little more than political damage control. Assault weapons available on the civilian market today are modified, as they are limited to semi-automatic-only firing, although they are now available in a wide range of configurations and styles. They are typically made with interchangeable parts, such that they may possess only one or two of the traits that define assault weapons by law, all the way to those that are nearly identical to military weapons that are now legal since the lapse of the 2004 federal law. Weapons manufacturers have, of course, done this deliberately, to obfuscate the line between military and civilian (in part, to complicate and perhaps thwart any future regulatory schemes), to illustrate (and contribute to) the practical problem of defining assault weapons as distinct from other types of weapons, to avoid either actual or anticipated restrictions imposed by the federal government or the states, and of course to market and sell as many (and generate as much profit) as possible—which is, after all, the purpose of a for-profit company in a capitalist system. Leaving the military provenance aside, not all military weapons are by any means beyond the bounds of civilian access; for example, a semi-automatic handgun, long standard issue in the military,[94] is a type of weapon expressly protected under *Heller.*

But are assault weapons unusually destructive—that is, "dangerous or unusual"? If widespread criminal use of the weapons is a key criterion, the answer, as best as can be determined, is "no," with three specific but notable exceptions: use by criminal and drug gangs, use against police, and use in mass shootings. One may argue that these exceptions are too narrow to justify nationwide regulations, given that all these killings, taken together, amount to a statistical percentage of all firearm-related injuries and deaths that is vanishingly small. Yet each poses special public safety concerns, because the behavior of gangs—a type of organized crime—is typified by its organized nature and potential to control segments of society through the systematic use of terror and force—a frontal assault on civil society and on the government's monopoly on the use of force, as discussed in Chapter 1. The killing of police warrants special concern because lethal attacks against police are not just murders but murders of the frontline agents of the government (like attacks against judges and prosecuting attorneys), who are charged with enforcing the laws that govern modern society and therefore make it habitable. Criminal law consistently penalizes the murder of police and other law enforcement / criminal justice officials as an even more serious offense than other murders. Mass shootings are unusually heinous precisely because of their mass nature and because they often involve children, to whom society seeks to extend extra protections, or other innocents. Mass shootings are also an assault against the public, not merely against individuals, which is a key reason why they are viewed with special horror by the public. Indeed, these three categories of crimes invoke an assault on the power and authority of government of the sort discussed in Chapter 1 and the line of democratic theory spanning Bodin, Locke, and Weber. Thus, a reasonable case (although not necessarily a definitive case) can be made to buttress assault weapon restrictions because of their consequences for these targeted populations.

The relative ubiquity of assault weapons in civilian society also merits attention. As noted earlier, significant civilian sales of these weapons only became notable in the late 1980s. By 1994 there were an estimated 1.5 million in circulation. Today, there are no precise statistics on how many are in circulation, largely because no such counts are maintained (and also because of varying definitions of what weapons belong in this category). A ballpark number of roughly 4 million assault weapons in civilian hands in 2012 has been offered up by a variety of sources—a little over 1 percent of all guns in the U.S.[95] Clearly, assault weapons have sold briskly in recent years and have even become top-selling;[96] prices have shot up, and manufacturers have been having difficulty keeping up with demand, generated in part by the concern that such weapons might be subject to restriction in the future, and as a political act in reaction to Barack Obama's moves in support of stronger gun measures and similar moves in a number of states. Even so, these brisk sales still represent a tiny fraction—a little over 1 percent—of all guns in America. These numbers belie hyped claims that assault weapons are "the most popular rifle in America,"[97] as compared with 200 million long guns already in circulation (although assault weapons probably do rank high in recent new gun sales). The problem is that popularity is defined by recent sales figures (in the range of several million), not as a proportion of total guns in society (300 million in all), where the vast majority of guns owned and used have been in circulation for a long time. Given that assault weapons' civilian ownership dates to the 1960s, that measurable ownership dates to the late 1980s, and that as of 2012, only about 4 million such weapons were owned by civilians, it would seem a stretch to argue that their availability is either long-standing or widespread, even given the concerted effort, for sales and political reasons, to spread such guns into society as widely as possible. On the other hand, assault weapons sales have shot up in recent years, and assault weapons have recently led all new gun sales. In the absence of any agreed-upon definition of guns in "common use," this is at least a plausible argument.

The "common use" metric raises at least one other question: does the government ever use a similar standard in determining whether to regulate other consumer products?

The answer to that question is beyond the scope of this discussion, but one is hard pressed to think of any other examples.

Regarding the "dangerous and unusual" and historical provenance standards, as Chapter 2 discussed, up to ten states enacted laws as early as the 1920s that barred semiautomatic weapons (see Table 2.2), in addition to barring fully automatic weapons, precisely on the argument that both fully automatic and semi-automatic weapons were similarly dangerous and used too frequently by gangsters and other lawbreakers. So, for example, in 1927 Michigan barred any weapon that fired more than sixteen times without reloading (covering both semi- and fully auto); Minnesota in 1933 outlawed "any firearm capable of automatically reloading after each shot is fired, whether firing singly by separate trigger pressure or firing continuously by continuous trigger pressure."[98] On the other hand, most states moved to bar fully automatic weapons only. Civilian access to fully automatic weapons was regulated by national law in 1934.

Finally, returning to the core holding in *Heller*—the use of firearms, and specifically handguns, for personal self-protection in the home—recent efforts to argue that semi-automatic assault weapons are well suited for home defense needs are contradicted by the very fact that the primary reason cited for handgun ownership is personal self-defense, a rationalization not chiefly applicable to the purchase of long guns, including assault weapons (despite a recent furious campaign to argue that weapons like the AR-15 are, in fact, good for home self-defense). In general, assault weapons purchasers typically cite their use for target shooting, small game or pest hunting, and recreation, not personal self-defense. Further, the ability of assault weapons to receive large-capacity magazines, cited by some as a capability for enhancing personal self-defense,[99] is already available for semi-automatic handguns that also can receive magazines holding up to thirty bullets. And some argue that the Supreme Court's recent Second Amendment rulings buttress the case for the constitutionality of an assault weapons ban.[100]

This argument is supported by not only the history of semi-automatic rifle regulation but also the math of both the 1994 law and the 2013 assault weapons bill described earlier. By the terms of the 1994 law, access was restricted to a total of roughly 60 types of weapons—but the law also specifically exempted from restriction 661 other named types of weapons, meaning that fewer than 10 percent of guns mentioned in the legislation were subject to restriction. The 2013 bill proposed barring over 150 weapons, but exempted 2258, meaning that the restriction rate was about 7 percent. Between the two measures, with 90 to 93 percent of guns available by law to civilians, as well as innumerable types of handguns specifically protected by *Heller*, it is difficult to mount any argument that any citizen's right of self-protection through the acquisition and use of a gun would be infringed or inhibited by an assault weapons ban.

Many in the gun community share some disdain for assault weapons, especially in connection with traditional hunting/sporting activities, where, according to one sportsman, "Hunting is taking one shot. It's not pumping round after round."[101] A well-known hunter and sportsman, Jim Zumbo, incurred the ire of many in the gun community when he wrote about assault weapons' use in hunting. Writing on his *Outdoor Life* blog in 2007 (he was hunting editor for the publication), he said of AR and AK-type weapons, "I see no place for these weapons among our hunting fraternity. . . . [T]hese have no place in hunting. . . . I've always been comfortable with the statement that hunters don't use assault rifles. We've always been proud of our 'sporting firearms.' "[102] In the wake of a furious reaction to his comments, Zumbo promptly lost his television show, magazine deals, and sponsors. Some sportspeople came to his defense, however, and he eventually returned to television.[103]

Yet this gets to what may be the chief reason, or set of reasons, for the desire by many to own assault weapons, especially those that more closely resemble classic military weapons. These are reasons that have nothing to do with the Second Amendment as law, or personal self-protection, or any special utility in connection with hunting. While these other reasons are often mentioned in passing, they are rarely offered as express justification for opposing assault weapons restrictions.

The reasons are, first, assault weapon acquisition as a political statement or form of political expression. Many have noted that spikes in firearms sales in recent years, specifically in assault weapons, have been keyed to both the election cycle (specifically the election and reelection of Barack Obama in 2008 and 2012) and, ironically, mass shootings. Both events have been tied to popular revulsion over shooting incidents and the increasing prospect of greater gun regulation. The very purchase of guns, especially assault weapons, is a way for some gun owners to express through their purchases their belief that such purchases should remain legal and unregulated and that guns themselves are not the problem, as well as their opposition to Obama. In fact, these sales patterns have been referred to as "political sales" by industry analysts.[104]

Second, some purchasers of these weapons do so simply because they can. While the politicized environment surrounding talk of regulation invokes, in part, a political response, it also attracts those who are enticed by the controversy surrounding such weapons simply because of the controversy, especially concerning those firearms that were illegal to own from 1994 to 2004. Imagine, for example, if the government announced that the speed limit on interstate highways would be raised for 24 hours from 65 to 120 miles per hour. Undoubtedly, some enthusiastic or curious drivers would be immediately inspired to test out the new law, for the sheer sake of the experience and the thrill of doing something that is normally illegal. While such driving would be, at the least, less than prudent (automobile accidents are more likely and more serious at higher speeds), the very fact of a brief window of opportunity would attract many. The once-forbidden fruit of assault weapons holds some similar appeal to gun owners. If it's legal, why not buy one? Or as one gun dealer recently noted about sales of the AR-15 assault weapon: "When you tell the American public that they're not going to have something, they want it."[105]

The third reason appears everywhere,[106] yet provokes relatively little sustained attention. To a certain segment of the gun-owning public, assault weapons, especially those with larger-capacity magazines, are sheer fun to shoot. The owner of an AR-15 commented to the *New York Times* recently that he found firing it to be "very stress-relieving."[107] Accounts of shooting events at firing ranges invariably underline the fact that some gun owners derive great satisfaction and pleasure from firing multiple rounds rapidly. One such account of a range in Arizona reported that participants found the experience "just *so much fun*," "so much fun to shoot," and an experience on which people get "hooked." Even the author of the article, a professional female journalist who had little exposure to firearms, concluded her extended narrative of the experience with her own weapons firing, saying, "Man, was that fun."[108] Much of this "fun" writing invokes not only implicit but also explicit expressions of male sexuality.[109]

Groups at the forefront of the political conflict over gun regulation note the fun factor as well. The NSSF information card discussed earlier lists as a "Modern Sporting Rifle Fact" that "they are a lot of fun to shoot!" In fact, an NSSF survey of gun owners reported that the most frequently cited reason for owning an assault weapon, which the NSSF carefully relabels a "modern sporting rifle," is recreational shooting.[110] Legal writer Adam Winkler disdains the notion of regulating assault weapons, in part, by stating that assault weapons are a type of gun "that millions of American gun enthusiasts love to shoot."[111] Even a hard-bitten reporter like Craig Whitney of the *New York Times*, in his book on gun control in America, admits: "I can attest that AK-47 'assault weapons' are great fun to shoot at a firing range."[112] Little wonder that gun enthusiasts refer to assault weapons, especially the AR's, as "Barbie Dolls for men"[113] (dolls, popular with girls for decades, that include innumerable interchangeable outfits).

The three aforementioned reasons cited on behalf of civilian assault weapon ownership—to make a political statement, because it is possible to own it, and because it's fun—are perfectly legitimate in their own right. But they amount to little more than the elevation of personal preference. Dramatic invocations of constitutional rights, American heritage, or direly expressed needs related to self-defense, on the other hand, have more cachet in this or any national debate. But when it comes to assault weapons, those arguments are mostly posturing to conceal a much more narrow, self-satisfying, pedestrian motivation, and that is why gun rights spokespeople, when asked to comment after the latest mass shooting committed with an assault weapon, will never say that such weapons should remain legal because they're so much fun to shoot.

One final component of this regulatory picture merits attention: large-capacity magazines. The case for constitutional regulation (and, arguably, political consensus) here is even stronger, since any and all weapons can still operate with magazines that hold fewer rather than more bullets, because bullet-feeding devices were widely and routinely regulated back to the nineteenth century (see the previous chapter), because larger-capacity magazines have been used commonly in mass shootings, and because the arguments on behalf of civilian possession of larger-capacity magazines are, at best, weak. Aside from absolutist arguments that any gun regulation violates the Second Amendment, opponents of magazine regulation argue that shooters can rapidly and easily interchange multiple magazines with smaller capacities (e.g., three ten-round magazines vs. one thirty-round magazine), inferring that a larger-capacity magazine really makes no difference.

This argument scarcely withstands scrutiny, as it does not offer a reason against restricting access to them but merely proposes that it makes no difference. Yet their prolific use in mass shootings undercuts that assertion: If larger magazines made no difference, why would mass shooters prefer them? By definition, the prospect of more shots fired and fired with greater rapidity raises the degree of mayhem in any shooting. Moreover, the exchanging of empty for full magazines can be done with efficiency in practice, but it still takes time and a modicum of skill. Some instances of mass shootings ended when the shooters were set upon when changing clips, such as the Long Island commuter railroad shooting in 1993 and the shooting of Representative Gabrielle Giffords in Arizona in 2011.[114] In

2013 Giffords's husband Mark Kelly (a former Navy captain and astronaut) offered this account of his wife's shooting:

> The shooter in Tucson showed up with two 33-round magazines, one of which was in his 9 millimeter. He unloaded the contents of that magazine in 15 seconds. Very quickly. It all happened very, very fast. The first bullet went into Gabby's head. Bullet number 13 went into a nine-year-old girl named Christina Taylor Green, who was very interested in democracy and our government, and really deserved a full life committed to advancing those ideas. If he had a 10-round magazine—well, let me back up. When he tried to reload one 33-round magazine with another 33-round magazine, he dropped it. And a woman named Patricia Maisch grabbed it, and it gave bystanders time to tackle him. I contend if that same thing happened when he was trying to reload one 10-round magazine with another 10-round magazine, meaning he did not have access to a high-capacity magazine, and the same thing happened, Christina Taylor Green would be alive today.[115]

Further, in a live shooting situation, shooters often succumb to the tension and confusion of the moment and take extra time, fumble, or drop a magazine (as did the man who shot Giffords) or commit other errors that open the door to intervention. Even some gun rights supporters draw the line at large-capacity magazines. As one such writer, otherwise critical of the assault weapons ban, mused: "Can anyone think of a really good reason to have a magazine that holds more than 10 rounds?"[116] Even for military use, American soldiers are issued 30-round magazines for their semi-automatic rifles (formerly, they were issued 20-round magazines).[117] This question came to the fore most dramatically in a 2012 Colorado movie theater shooting, where the shooter used an assault weapon with a legally obtained 100-round bullet magazine (drum) to kill 12 and wound 58. As one gun rights writer, otherwise dubious about gun regulations, concluded: "Personally, I see no justification for the sale to civilians of the sort of 100-round drum magazine employed by the Aurora movie theater killer."[118] And as for firepower, instead of entering the Colorado movie theater with an assault weapon and a semi-automatic handgun with a large-capacity clip, suppose he had instead fired a bolt-action rifle (a firearm that requires two hands in order to advance the next round) and a six-shot revolver? Chapter 5 of this book examines the case of New York State, which has recently strengthened its assault weapons ban. It confronts many of the arguments discussed here.

The next chapter extends this analysis to the specific and central issue that lies at the core of Second Amendment rights: self-defense. Yet this concept has not been immutable in our history. While it has existed in law for centuries, self-defense has evolved in ways that bear directly on the intersection of guns and self-protection and interpersonal violence. In recent years, that definition has changed significantly, dramatically, counterintuitively, and ahistorically.

CHAPTER 4

Stand Your Ground: How Did We Get from Self-Defense to Shoot First?

The man who stood accused of murder was firm in his defense: "I enjoyed helping a friend if I could. I would rather be considered a vigilante. . . ."[1] By way of explanation, he added, "I was always taught to take care of my family and my friends. Family and friends come first. My father always taught me that." A vigilante, he said, was "somebody that would hurt somebody that was doing wrong." His favorite gun, he said, was a snub-nose .38 revolver, because it slipped conveniently into and out of his pocket. Under questioning, the man was asked, "Is there any honor and integrity in what you did?" "I thought so," he replied.[2]

Another man, in another shooting incident at another time, offered a very different explanation for why he shot four men: "I wanted to kill those guys. I wanted to maim those guys. I wanted to make . . . them suffer in every way I could."[3]

The man in the first case was John Martorano, a career criminal referred to as "The Executioner," who was testifying against another accused gangster, James "Whitey" Bulger, at Bulger's 2013 trial. Bulger, Boston's reputed crime boss during the 1970s and 1980s, had eluded capture for years. While Bulger stood accused of killing at least 19 people during his nefarious career (he was convicted of 11 murders), Martorano was no saint, having admitted to at least 20 murders himself. Yet in a 2008 interview, a news correspondent reported this: "If you believe Martorano— and the Justice Department does—he killed out of a sense of loyalty and duty. He sees himself as a stand-up guy, a man of his word. . . ."[4]

The man who told authorities that he wanted to kill and maim "those guys" was neither a felon nor a murderer. While riding a New York City subway in December 1984, Bernhard Goetz was approached by four teenage African American males, one of whom asked him for $5. Goetz, who had been injured in a mugging three years earlier, had started carrying an unlicensed handgun. Feeling threatened by the men and convinced that they planned to attack him, Goetz pulled out his gun and shot at all four (even though, by his own admission, he could have avoided a confrontation). Apparently missing one, he approached that man, saying, "You seem to be doing all right, here's another" whereupon he fired a bullet into the man, which paralyzed him for life. Goetz, dubbed the "Subway Vigilante," was tried on four counts of attempted murder (all four survived) but was acquitted by a New York jury in 1987. He was, however, found guilty of illegal weapons possession and served six months in prison.[5] In the aftermath of a 2012 shooting in Florida by a neighborhood watch volunteer, George Zimmerman, many drew parallels between him and Goetz; Zimmerman shot (but killed) an unarmed African

American teenager whom Zimmerman claimed posed a direct and dire threat to him (more on the Zimmerman case later).[6]

No one would confuse professional hitmen and career criminals with average citizens who, for more honorable reasons, would use violence—even lethal violence—to protect themselves or others. Yet Martorano's less-than-persuasive justification for his killings bears an all-too-close resemblance to the justifications often heard from those who use violence in instances they claimed justified their actions. Goetz was dubbed a vigilante by the media; Martorano claimed the vigilante label for himself, in a likely effort to cast his nefarious actions in a more positive light. But at least two important lessons emerge from these very different cases: first, self-defense claims are often defined by the person's own perceptions of danger and the need to use force; second, in the real world, it is often difficult to discern anything resembling full, unambiguous truth.

This chapter examines the antecedents and development of what has come to be known as the "stand your ground" defense, which condones the use of force, including lethal force, by individuals in public places who feel threatened. While the idea seems to be as old as America, it did not receive systematic legal blessing until the end of the nineteenth century. Some states retained stand your ground for people in public places, while others emphasized the principle of safe retreat, meaning that a person feeling threatened in a public place had a legal (and arguably moral) obligation to avoid violence if it was possible to do so without injury. The stand your ground principle arose as an extension of the "Castle Doctrine," an old legal principle protecting the right of people to meet force with force if attacked within their own home rather than leave their home.

While stand your ground would seem to be largely a vestige of a bygone, romanticized version of Old West justice, the principle has not only persisted in many states but also in 2005 was expanded, first in Florida, and then in roughly half of the states, thanks to vigorous pressure from gun rights organizations and a little-known corporate-funded group that advances conservative state laws called ALEC. The purpose and consequences of this change—coming at a time when the need for stand your ground had receded, not advanced—have little or nothing to do with legal inequities in the administration of self-defense cases and much to do with gun politics. Here, as in the other subjects examined in this book, romanticized, if not fictionalized, versions of America's past eclipse reality. Integral to this notion is its questioning of government authority, as discussed in Chapter 1. Americans have a long tradition of suspicion of an overweening government, but the modern translation of that tradition contradicts, more than conforms with, our own past.

THE EMERGENCE OF SELF-DEFENSE

Murder is the worst crime.[7] The taking of another life has been considered among the ultimate and most serious of crimes since ancient times. Among the biblical Ten Commandments, "Thou shalt not kill" is not the only prohibited act on the list, but it is the one that carries societies' strongest opprobrium.[8] In the eighteenth century, the great British jurist William Blackstone referred to "destroying" a life as "the principal crime or public wrong that can be committed against a private subject. . . ."[9] As one modern text notes, "To be free of physical attack is of paramount value to all members of society. The right to life and physical security is the matrix of all the other inalienable rights of a person."[10]

Yet there are exceptions to the prohibition against taking another life. First and foremost, the government retains a monopoly on the use of deadly force. This principle has long been understood to be a cornerstone feature in the development of the modern state, as discussed in Chapter 1.[11] As the sociologist and political thinker Max Weber noted, "A state is a human community that (successfully) claims the *monopoly of the legitimate use of physical force* within a given territory."[12] A police officer may take a life in the line of duty if the circumstances warrant (a power subject to constraints and checks to prevent abuse), or the state may take the life of a person convicted of a crime sufficiently heinous to warrant the ultimate penalty, based on the state authority that stands behind these acts. In the words of Henry C. Black, this power arises from "the sovereign right of a government to promote order, safety, security, health, morals and general welfare within constitutional limits and is an essential attribute of government."[13]

State power aside, the taking of another life is also allowable when the circumstances involve a legitimate claim of self-defense to an individual if the threat to the defender is considered sufficiently dire and great. As the legal thinker H. L. A. Hart wrote, "Killing in self-defence is an exception to a general rule making killing punishable; it is admitted because the policy or aims which in general justify the punishment for killing (e.g. protection of human life) do not include cases such as this."[14] Self-defense, even if clearly established, was not always a kind of legal safe haven. In Britain, in fact, "the right to kill in self-defense was slowly established, and is a doctrine of modern rather than of medieval law."[15] Yet even by the time of King Henry VII at the start of the

1500s, those found to have killed in self-defense were still convicted of murder but were also routinely pardoned by the monarch.

By the time of Blackstone, self-defense was well established as a valid defense in law, but it was treated differently than justifiable homicide, which pertained to a killing to advance, or in the name of, government justice (even by private citizens under certain circumstances). Self-defense cases, according to Blackstone, are "excusable, rather than justifiable. . . . This right of natural defence does not imply a right of attacking. . . . They cannot therefore exercise this right of preventive defence but in sudden and violent cases, when certain and immediate suffering would be the consequence of waiting for the assistance of the law . . . it must appear that the slayer had no other possible (or at least probable) means of escaping from his assailant."[16] One might well ask why a person claiming self-defense would not be treated in the same way as someone committing a justifiable homicide, since the very self-defense claim, if sustained, is predicated on the idea that a crime—perhaps the murder of the survivor—was thwarted or stopped. The key reason, as Blackstone noted, was because "both parties may be, and usually are, in some fault, and it scarce can be tried who was originally in the wrong."[17] As a contemporary legal analyst noted, "Homicide in self-defense rarely arises without fault on both sides."[18]

Because of the ambiguity too often found in real-life self-defense cases, the British tradition emphasized a valid self-defense claim as one where the individual could only invoke self-defense if two conditions applied: the encounter was in some manner necessary, and safe escape or retreat was not possible. The purpose was to ensure, to the extent possible, that the only alternative to the violent confrontation giving rise to the self-defense claim was itself serious injury or death.[19]

THE CASTLE DOCTRINE EXCEPTION

The one circumstance where a person attacked need not abide by the retreat rule was when attacked in his or her dwelling, where "he might defend his castle against felonious attack without retreating from it, since that would be to give up the protection of a 'castle,' which the law allows him."[20] The reference to one's castle is the medieval equivalent of one's home today, giving rise to the familiar expression, appearing as early as the 1600s in a British court case, that "a man's home is his castle."[21] Contrary to the common contemporary impression, the special status accorded the home in this doctrine did not arise from any belief that a person's homestead or possessions were of such value that they merited the use of violence to protect them (although such a notion did emerge later), but rather because a person's home was the ultimate refuge of a person attempting to escape harm or avoid conflict; thus, with a person who has "retreated to the wall" of, in this case, the home, an attack against an aggressor there merited special protection under the self-defense doctrine.[22] By the early seventeenth century, a British court ruled in *Seyman's Case*:

> That the house of everyone is to him as his castle and fortress, as well for his defence against injury and violence, as for his repose; and although the life of man is a thing precious and favoured in law so that, although a man kills another in his defence, or kills one *per infortunium* [by misfortune] without any intent, yet it is felony, and in such case he shall forfeit his goods and chattels for the great regard which the law has to a man's life, but if thieves come to a man's house to rob him, or murder, and the owner or his servants kill any of the thieves in defence of himself and his house it is not felony, and he shall lose nothing. . . .[23]

While the British legal tradition played a key role in the development of American law on this and many other subjects, American self-defense law soon diverged in important respects from that of Britain. Values of individualism, the persistent strain of antigovernment sentiment, actual and fanciful notions of behavior in America's unsettled western lands, and the "true man" doctrine all contributed to elevation of the notion that citizens had a right to meet force with force not only in their home, but even in public places—and without the need to retreat (an option viewed by some as cowardly and therefore incompatible with the behavior of a right-thinking American). Lest the phrase "true man" be misunderstood, it is not a reference to some kind of John Wayne–like heroic figure but rather to individuals with clean legal records who have not run afoul of the law or are free from legal fault. The phrase is akin to a similar old-fashioned expression, "good men and true," a phrase from the Middle Ages referring to those eligible to serve on a jury.[24]

In the late nineteenth century, courts in many states issued a series of rulings that projected the Castle Doctrine principle into public places, concluding that the "true man" (what today might be labeled an "honest man" or a "good guy"[25]) had a right to defend himself in public without need to retreat if he had a right to be where he was.[26] Historian Richard Maxwell Brown referred to this change in American legal doctrine as "a proud new tolerance for killing in situations where it might have been avoided by obeying a legal duty to retreat." Brown's verdict about the effect of this change was that it "undoubtedly had an impact on our homicide rate, helping to make it the highest on earth among our peer group of the modern, industrialized nations of the world."[27]

The many state court rulings[28] beginning in the late 1800s that grappled with applying the stand your ground versus safe retreat options for violent interpersonal confrontations outside of the home contributed to several Supreme Court rulings. In *Beard v. U.S.* (1895),[29] the Supreme Court overturned a lower court ruling upholding the conviction of a man, Babe Beard, who had killed another by whom he felt threatened while the man was on Beard's property (though not in his house). In this instance, the High Court decision rejected the notion that Beard had a duty to retreat from his own property. In *Allen v. U.S.* (1896),[30] the Supreme Court concluded that a man attacked by another could defend himself lawfully, even to the extent of killing the other person, if he felt in danger of losing his life or suffering serious bodily harm "provided he use all the means in his power otherwise to save his own life or prevent the intended harm, such as retreating as far as he can. . . ."[31] Other cases from the High Court around this time seemed to favor a more expansive view of the self-defense privilege as one that could be invoked when defendants were standing their ground in places other than their home or property.[32] In 1921 the Supreme Court again took up a self-defense case in *Brown v. U.S.*[33] In a ringing decision written by Oliver Wendell Holmes, the Court overturned the conviction of a man who had killed another with whom he had had a long-standing feud. The trial judge had instructed the jury that the man had a duty to retreat before killing his assailant (the incident occurred in a public place), and so the jury convicted him. Appeals courts upheld the verdict.

In his opinion, Justice Holmes noted that "the failure to retreat is a circumstance to be considered with all the others" in order to reach a verdict. But, he continued,

"Many respectable writers agree that if a man reasonably believes that he is in immediate danger of death or grievous bodily harm from his assailant he may stand his ground and that if he kills him he has not exceeded the bounds of lawful self-defense."[34] Unlike the *Beard* case, Brown was not on his own property, said Holmes, but nevertheless was "at a place where he was called to be, in the discharge of his duty."[35] (Both men were working on the construction site of a federal post office facility.) While Holmes's decision championing the stand your ground principle would seem at odds with much of his civil liberties jurisprudence, it did reflect a clear expression of the "true man" exhibiting masculine bravery by standing his ground in a public place.[36] In application, this ruling applied to the federal government, not the states.

Yet this view was not, and has not been since, universally embraced. At the start of the twentieth century, only nine states abandoned the safe retreat principle, but even in these nine, an individual making a stand your ground claim had to demonstrate that his or her actions were reasonable. Another fourteen states required individuals to establish that they faced "imminent" threats in confrontations in public places, and eleven states retained safe retreat.[37] In recent decades, state laws did and do continue to be divided on the stand your ground versus safe retreat views of justifiable self-defense in public places. The Model Penal Code of the American Law Institute emphasizes safe retreat over physical confrontation, although the authors also recognize that more jurisdictions around the country have favored some version of standing one's ground as opposed to safe retreat.[38] So things stood until 2005.

ENTER THE HAMMER

Since the early 1980s, the National Rifle Association (NRA) has devoted much of its political resources to advancing its policy goals in state legislatures. The state legislative strategy fit well with the NRA's ability to press its agenda most successfully in a low-visibility way in more conservative jurisdictions, as citizens generally pay less attention to their state governments than they do to national politics (which are the focus of most news coverage) or to local politics, where snow removal, garbage pickup, zoning laws, and many other local government responsibilities affect citizens most directly in their daily lives. Under such circumstances, narrow, focused, low-visibility interest-group pressure can have maximum effect. In addition, the majority of states and therefore state governments are more conservative than the country as a whole because of demography (in particular, more rural and more white) and their political and social traditions.

The NRA's most decisive political victory in the states has been reflected in a sea change in state "concealed carry" laws. In 1981 only two states (Maine and Washington State) had so-called shall issue concealed handgun carry laws on the books, meaning that applicants had little difficulty obtaining a permit to carry a handgun concealed on their person unless something in their record, like a felony conviction, barred the permit. (One state, Vermont, had no permit requirement.) Nineteen states barred concealed carry entirely, and 28 states had "may issue" laws, which gave states great discretion over the issuance of carry permits. As Chapter 2 showed, many of the so-called Wild West states were among those with the toughest concealed carry standards. States that barred concealed carry entirely in 1981 included the "Old West" states of Arkansas,

Arizona, Kansas, Missouri, Nebraska, New Mexico, North Dakota, Oklahoma, Texas, and Wyoming. By 1988, owing to NRA lobbying efforts, "shall issue" laws existed in 9 states. By 2011 (and as of 2014), 36 states had "shall issue" laws, and 4 states had no permit requirements (Alaska, Arizona, Vermont, and Wyoming), with the remaining 10 states and the District of Columbia retaining the stricter "may issue" standard.[39]

In 2005 a Floridian, the former NRA national president Marion Hammer, spearheaded a new initiative—to expand in Florida state law the right of citizens to use deadly force in circumstances where individuals feeling threatened could stand their ground in a public place rather than first seek safe retreat, as Florida law stipulated up to that time. Acting rapidly and with little public fanfare, the measure won ready enactment through the state legislature, despite opposition from police and prosecutors.[40] One indication of the relatively little attention that this effort attracted outside of the state capital was the reaction of the head of the pro–gun control Brady Center to Prevent Gun Violence, Sarah Brady, who said that she was "in absolute shock" over the law's enactment, adding, "If I had known about it, I would have been down there."[41] This extension of the Castle Doctrine to public places was, as we have noted, hardly a new idea. But this new initiative did more.

As Hammer and other bill supporters stated, this legislation was not proposed in response to any pattern of wrongful convictions based on existing state law. In fact, the case of a mistaken shooting in 2004 was the one example offered to justify the need for a new law, even though the man who claimed self-defense was not prosecuted; nevertheless, it proved to be a key impetus to this change. After a hurricane ripped through Florida, a stranger attempted after dark to enter an RV damaged in the storm and owned by

77-year-old James Workman. Workman fired two shots and killed the man, who turned out to be a temporary employee of the Federal Emergency Management Agency (FEMA) who had been checking for looters and homeowners in trouble and who had also been experiencing behavioral problems that seemed to exhibit themselves on the night of the shooting. Workman never hired a lawyer and was cleared of any wrongdoing, but the investigation took three months—a period of time dubbed appallingly long by Florida legislators who allied themselves with Hammer. During legislative debate over the bill, proponents repeatedly cited and misrepresented the facts of the Workman case to imply that the state law needed to be changed.[42]

According to one bill cosponsor, the purpose of the bill was to "curb violent crime and make the citizens of Florida safer" and to support "victims of violent attacks when the law is in their favor."[43] In an article published shortly after the passage of the Florida law, Hammer wrote: "That's what this law is all about: restoring your right under the Castle Doctrine and the Constitution to protect yourself, your family and others. Your home is your castle, and you have a right—as ancient as time itself—to absolute safety in it."[44] As a factual matter, almost none of those things was true about the new law: it did not "restore" a right (more properly, a "privilege" under law), but created a new one for behavior in public places; it did not involve any constitutional protection; the right to self-protection in public places already existed under Florida law;[45] and the initial formulation of the Castle Doctrine pertained to the home, where Florida law already provided appropriate protection and no need to retreat, not public places—ergo its very name.

The selection of Florida as the first state to press for this change in law was neither an accidental nor arbitrary decision: in recent decades, Florida has been highly receptive to the enactment of gun-friendly laws and has been selected by gun rights groups as a kind of testing ground.[46] Still, the success in Florida emboldened the NRA to press its efforts in the other states. As NRA Executive Director Wayne LaPierre said after the bill's enactment, "We will start with red and move to blue"[47] (a reference to conservative "red" states and liberal "blue" states). A few months after Florida acted, the NRA approached the American Legislative Exchange Council (ALEC), a national group of corporate-funded conservatives that drafts and presses for enactment of state laws to advance many conservative causes, to include its new stand your ground law as a model to be pressed in other states. ALEC accepted the proposal; within a year, 8 more states had adopted Florida-style stand your ground laws. And 26 states had adopted similar laws by 2012.[48] (ALEC withdrew its support for stand your ground laws in 2012 as a result of the adverse publicity that followed the Zimmerman–Martin shooting case, discussed next.) Of these states, at least 10 adopted laws almost identical to Florida's.[49]

Advocates of modern stand your ground laws emphasize that their purpose is to protect law-abiding citizens' ability to defend themselves in public places where retreat may be dangerous (especially if an attacker has a gun), that citizens should not have to leave a public place where they have a right to be,[50] and that these laws have been around for a very long time. As the account in this chapter demonstrates, the Castle Doctrine is hundreds of years old, and the stand your ground principle has existed in American law for over a hundred years. So why all the fuss?

STAND YOUR GROUND OR SHOOT FIRST?
THE CASE OF FLORIDA

The answer to the preceding question may be found in the added immunities and protections in the Florida and subsequent similar state laws extended to anyone who makes a self-defense claim in a public place. Above and beyond applying the Castle Doctrine self-defense principle to public areas (the wisdom of which is, at the least, debatable), Florida's 2005 law gives to a person claiming self-defense "an absolute and irrebuttable presumption that an individual who kills or harms another . . . has acted in self-defense and cannot be prosecuted."[51] Law enforcement must thus presume that an individual making a self-defense claim acted out of reasonable fear, a standard met by nothing more than the individual's claim to such a fear. In addition to eliminating the requirement that people feeling threatened in public places must first attempt safe retreat, these two provisions profoundly changed the manner in which Florida's criminal justice system handles such cases. The critical portion of the law from Florida Statutes, Section 776.013(3), states:

> A person who is not engaged in an unlawful activity and who is attacked in any place where he or she has a right to be has no duty to retreat and has the right to stand his or her ground and meet force with force, including deadly force if he or she reasonably believes it is necessary to do so to prevent death or great bodily harm to himself or herself or another or to prevent the commission of a forcible felony.

Note that the standard for establishing a viable self-defense claim is that the person making a self-defense claim after applying violence is the individual's reasonable belief—not externally examined or verified facts (although such information can be introduced later if it is uncovered). In other words, persons who report feeling threatened by "death or great bodily harm" have met the necessary legal standard—even if they could have safely retreated or called the police.

Coupled with this is the law's provision of immunity from "criminal prosecution and civil action for the use of such force" (Section 776.032), which extends to immunity from arrest, custodial detention, and the bringing of charges against the person. According to the Association of Prosecuting Attorneys, this blanket immunity "is greater than the legal protections afforded police officers who are involved in a shooting in the line of duty."[52] Police may not arrest the person in question, according to Section 776.032(2), "unless it determines that there is probable cause that the force that was used was unlawful." As this has played out in such cases, the police are obliged under the law to ask only three questions: whether the defendant had a right to be where he or she was; whether the person was engaged in lawful activity; and whether the person claimed fear of death or imminent bodily harm.[53]

In practical terms, law enforcement is restricted in its ability to conduct an investigation and gather evidence, because police must accept the individual's assertion (bundled with the immunity protection), without the need for corroboration or any actual evidence of an objective threat, that he or she felt threatened. Before the law change, police were not constrained from investigating acts of violence, much less acts that resulted in a person's death. But since such individuals cannot be detained or arrested under the new law, it is difficult for the police to establish probable cause—the basis for proceeding with an investigation. Law enforcement finds itself left to disprove the person's presumption of "reasonable fear" rather than to establish a case; nor can it turn the matter over to prosecutors, judges, or juries. These constraints "can affect how thoroughly police investigate"[54] self-defense claims.

According to Florida lawyers involved in cases after the law took effect, many thought that the stand your ground principle would have a significant impact on trials, with more defendants bringing in a stand your ground defense. Yet that seems not to have been a significant trend. What has been a notable change, according to the former president of the Florida Association of Criminal Defense Lawyers, was this: "The real impact has been that it's making filing decisions difficult for prosecutors. It's causing cases not to be filed at all or to be filed with reduced charges."[55] That view is also shared by prosecutors around the state.[56]

According to Florida state attorney William Meggs, despite the fact that the law is designed to exclude from protection those who are participating in unlawful activity, in practice "defendants engaged in unlawful activity are able to effectively use this law as a shield from prosecution."[57] According to the national Association of Prosecuting Attorneys, the new stand your ground laws have imposed "a barrier to prosecution of genuine criminals." The organization's vice president, Steven A. Jansen, said that "it's almost like we now have to prove a negative—that a person was not acting in self-defense, often on the basis of only one witness, the shooter."[58] Another critic described the effect of the Florida law by saying that it "redefined self-defense—its nature has fundamentally changed. It is no longer an affirmative defense requiring admission of guilt before claiming justification. Rather, the law decriminalizes homicide and other violent acts by declaring certain actors innocent and not culpable for their violent behavior."[59]

While the law in general has an abiding interest in protecting people who legitimately exercise self-protection, the value of protecting human life—traditionally placed on an even higher pedestal—loses its preeminent status under the Florida stand your ground law because the state is impeded in its ability to fully investigate an incident, to the extent that would be otherwise possible, and then turn investigative findings over to prosecutors, who in turn have been less likely to prosecute or prosecute vigorously.[60]

Many cases in Florida and in other states that have adopted this law have emerged which underscore the fears of critics. But no case garnered more attention in the first eight years after the enactment of the Florida law nor did more to draw it to the attention of the nation than the shooting death of a 17-year-old African American teenager, Trayvon Martin, by neighborhood watch volunteer George Zimmerman in 2012.[61]

Zimmerman was patrolling a local neighborhood in Sanford, Florida, on a rainy night in February 2012 when he saw a tall African American male wearing a hooded sweatshirt wandering the neighborhood. When Zimmerman called in the sighting to 911, the dispatcher advised him to remain in his vehicle. Instead, Zimmerman left to follow the person he had seen. Zimmerman was armed with a handgun, which he carried legally (although police authorities urge neighborhood watch volunteers not to carry firearms). Within minutes, the two had some kind of encounter, during which Zimmerman shot and killed Martin with a single bullet to the chest at close range. Martin was unarmed; Zimmerman suffered cuts to his head and face. Martin had been visiting his father in the neighborhood where he had been seen wandering and had gone to a local store to purchase a drink and a bag of candy but had become disoriented in the darkened, unfamiliar neighborhood. Zimmerman was charged with murder but was found not guilty in a jury trial in July 2013.

As many noted, Zimmerman's lawyer did not expressly invoke Florida's stand your ground law in his defense, but rather relied on a classic and standard self-defense claim; however, the new Florida state law had a significant effect on the case from start to finish. First, while Zimmerman was read his Miranda rights and questioned on the night of the shooting, he was not arrested and held, because police are not allowed to do so if there is probable cause that Zimmerman acted in self-defense. Under the law, his claim to such defense, which he made from the start, forestalled that possibility in the absence of substantial contrary evidence (evidence that was not gathered, in part, because of a less-than-full-bore investigation). While we do not know whether Zimmerman lied to the police about his self-defense fears, he surely had an abiding self-interest to lie, as would anyone in such a situation.

Second, news reports noted that the initial police investigation was not as thorough as it could have been (neighborhood canvassing, witness interviewing, crime scene preservation were all considered inadequate, e.g.[62]). While initially attributed to police incompetence or lack of zealousness, it was later attributed, at least in part, to the potency of the self-defense claim as set out in the law and the attendant reluctance of police to proceed with a full-bore investigation under such circumstances. It is also the likely reason the local prosecutor declined to bring any criminal charges against Zimmerman.[63] Charges were eventually brought six weeks after the shooting when the governor named a new prosecutor.

Third, defendants claiming self-defense are entitled to a pretrial immunity hearing; if the court finds the person entitled to immunity, no criminal trial occurs. Even though charges of criminality are at stake at immunity hearings, the legal standard of proof for the defendant is "preponderance of the evidence," a lower legal standard (it is the one used in civil cases) than the higher standard applicable in criminal cases, "beyond a reasonable doubt." The person so granted immunity is also entitled to damages, including all fees, expenses, and lost income. In addition, law enforcement authorities are subject to penalties if they do not prevail, in that they can be held liable for damages (stripping them of the immunity normally shielding law enforcement). In other words, law enforcement faces a heavy price for failing to make its case.[64] In Zimmerman's case, his lawyer decided against seeking a preliminary hearing, instead moving straight to trial to confront the charge of murder or manslaughter. This was seen by legal experts as a shrewd move by Zimmerman's lawyer, because it avoided exposing their case and strategy to the prosecution, which could have then adapted its strategy in the criminal trial. Early exposure of the defense's case would have been moot had the pretrial hearing gone Zimmerman's way, but the political pressures and national attention focused on this case made the likelihood of the case ending at a pretrial hearing remote indeed.[65]

Fourth, the judge's instructions to the jury included the statement that if Zimmerman "was not engaged in an unlawful activity and was attacked in any place where he had a right to be, he had no duty to retreat and had the right to stand his ground and meet force with force, including deadly force if he reasonably believed [it justified]."[66] Lawyer Jonathan Turley, among others, argued that this instruction was not related to stand your ground, because it reflected the common law tradition that countenances such actions in many states (as discussed earlier). Yet before 2005, as noted, Florida law called for safe retreat in public places.

This is clear from the jury instructions read to Florida juries in such cases before the 2005 law change, which included asking whether the defendant "used every reasonable means within his power and consistent with his own safety to avoid the danger before resorting to that force. The fact that the defendant was wrongfully attacked cannot justify his use of force likely to cause death or great bodily harm if by retreating he could have avoided the need to use that force."[67] When that wording was dropped in 2005, it resulted in an important added benefit to Zimmerman's case. And one of the Zimmerman jurors said after the trial that the stand your ground law was a factor in their decision.[68]

Fifth, Florida's law protecting individuals making self-defense claims from civil suits makes such an action by Trayvon Martin's family highly unlikely. Zimmerman can still claim immunity to protect himself from civil action; if a civil suit proceeds, the plaintiff (i.e., the Martin family in this case) must pay the defendant's costs if the plaintiff loses. As one legal expert concluded, "If there is a civil suit filed, it will be dismissed, and future ones will be barred."[69]

Sixth, when a Florida-style stand your ground law is combined with citizens carrying concealed handguns, the circumstances become even more complicated, because in an altercation, it becomes more likely in a state like Florida (which has issued more than a million concealed carry permits and where handgun ownership is higher than other places in the country) that the opponent may also be carrying a gun, and if the survivor believes that the opponent is reaching for a gun—or reaching for that of the survivor—that provides the basis for the perceived fear that the survivor's life was in danger. As one analyst noted, "Since your fear needs [sic] only be reasonable, not correct, a mistaken but reasonable fear that the other person is reaching for a gun legally justifies killing an unarmed person."[70] This was just the set of events described by George Zimmerman. In Florida, at least, the Zimmerman case is not unique. "In case after case" in the first six years after the law's enactment, "Floridians who shot and killed unarmed opponents have not been prosecuted."[71] Voices calling for modification or repeal of Florida's law swelled after the Zimmerman trial, eventually yielding hearings in the Florida state legislature. In late 2013, however, after several hours of committee hearings, an effort to repeal the law failed by a wide margin in a state house committee vote.

While the Zimmerman case might have been taken as a cautionary tale for similar situations in Florida and other states, it seems to have had no effect on either law or behavior. For example, a 47-year-old white man, Michael Dunn, was charged with one count of murder and three counts of attempted murder when Dunn pulled into a gas station in Jacksonville, Florida, in late 2012 next to a vehicle containing four African American teenagers. With loud rap music—what he called "rap crap"—coming from the youths' vehicle, Dunn told them to turn down the music. One did, but another occupant of the car objected and reportedly exchanged words with Dunn, whereupon Dunn retrieved a legally owned handgun from his glove box and shot the teen he was arguing with, hitting him three times and killing him. As the car sped away, he fired seven more rounds. At trial, Dunn claimed that one of the teens had pointed a barrel of a shotgun at him through an open window, but no gun was ever found, and no other shots were fired by anyone other than Dunn. In early 2014 Dunn was convicted of three counts of attempted murder, but the jury failed to deliver a verdict on the murder charge, resulting in a mistrial. Prosecutors sought a new trial on the murder charge, and in late 2014, he was convicted of murder and sentenced to life without parole.[72] In January 2014 a 71-year-old man, Curtis Reeves Jr., and his wife entered a movie theater in the Tampa, Florida, area and sat behind 43-year-old Chad Oulson and his wife. Oulson was texting his babysitter during the movie previews. Reeves tapped Oulson on the shoulder and asked him to stop texting; Oulson refused. Reeves then left the theater but returned. Loud words were exchanged as the men stood, and Oulson apparently threw popcorn at Reeves, whereupon Reeves pulled out his legally owned .380 caliber handgun and shot Oulson once in the chest, killing him. Reeves claimed he had felt threated by Oulson and was just defending himself. Both men were military veterans, and Reeves was a retired Tampa police captain.[73]

In April 2014 a Montana man who had left his garage door opened detected the presence of someone in his garage around midnight thanks to a motion detector. Grabbing his shotgun, 29-year-old Markus Kaarma rushed outside, aimed into the garage, and fired four times, killing a 17-year-old German exchange student, Diren Dede. A second student who had accompanied Dede did not enter the garage. While all agreed that the boy was trespassing and that items had been taken from Kaarma's garage in the past, the law historically would not justify death for the crime of petty theft. But in 2009, Montana adopted a Florida-style stand your ground law. While state law had formerly justified the use of force in one's home if an intruder behaved in a "violent, riotous or tumultuous manner," the 2009 law changed that standard to one where force, including lethal force, is justified as long as the person believes it necessary to prevent an assault.[74] In December 2014, Kaarma was found guilty of deliberate homicide, as he entrapped the victim, and ballistic evidence showed that he was not in danger when he fired the fatal shot.

THE CONSEQUENCES OF STAND YOUR GROUND

The widely followed Zimmerman case illustrates some of the nuances in the Florida law and similar laws in other states. But it is only one case. How has it played out throughout the state?

A Florida newspaper, the *Tampa Bay Times*, conducted an extensive and intensive analysis of self-defense claims in the state following enactment of the 2005 law, identifying almost 200 cases involving self-defense claims. The paper's detailed investigation drew on many sources, including news reports, police reports, court records, and numerous interviews with prosecutors and lawyers. By examining the facts of each case, they were able to make substantive judgments about the circumstances of each. In summary, they found that stand your ground claims were successful 68 percent of the time. In those, 35 percent of claimants were not charged; 23 percent won immunity at an immunity hearing; and 10 percent were acquitted by juries. Of those found guilty, half accepted a plea bargain, and the other half were convicted by a jury. Those making such claims were more likely to be successful if the victim was African American (73 percent) than if the victim was white (59 percent), although in follow-up investigation, the *Times* reported that it found "no obvious bias" in the treatment of African Americans versus whites.[75] Two-thirds of the defendants used guns.

Beyond these numbers, the *Times* found that the law was administered in widely varying ways across the state, such that circumstances where persons were found not guilty in some jurisdictions were convicted in other cases involving virtually identical circumstances. According to the paper, which called these outcome disparities "shocking," defendants who have benefited the most from the stand your ground law have been "those with records of crime and violence": almost 60 percent of those claiming self-defense when a death resulted had been arrested at least once before; about a third had been accused of violent crimes or drug offenses in the past; and over a third had threatened others with a gun in the past or had been found to carry guns illegally. In "dozens" of cases, both the defendant and victim had criminal records. In the prosecution of these cases, the results varied widely from county to county as to whether they resulted in charges, trials, convictions, or acquittals. Defendants with prior criminal records were less likely to have their self-defense claims upheld (59 percent acquitted for those with at least one arrest, and 45 percent acquitted for those with three or more prior arrests).[76]

Aside from this detailed study, a Harvard University researcher drew on the data used by researchers studying stand your ground laws nationwide (see the discussion that follows) to measure the impact of the Florida law on its state homicide rates, but did so by employing different statistical techniques. That study concluded that the enactment of Florida's law not only did not deter homicides but instead resulted in between 1 and 1.5 extra homicides per year from 2006 to 2010.[77]

What about the larger question of the effects of recent stand your ground laws and gun carrying by civilians, across the country? Several studies have sought to shed light on this question.

A study of gun carrying in Philadelphia from 2003 to 2006 set out to examine the connection between being hurt by gunfire in an assault and individuals' possession of a gun at the time of such an injury. According to the results of this case-control study of 1361 gun assaults after controlling for confounding factors, people in possession of a gun were 4.46 times more likely to be shot in an assault than those who were attacked while unarmed. Individuals were 4.23 times more likely to be shot and killed if they were armed than if not. And in instances where the armed person had at least some chance to offer resistance, those individuals were 5.45 times more likely to be shot. The researchers offered several possible reasons for these significantly elevated rates of gun injury and death for those who were themselves armed.

First, the victims may have felt themselves unjustifiably empowered because they were armed, causing them to react or respond more aggressively or recklessly where they might not have had they not been armed. Second, armed individuals may have been more likely to enter dangerous situations or environments that they would have otherwise avoided had they not been armed. Third, some armed individuals may have had their guns stripped from them and then turned against them. Fourth, many of the shootings studied involved participants who had had a prior dispute, so there was both an escalation of arms and a greater proclivity to use them. Fifth, in the smaller number of incidents when the perpetrator was not armed but the victim was, the element of surprise may have worked to the disadvantage of the armed person. And sixth, some shootings occurred when the armed victims had no opportunity to effectively use their firearm, when events happened too suddenly, when they were fired at from a long distance, or even when physical barriers existed between the shooter and the armed victim (e.g., when a bullet passed through a wall). The authors concluded that while successful defensive gun uses do occur annually, "guns did not protect those who possessed them from being shot in an assault" and "the probability of success may be low for civilian gun users in urban areas."[78]

While this study addressed and was critical of the gun carry practices facilitated by Castle Doctrine–type laws, it did not specifically examine the impact of the law changes that occurred in the last decade. But other studies have. An analysis of killings dubbed "justifiable homicides" by the *Wall Street Journal* in 2012 found that, from 2000 to 2010, they nearly doubled. While the nation experienced an average of 16,000 total killings annually during this period (a majority of them from guns), a total of 2285 of those were considered justifiable. On a per capita basis, the annual overall homicide rate declined during this period, whereas justifiable homicides increased 85 percent, from 176 cases in 2000 to 326 cases in 2010. The increase could be the result of more citizens killing each other given the new laws, or they could simply be killings that would have occurred anyway but that are now labeled "justifiable" because of the new laws (or a combination of the two)—except that proposition is contradicted by the slight decline in overall killings over this period. Among the states that enacted Florida-style stand your ground laws, justifiable homicides doubled in Texas and Georgia and tripled in Florida (from an average of 12 per year in the five years before the new law to 33 per year in the five succeeding years). Florida and Texas alone account for a quarter of all justifiable homicides during this ten-year period. On the other hand, in five other states that enacted the new stand your ground laws during this period (Alabama, Kansas, Mississippi, Montana, and West Virginia), justifiable homicide rates did not appreciably change. In Michigan, the rate actually declined. As reported by the *Journal*, homicides are considered justifiable if prosecutors decline to press charges or if a judge or jury concludes that the use of lethal force was warranted as an act of self-defense. The *Journal* also reported that justifiable homicide cases differed from murders in that in the case of the former, the victim and killer were strangers in about 60 percent of the cases, whereas in nonjustifiable cases the victim and killer knew each other in more than 75 percent of the incidents. Firearms were used in over 80 percent of the justifiable killings, compared with 65 percent of unjustifiable killings.[79]

Two researchers from Texas A&M University drew on FBI Uniform Crime Report data from the U.S. Department of Justice to examine the effects of newly enacted stand your ground laws. Their analysis of the period from 2000 to 2010 found no evidence that such laws deterred crimes, including burglary, robbery, or aggravated assault. They did, however, find an increase in the homicide rate of about 8 percent (about 600 additional homicides per year) in states with the new stand your ground laws and an approximate increase in justifiable homicides of between 17 and 50 percent, leading them to conclude that "a primary consequence of castle doctrine laws [when applied to public places] is to increase homicide by a statistically and economically significant" [80] rate. At the same time, they found little evidence that criminals were more likely to carry guns than before the enactment of these laws. In all, they concluded that stand your ground laws reduce the costs associated with the use of lethal force, thereby encouraging more of it.

A 2012 study from the National Bureau of Economic Research applied a variety of statistical techniques to examine the effect of stand your ground laws on homicides and gunshot injuries. Drawing on data from the U.S. Vital Statistics, that study found that the enactment of such laws (looking at those states that enacted more expansive, Florida-style laws, compared with the rest of the country) was associated with a significant increase in homicides, averaging from 336 to 396 additional white male deaths per year, or a 6.8 percent increase in the homicide rate (a figure very close to that found in the Texas A&M study, even though it drew on different data). Statistically speaking, that increase occurs almost entirely among white males (the researchers found no statistical effect on white females, and virtually none among African Americans, either male or female). The authors speculate that the racial disparity may be accounted for by the fact that the overwhelming majority of those with concealed gun carry permits are white males, who are also most likely to own guns and to have purchased more guns in recent years as news of liberalized carry laws and the enactment of stand your ground laws has spread. The researchers conclude that there is "no evidence" that stand your ground laws "result in a reduced number of deaths among citizens in the states that have introduced such laws. On the contrary, these results indicate that the number of firearm related homicides . . . increase significantly as a result of these laws."[81] The study also examined the connection between stand your ground laws and nonfatal firearm injuries and found that stand your ground states experienced higher rates of emergency room admissions and hospitalizations for gunshot wounds than in non–stand your ground states.

A pro-gun control group, Mayors against Illegal Guns, conducted its own detailed analysis of homicide rates in stand your ground states as compared with states without such provisions. Drawing on FBI data, it found a 53 percent increase in justifiable homicides (not in the overall homicide rate) in states that enacted such laws in the years that followed compared with a 5 percent decrease in justifiable homicides in states that did not enact these laws during this period of time. Increases were particularly significant in Arizona, Florida, Georgia, Kentucky, and Texas.[82]

The intersection of race and stand your ground laws was examined in a report by the Urban Institute. Drawing on data from the Supplemental Homicide Reports compiled by the FBI, researcher John Roman found significant racial differences in the adjudication of stand your ground laws. Looking at data on all homicides and all gun homicides from 2005 to 2010 (see Table 4.1), Roman found that when the killer and victim (for all homicides) were both white in non–stand your ground states, the killing was ruled justified in about 1.7 percent of instances; when the shooter was African American and the victim white, the justifiable rate was about 1.1 percent; when the shooter and victim were both African American, the justifiable rate was about 2.1 percent. When the killer was white and the victim black, however, the justifiable rate was 9.5 percent. In stand your ground states, the justifiable rates for black on black, black on white, and white on white killings were within 1 to 2 percent of each other when compared with non–stand your ground states. But when the killer was white and the victim black, the rate rose to almost 17 percent.

These differences are more pronounced for gun homicides. Rulings of justifiability for black on black and black on white cases are within 1 to 2 percent of each other in non–stand your ground and stand your ground states. When whites shoot whites in non–stand your ground states, the figure is nearly 8 percent, but 15 percent in stand your ground states. When the shooter is white and the victim black, the justifiable rate is over 29 percent in non–stand your ground states and almost 36 percent in stand your ground states. It may simply be that more acts of homicide considered justifiable involve African American victims. Still, the correlations raise a legitimate question regarding the impact of race on the administration and prosecution of self-defense claims in the criminal justice system. These statistics do, however, find parallels in studies of other aspects of the criminal justice system that have found race-based

Table 4.1 All Homicides, and Gun Homicides, Ruled Justifiable, 2005–2010

Homicides

Non–Stand Your Ground States				Stand Your Ground States			
Black perpetrator, black victim	Black perpetrator, white victim	White perpetrator, black victim	White perpetrator, white victim	Black perpetrator, black victim	Black perpetrator, white victim	White perpetrator, black victim	White perpetrator, white victim
2.15%	1.13%	9.51%	1.68%	3.16%	1.4%	16.85%	3.51%

Gun Homicides

Non–Stand Your Ground States				Stand Your Ground States			
Black shooter, black victim	Black shooter, white victim	White shooter, black victim	White shooter, white victim	Black shooter, black victim	Black shooter, white victim	White shooter, black victim	White shooter, white victim
4.62%	2.88%	29.33%	7.77%	6.22%	3.38%	35.88%	15.15%

Source: John Roman, "Is American Criminal Justice Color-Blind? The Statistics Say No," *Metro Trends* Blog, Urban Institute, July 16, 2013, at http://blog.metrotrends.org/2013/07/american-criminal-justice-color-blind-statistics/. Data from Supplemental Homicide Reports, FBI.

bias when other factors are controlled for. Specifically, considerable evidence has found systematic race bias against African Americans not only in death penalty cases but also in jury selection and the prosecution and administration of drug cases.[83]

CONCLUSION: STAND YOUR GROUND ON STEROIDS

None of these studies closes the book on the consequences of stand your ground laws, but they all point to the same conclusions. First, there was and is no identifiable benefit to be had by their enactment or the gun carrying that has typically accompanied it.[84] There is no evidence that they reduce or suppress crime or generate any societal benefit beyond perhaps a feeling among gun carriers that they are acting justly or beneficially when potential self-defense situations arise. Second, there is considerable evidence that these laws have generated an increase in homicides— more killings that would not otherwise have occurred absent the change in law. Third, self-defense killings are anomalous as compared to all killings in that they are different as to their frequency—that is, they have shown an increase nationwide and in states with wide-open stand your ground laws (notably Florida and Texas)—whereas the overall murder rate has undergone a slight decline over the same period. Fourth, they are also different as to their nature, as self-defense killings usually involved strangers whereas murders usually involved people known to the killers. Firearms were more likely to be used, and the consequences for the manner in which self-defense cases were handled through the criminal justice system seem to be worrisomely adverse for African Americans as compared with whites. As the case analyses published by the *Tampa*

Bay Times indicate, at least in Florida, those with a past of criminality and violence have benefited significantly from the stand your ground law—an outcome sharply at odds with the "true man" or (to use a more contemporary term) "good guy" mythology that is often extolled as a justification for such laws.

Again, the principle that citizens have a right to defend themselves when under legitimate attack or threat is as old as America. That right, while administered somewhat differently from state to state, was neither under siege or threat. In addition, the stand your ground principle is not new, but in its contemporary "stand your ground on steroids" version, it cannot be said to have improved safety or facilitated the job of law enforcement, prosecutors, and courts, and authorities have continued to speak out against these laws. The administration of stand your ground / self-defense cases has, in practical terms, resulted in less scrutiny than traditional wrongful death investigations. That is problematic for the very reason cited by Blackstone and many others: self-defense cases are unusually complex and complicated to resolve (this fact is certainly one lesson to emerge from the Zimmerman-Martin shooting, where despite the not guilty verdict, we will never know exactly what happened, partly because of the incomplete initial investigation and initial reluctance to bring charges) and because the only other witness was killed. For that reason alone, they require extra scrutiny by those who are charged with investigating deaths that are neither natural nor accidental. Writing over a century ago, the British legal thinker Albert V. Dicey observed that self-defense "does not admit of being given with dogmatic certainty; nor need this uncertainty excite surprise, for the rule which fixes the limit to the right of self-help must, from the nature of things, be a compromise between the necessity, on the one hand, of allowing every citizen to maintain his rights against wrongdoers, and the necessity, on the other hand, of suppressing private warfare."[85]

This, in turn, returns us to the question of why such laws have swept across roughly half the states since 2005, especially at a time when crime in nearly every category, including violent crime,[86] continues to drop throughout the nation (continuing a twenty-plus-year trend), when police are more highly respected and more effective than ever, and when fear of crime among the public has also declined. As this book argues, recent more aggressive stand your ground laws question the authority of the state (as discussed in Chapter 1) and seek to appropriate some of that authority by placing it directly into the hands of armed citizens, yet without any coherent, much less persuasive evidence that such a transfer is necessary or beneficial.

More specifically, however, we can identify a more focused reason for this policy change, and it is, in short, politics. The chief instigator of this and other efforts to make gun possession, carrying, and use easier has been what is generally termed the "gun lobby"—mostly the NRA. Its chief political difficulty is a long-term existential threat to its recruitment base. The base of support of the gun rights community is America's roughly 80 million gun owners. Yet demographically, that base is declining.

In the early 1970s, about half of all homes reported one or more guns in it; by the end of the first decade of the twenty-first century, that percent had declined to a third. Gun ownership is highest among the oldest age cohorts and lowest among the youngest. So according to the 2012 National Opinion Research Center's (NORC) general social survey, 47 percent of those ages 65 and older own one or more guns; among those under 39, gun ownership is 28 percent. Related to this is the fact that a steadily declining proportion of Americans participate in hunting and sporting activities, which historically is the most common basis for gun familiarity and most common reason for gun ownership. Hunting/sporting gun activities are the primary means by which young people are traditionally exposed to guns. It bears noting, however, that recent polls have shown personal safety / self-protection as the most common reason for gun ownership. A 2013 Gallup poll, for example, reported that 60 percent of respondents cite this as the most important reason for gun ownership compared with 57 percent who cite recreational reasons.[87] A 2013 Pew Research Center poll found similar results.[88] While this recent increase in self-defense-based reasons might reflect heightened concerns by gun owners, it could instead be a consequence of continuing decline in hunting/sporting activities rather than an objective rise in self-defense concerns.

Closely related is the decline in the nation's rural population (gun ownership is highest in rural areas, lower in suburbs, and lowest in urban areas). In the 1970s, 27 percent of the country lived in rural areas; in 2012 that figure was 17 percent. In addition, immigrants, women, political independents, and Hispanics are all less likely to own firearms, and except for women, all represent growing segments of the population. Demographically speaking, despite aggressive efforts to market guns to segments of the public less likely to own or use guns, gun ownership continues to be most common among older white males, which is also a declining demographic group in relation to the population as a whole. Even in those regions of the country with the highest gun ownership—the South and the western mountain states—gun ownership has been falling off.[89]

Those unhappy with these trends have pointed to flurries of gun purchases in recent years, including assault weapons, and increases in gun-training class enrollments and increases in pistol permit applications as indications that the overall statistics must be wrong. While these trends are indeed real,[90] the larger problem with this argument is that these upticks are relatively small, probably isolated, episodic, and reflective of small variations over the years that do not contradict or alter the long-term decline consistently seen in national data. Thus, for example, nationwide gun ownership rates reported by the NORC were 32 percent in 2010 and 34 percent in 2012. If this 2 percent increase is not a statistical anomaly, it may reflect a short-term spurt in gun purchases. In addition, the widely reported surges in gun purchases of the last few years, especially after the election and reelection of Barack Obama in 2008 and 2012, were most likely purchases by those who already own guns and who decide for personal or political reasons to increase their collections.[91]

With the long-term decline in gun ownership as a backdrop, the NRA's aggressive push to make it easier to get, have, and carry guns is logical not because of crime, safety, or rights but as a matter of political strategy and base-building. The other political piece to this puzzle is the NRA's ally and financial backer, the gun industry. Both have an abiding interest in one objective: pressing as many guns into as many hands as possible.

Given a business predicated on product sales, gun manufacturers face a very specific sales problem: the product they produce generally has a long shelf life. After all, a gun, properly maintained if used regularly, can easily last decades, and an unused firearm placed in a drawer or closet can be perfectly serviceable decades later. Thus, the gun industry faces the double whammy of the relative durability of its product compared to other consumer products and declining public interest in its product. The obvious remedy is to seek new markets, such as women (an effort that has met with little success[92]) or children,[93] international trade (the U.S. is already the world's largest exporter of guns), or increased sales among existing owners (who are, after all, a proven market, given that they already own guns). The NRA sealed its decades-long political hold on the gun industry when it spearheaded enactment of national legislation that provided the gun industry with unique protection from lawsuits, the Lawful Commerce in Arms Act of 2005.[94] The $12 billion per year gun industry, in turn, has poured money into NRA coffers for political and other activities. While the industry's sales and profitability were fairly flat in the 1990s, it has turned significant profits in recent years with sales of semi-automatic assault weapons, the most well-known and profitable of which has been the AR-15. The political maelstrom surrounding the attempt to reenact an assault weapons ban in 2013 in the aftermath of the Sandy Hook Elementary School shooting in December 2012 (and other mass shootings where the shooters used assault weapons) also served as the springboard to enhanced sales—a political reaction by gun owners to the pending legislation, as discussed in the last chapter. In 2012 civilian gun and ammunition sales amounted to $5 billion.[95]

In at least some states, liberalized concealed carry laws and Florida-style stand your ground laws have prompted significant increases in the number of people seeking concealed carry permits. In Florida, between the 2005 stand your ground law's enactment and 2012, the number of concealed carry permits issued to residents tripled, to 1.1 million.[96] A *Wall Street Journal* survey of twelve states with enhanced stand your ground laws also found increases in concealed carry permits after they enacted new stand your ground laws, including in Nebraska, Ohio, Oklahoma, Tennessee, Texas, Utah, Wisconsin, and

Wyoming enacted new stand your ground laws. According to the president of the International Association of Chiefs of Police, his experience led him to conclude that such gun carrying almost never resulted in actual self-defense, but instead resulted in "a whole lot of cases of guns being used not in ways they're designed: kids shooting themselves, gun-cleaning accidents, crimes of passion, that sort of thing."[97]

Finally, even if there were no evidence that the new stand your ground laws resulted in an increase in killings, such enhanced laws would be, and are, deeply problematic for two reasons. The first, as mentioned earlier, is the complexity and subjectivity of self-defense cases in real life—especially when they result in the death of one of the persons involved. Such circumstances cry out for more investigation, not less. Stand your ground laws impede investigation, which is antithetical to the state's overriding interest in protecting the lives of its citizens.

Second, the very principle of stand your ground, even in its pre-2005 form, rests to a great degree on values that are largely incompatible with a mature society, including often fanciful notions of masculinity, bravery, vigilantism, and idealized images of individuals taking the law into their own hands long depicted in popular culture and the Old West ethos. One critic concluded about Florida's law that it "promotes, if not outright encourages, the use of violence to resolve disputes. It permits conflicts to escalate, even to the point of death because it empowers each person to stand ground in the face of fear of death or imminent bodily harm . . . . [T]he law . . . immunizes violent offenders from prosecution under such circumstances, eliminating any accountability whatsoever for the loss of life in a given circumstance."[98]

Writing in 1991, historian Richard Maxwell Brown asked whether stand your ground's "jurisprudence of

lawlessness" was becoming "out of date"[99] in modern
America. As discussed here, the evidence says "yes," even
as the politics says "no." The enactment of recent "stand
your ground on steroids" laws represents a movement
without a coherent justification, aside from a narrow
political calculus that hardly justifies these changes in law.
The final chapter focuses the book's analysis on the case
of a place where, unlike Florida and most of the rest of
the states, gun laws were already strict and have recently
become significantly stricter. Yet far from being a historical anomaly, New York State's strict gun regulation regime
is a more logical extension of America's gun and gun-
regulation tradition than is true in much of the rest of the
country, as Chapter 2 established. We look to New York
to answer this question: How, in practice, does a relatively
strict gun-regulatory regime function, bearing in mind the
relationship between the citizen and the government set
out in Chapter 1?

CHAPTER 5

The Case of New York

I built a gun. No kidding.

On a bright spring afternoon, I visited the home of a friend and colleague, a gun owner and outdoors enthusiast, to build the "lower receiver" of an AR-15. Our goal was to construct a "featureless" AR-15, meaning a weapon that would be legal under New York's recently enacted law that imposed new restrictions on civilian ownership of assault weapons.

The AR-15 was first produced by the ArmaLite Company in the late 1950s. According to one of its designers, Jim Sullivan, the weapon was "designed for full automatic military use. It wasn't really designed as a sporting rifle."[1] ArmaLite sold the rights to the gun to the Colt Company in 1959. A few years later, the weapon was adopted by the American military and produced as the M16, where it gradually came in to use during the Vietnam War in the 1960s. Colt received permission to market a semi-automatic version of the AR-15 to the civilian market, but as noted in Chapter

3, civilian sales of these types of weapons only began to expand significantly in the late 1980s. Today, the AR-15 type of weapon is manufactured and sold by over thirty companies, including Smith and Wesson, Bushmaster, and Sig Sauer. According to one longtime gun specialist, "The AR-15 is like Legos for grownups because you can adapt them for different calibers, different barrel stocks, with just a few simple tools."[2] Another gun enthusiast analogized the modular nature of the weapon this way: "This is the man's Barbie doll—you know, the Mr. Potato Head of firearms."[3] (Both of these children's toys have been popular because of their many interchangeable parts and accessories.)

The Legos-like modular quality of the AR-15 is what I encountered working on the assembly of this weapon. In less than two hours, we were able to complete the assembly of the lower receiver. This element of the gun cost about $160 and had to be purchased either from or through a dealer with a federal firearms license, or FFL, which calls for completion of the Bureau of Alcohol, Tobacco, Firearms, and Explosives form 4473. In this instance, my friend ordered the item from an out-of-state dealer, who sent it to a local FFL, where he picked it up and completed and submitted the federal form.

Our assembly efforts included installing the magazine release (a lever that releases the bullet magazine), the trigger guard (a piece of metal that keeps the trigger from being bumped), the trigger assembly (the operation of which actually fires the weapon), and the selector switch and safety (the device that prevents or allows the gun to fire). The significance of the lower receiver of the AR-15 is that it is the component that possesses a unique serial number—the number that defines this as a traceable, identifiable firearm. The other parts, including the "upper" mechanism that feeds bullets, the stock, and the barrel, are essential but interchangeable components that do not change the identification of the weapon. They are, however, essential to how these weapons are treated under New York law.

After assembly of the lower receiver, there were two ways to construct (or modify) this firearm to produce a legal weapon. The first was to retain the detachable magazine feature but to then make sure it possessed no more than one other named trait, such as an adjustable stock[4] (the portion of the gun that rests against the shoulder). Alternately, we could modify the magazine-receiving mechanism to make the magazine a fixed, permanent feature of the weapon, which can be done by removing the magazine catch button and spring, installing a simple added part, a $2 "tee nut" fastener plus washer, and then welding or gluing the modified piece in place permanently. The standard ten-bullet magazine would then become a permanent feature of the weapon (a spacer could also be inserted to limit its bullet capacity to seven, a restriction established in state law in 2013).

How, then, could one load the weapon if the magazine could not be ejected for loading or replacement? The answer is that it can be loaded from above by pulling a pin and lifting up the upper (it is hinged at the front), which exposes a space through which bullets can be inserted one at a time. Alternately, one could install a bolt-action upper as a slightly smoother way to feed in bullets. Since this weapon, as modified, would no longer have the ability to accept detachable bullet magazines, it would no longer be considered an assault weapon under state law and therefore the owner would no longer need to register it with the state or worry about the other listed features.

This experience made clear to me that, for those interested in acquiring one, a legal assault weapon under the state's strict new law enacted in 2013 is accessible, available, and feasible. For those who already own a weapon implicated by the new state law, the picture becomes more complicated. For example, one local law enforcement officer with whom I spoke expressed considerable personal irritation. He owns a Remington Sportsman semi-automatic shotgun, which includes a thumbhole stock (a hole in the stock of the weapon that makes it easier to grip with one hand), and it therefore comes under the state's new definition of an assault weapon. An owner like him can keep the weapon but must register it with the state, although as a police officer he is exempt from this requirement. He likes the thumbhole option because, he said, "it makes a big difference" when he goes turkey hunting because it helps him keep the gun more steady using one hand. Still, the average owner can keep the weapon.

As for the AR-15 assembly, aside from acquiring a greater appreciation for the elegant mechanical and design simplicity of this weapon, I experienced a certain demystification of it as well. The act of deconstructing something that is complex, inscrutable, or menacing has the effect of pushing aside its cumulative effect or consequences.

To explain this more clearly, think for a moment about an open heart operation. A heart surgeon begins by using an oscillating electric saw to cut through the sternum or breastbone in the middle of the sedated patient's chest. Then, a retractor is used to pry the cut apart halves of the rib cage in order to get access to the still-beating heart. Bones are invariably broken in the process, although advances in technology have reduced this problem. Thereafter, the surgeon begins the multihour process of operating on a live, beating heart. My point here is that anyone witnessing an open heart operation would likely be repelled, if not horrified, by observing the process of prying open the chest of a living human being, even while understanding that it is a lifesaving procedure. But for the medical specialist, an immersion in the technical details of the procedure, the focus on each particular step in the hours-long process, has a demystifying effect, as it must. One expert put it this way: "Becoming a cardiac surgeon means getting over a huge mental block: 'You've got to get comfortable putting stitches into a beating heart.'"[5]

In a certain respect, the experience of assembling an AR-15 from a bunch of small parts has a similar effect. When a fearsomely destructive weapon is disassembled and laid out on a table in parts and one focuses on the mechanics of assembly, it becomes a problem-solving exercise that has the effect of distancing an awareness of what such a weapon, when assembled, can do. It is not only unsurprising but logical that weapons enthusiasts for whom firearms assembly and use are routine would shrug at the dismay expressed by others when weapons like the AR-15 are used in mass shootings, for example, because firearms owners have both greater technical knowledge (and familiarity) and a lessened sense of mystery. That is both the value and the danger of intimate acquaintance with guns: demystification is of value, but the loss of appreciation of firearms' destructive capabilities is indeed a danger. British scholar Peter Squires offered a similar observation about how an emphasis on the "properties and capacities of firearms," "dispassionately examined," has the effect of divorcing them "from any reference to the social purposes embodied in a weapon's design, the uses to which it may be put or, indeed, the consequences of its use."[6]

The purpose of this chapter is to examine the case of New York—a state that has long been in the forefront of tougher gun laws[7] and that has, in the minds of some, become a gun owner's nightmare. But has it? With so much hand-wringing among gun rights activists nationwide about the reputedly adverse effects of stricter gun laws, it is not only useful but instructive to examine a place that already has such laws. As the analysis in Chapter 2 suggests, New York, with its strict gun regime, has in many respects a stronger link to the American gun tradition than other places in the country that have rushed to loosen or eliminate gun regulations. And harking back to this book's first chapter, New York offers a both concrete and contemporary case study of how the relationship between the armed citizen and the government actually functions. As I will argue in this chapter, that relationship, while different than that of the majority of states, functions effectively to preserve gun rights in the context of a feasible regulatory scheme.

THE NEW NEW YORK GUN LAW

In January 2013 the New York State Legislature moved rapidly—too rapidly, said many—to enact a sweeping and tough new set of gun regulations, the New York Secure Ammunition and Firearms Enforcement (SAFE) Act of 2013, at the behest of Democratic Governor Andrew Cuomo. Two events were clear catalysts for this action: the elementary school shooting of twenty children and six adults in Connecticut the previous month and, less than two weeks later, the murder of two firefighters in Webster, New York, by a man who deliberately set a house on fire to draw first responders to the scene and then murder them (two others were injured).

Relying on a power provided in the state constitution called a "message of necessity," the Democratic governor was able to rush the bill through the legislature. Since 1938 the state constitution has stipulated that legislation must be presented to the members of the legislature at least "three calendar legislative days" before it can be acted upon—unless the governor certifies that, in his or her opinion, circumstances "necessitate an immediate vote," whereupon the three-day rule is waived.[8] While the obvious purpose of the "message of necessity" provision is to address bona fide emergencies, the constitution's language is broad enough to allow governors to define those circumstances as they see fit, and that is how governors have treated this power for decades.[9]

After huddling with legislative leaders, the bill was formally presented to both the State Assembly and State Senate on January 14. Both houses rapidly enacted the bill, by a vote of 104 to 43 in the Democratic-controlled Assembly and 43 to 18 in the Republican-controlled Senate. Cuomo signed the bill into law the next day, on January 15.

Critics from the state's gun community lambasted the bill for its strict new provisions but also for the rapidity of its passage, charging that the governor was abusing his powers by avoiding hearings and the opportunity for opponents outside of the legislature to make their case. Here, however, Cuomo was doing what New York governors often do, especially with controversial legislation. According to a good government group, Cuomo used messages of necessity 29 times in 2011 (his first year in office), only 5 times in 2012, and 3 times in 2013. Cuomo's two predecessors, both Democrats, averaged 41 per year, and their predecessor, Republican George Pataki, averaged over 53 such messages per year in his last term of office.[10] Such messages have been used for legislation of every sort, from the legalization of gay marriage, to the establishment of public school teacher evaluations, to enactment of the entire state budget. Still, the chief complaints revolved around the contents of the bill. (It takes no leap of faith to note that criticism of the process by which the bill was enacted would have been far,

far more muted had groups like the gun community agreed with the content of the legislation.) The SAFE Act consisted of what the governor boasted was the toughest set of gun laws in the nation.[11] Chief among its provisions was the imposition of new restrictions on assault weapons. State law first imposed limits on such weapons in 2000, but the new law tightened those restrictions by categorizing assault rifles as those that can accept detachable magazines and that have at least one additional characteristic (the earlier law specified two characteristics), including a folding or telescoping stock, a protruding pistol grip, a thumbhole stock, a second handgrip or protruding grip, a bayonet mount, flash suppressor, muzzle brake (erroneously spelled "break" in the legislation), a muzzle compensator, a threaded barrel designed to accommodate any of the above features, or a grenade launcher. Semiautomatic shotguns and pistols are also similarly restricted, as is the case with past assault weapons bans. In the case of shotguns, they fall within the terms of the new law if they possess at least one characteristic named in the law, even if the only feature they possess is a detachable magazine. New Yorkers who already lawfully owned assault weapons considered legal before 2013 under state law but that would now be restricted under the new law could keep them, but they had to now register them with the state (the registration must be renewed every five years) by April 2014.

Those who own an assault weapon, as defined by the law, that must be registered can also eliminate design features to exempt it from registration by, for example, removing the bayonet lug or grinding off threading on the barrel. A background check is also run during the registration process, and the state now maintains this information in a database. While the owners of these weapons may keep them for life, they may not transfer or sell them to anyone else, including family members. They can, however, transfer them to authorized sources, including the police, a firearms dealer, or someone out of state for whom ownership is legal in that state. A related new provision now requires surrogate's courts around the state (each county has one), which handle all probate and estate matters, to inventory a person's firearms separately from other possessions when people die, which will identify the existence of weapons in this category. The law also imposed new restrictions on high-capacity bullet-feeding devices (i.e., magazines). Under previous law, those obtained before 1994 of any capacity were grandfathered in (i.e., were legal to own). New magazines from 1994 on were limited to those that could hold no more than ten bullets. Under the 2013 law, however, all magazines, including pre-1994 versions, are now illegal to own if they hold more than ten bullets—however, they may be loaded with no more than seven bullets. That is, gun owners may not have more than seven rounds in any weapon's bullet-feeding device. Not surprisingly, this provision prompted particular ridicule and dismay. Owners could transfer now-illegal magazines to dealers or to individuals out of state or modify the magazine to reduce its capacity to seven rounds. (Owners were given until April 2014 to effect such transfers; police and police-issued firearms are exempted from this and some other regulations.) The law also noted that police have no presumptive right to inspect magazines unless they first have probable cause. Regarding pre-1994 magazines that were formerly legal but are now illegal to own, the 2013 law has a kind of forgiveness provision saying that if a person believes mistakenly that possession of such a pre-1994 magazine is still legal, that individual may avoid being charged under the law if he or she then disposes of it within thirty days. (Ignorance of the law is rarely a basis of avoiding prosecution, but it is in this case.) Noncomplying assault weapons and feeding devices more than fifty years old are exempted from these new restrictions as antiques, curios, or relics.

An additional significant change now extends background checks, formerly limited to commercial weapons sales, to private gun sales as well as ammunition sales. Under the new procedure, an individual wishing to make a private gun sale may still do so but must go to a licensed dealer, pay a fee of up to $10, and have the dealer run a background (NICS) check before the sale can be completed. The only sales or transfers exempted from the background check are those to immediate family members (spouses, domestic partners, children, and stepchildren). Direct sale of ammunition was barred as of 2014, although such sales can be routed through firearms dealers, as is already true with Internet gun sales. Ammunition sale records and checks occur at the state level (not through the NICS system), are required to be purged yearly by the state, and are exempted from freedom of information inquiries. This restriction would theoretically bar the sale or giving of even a few rounds between individuals, but the expectation is that there is no interest in tracking down, much less prosecuting, the sharing of ammunition between two hunters in the woods or two shooters at a firing range.[12]

The SAFE Act also requires pistol permits to be renewed every five years; formerly, they never had to be renewed. And while information concerning the identification of pistol permit holders is public, permit holders can now, under the new law, file for an exemption from any public disclosure with the state (this provision is under court challenge from newspapers and First Amendment advocates), which has been inundated with such requests. (In Cortland County, local officials report receiving 3000 exemption requests in 2013 out of around 7000 permits identified in the county.) This matter garnered considerable attention when, beginning in late 2012, reporters for local downstate county newspapers published the names and addresses of pistol permit holders in Putnam, Rockland, and Westchester counties. Permit holders were outraged, some county governments refused to release any permit holder information, and local reporters received death threats.[13]

Another significant portion of the new law requires certain categories of mental health professionals to report to state authorities any persons under their care whom they believe are "likely to engage in conduct that would result in serious harm to self or others."[14] Those persons are then to be checked to see if they are licensed to own firearms. If so, the state police are notified and a judgment made as to whether to suspend or revoke their licenses and then retrieve the guns. Beyond these measures, criminal penalties for firearms-related violations were enhanced, including possession or use of firearms while on school property, in connection with drug trafficking, straw gun purchases, and other felonies, including the killing of first responders (e.g., firefighters). The law also allows those under an order of protection issued by a court to have their gun license suspended or revoked and requires that firearms must be stored safely in homes where others with criminal backgrounds live; they must report stolen guns within twenty-four hours.

This new law put the Empire State at the forefront of those with tough or toughened laws. New York was the first state to act after the Sandy Hook Elementary School shooting. Only three other states (California, Hawaii, Massachusetts) and the District of Columbia have a ten-round magazine limit, and none has a limit as low as seven. In the balance of 2013, California, Colorado, Connecticut, Delaware, Hawaii, Illinois, Maryland, Massachusetts, New Jersey, and Rhode Island all toughened their gun laws. Moving in the opposite direction, however, over two dozen states moved to loosen gun regulations, including Arkansas, Indiana, Kansas, Kentucky, Louisiana, Maine, Mississippi, Missouri, South Dakota, Tennessee, Texas, Virginia, and Wyoming. These states enacted a variety of measures, including laws to make it easier for school personnel to bring guns to schools, to allow guns in churches, and to loosen concealed carry regulations. By one count, during 2013 states enacted thirty-nine laws of various types to tighten gun regulations and seventy laws that loosened gun regulations.[15]

THE POLITICAL REACTION

Opponents of the new state law were vocal, visible, and angry. The criticisms of the strict new assault weapons restrictions were similar to those of like measures (see the discussion in Chapter 3), arguing that such weapons are rarely used in crimes and that the new standard would restrict or bar legitimate hunting weapons. Many questioned the new seven-bullet limit on magazines, considering it an arbitrary number that did not readily conform to the capacities of existing magazines (e.g., semi-automatic handguns typically come with magazines holding more than seven rounds). And joining gun rights activists were many in the mental health community, who objected to the new reporting procedures pertaining to those with mental illness, fearing that the new law would drive away gun owners with mental health problems from treatment for fear of losing their firearms. They also objected to possible violations of patient privacy and to the substantial new reporting procedures.[16]

In late 2014, the *New York Times* reported that since the mental health provisions of the New York SAFE Act took effect in March 2013, mental health officials had filed 41,427 reports of mentally disturbed individuals who public health officials felt should not have access to firearms. This led to about 34,500 being barred from having guns. Of those, 278 had pistol permits, which were then revoked. According to the *Times*, the "overwhelming majority" of the reports came from hospitals dealing with mentally ill individuals in emergency rooms or providing inpatient psychiatric services, not from mental health therapists or clinics. Such individuals most often had been diagnosed with schizophrenia, psychosis, or major depression. By way of comparison, about 144,000 people are treated for mental disorders in public and private hospitals throughout the state annually—that is, such individuals had mental problems serious enough to warrant a visit to a hospital. In terms of new criminal offenses established by the law, about 3300 such offenses have been reported as of late 2014. About 92 percent of those offenses involved the newly established felony charge of criminal firearm possession.[17]

Leading the opposition, as is typical of gun politics rhetoric, was a chorus of charges that the new law was taking away people's rights. As one protest organizer said, there was "a whole spectrum of constitutional rights being infringed on."[18] Chief among them, of course, was said to be the Second Amendment (the New York State Constitution is one of six in the country that has no Second Amendment–type provision in it.) Many howled that the law would make criminals out of formerly law-abiding citizens.

The courts will ultimately sort out the constitutionality of the new law.[19] Without question, activities and items that were once legal would now become either illegal (e.g., possession of pre-1994 large bullet magazines and private, unrecorded gun sales) or subject to regulation (e.g., assault weapons registration). But as discussed in Chapter 1, the act of governance continually grapples with redefining the dividing line between freedom and government control. So how do these new restrictions stack up?

The short answer is that there is no simple answer. To gun owners, especially those who own any of the items subject to new regulations, such restrictions are both unnecessary and burdensome. One of the most frequently raised objections was that "only law-abiding citizens / gun owners are hurt by this new law, because criminals won't obey the new laws anyway, and the law makes criminals out of honest citizens."[20] As noted, the law does indeed impose new obligations on gun owners. But there is nothing new about this in the realm of public policy. The idea of something once legal becoming illegal has and does occur in many areas in law—when, for example, it became illegal to drive an automobile without wearing a seat belt when it formerly was legal to do so. More significant, however, is the omnipresent complaint from critics in the gun debate that gun laws generally are of no use because criminals disregard them.

The problem with such blithe assertions is that they are rarely examined. The very trait ascribed to gun laws—that criminals ignore them—is equally applicable to all law and laws. Every law ever written has been violated, from jaywalking to murder. Should those laws be repealed, vilified, ignored, or dubbed a failure because they are violated by "criminals" who, by definition, have become "criminals" because they have violated the law? While the questioning of laws' effectiveness is an appropriate inquiry (e.g., laws against marijuana possession and use have been gradually decriminalized or repealed entirely in some places in recent years, partly on the argument that they are widely ignored), gun laws as a whole are no less or more enforceable than most other laws. What sets them apart is the relentless political drumbeat against them—most easily understood as an effort to delegitimize if not repeal them. At the federal level, efforts by gun groups to weaken, water down, underenforce, emasculate, and roll back federal laws are well known and amply documented. And they are efforts designed to strengthen the very argument that such laws are ineffective—even as their ineffectiveness arises largely from political and legal efforts to make sure that they are as ineffective as possible.[21]

To return to the specifics of the New York law, the arguments regarding assault weapons and bullet magazines have been examined elsewhere in this book. Governor Cuomo did, however, run afoul of the seven-bullet magazine limit. As Cuomo admitted two months after the SAFE Act's enactment, manufacturers do not generally produce seven-bullet magazines (not that it would be very difficult to do so), obliging him to roll back this part of the law to continue to allow ten-bullet magazines to be sold, even though they must still contain no more than seven rounds.[22] According to manufacturers, however, the chief reason seven-bullet magazines are not available is simply because of a lack of demand.[23] New York's law would be likely to create just such a market. While many have questioned the selection of seven bullets as the cut-off as opposed to ten, Chapter 2 showed that states in the early twentieth century varied widely in their magazine bullet maximums.[24] And aside from production of new magazines holding seven rounds, larger-capacity magazines can be altered by insertion of a simple block to reduce a magazine's capacity (this can be done by gunsmiths or by enterprising gun owners).[25] Yet these considerations may ultimately prove moot, as a federal district judge struck down the seven-bullet limit (retaining the state's preexisting ten-bullet magazine loading limit) on the last day of 2013 in *New York State Rifle and Pistol Association v. Cuomo*.[26]

The provision ending private, non–background check gun sales addresses one of the most commonly cited reforms that could have beneficial effects on illegal gun trafficking and use, and it is one proposed change that has garnered support from elements of the gun community. In the U.S. Senate in April 2013, gun rights groups, including the Citizens Committee for the Right to Keep and Bear Arms, supported a universal background check bill sponsored by gun rights advocates Joe Manchin (D-WV) and Patrick Toomey (R-PA) (the measure garnered fifty-four Senate votes in favor, but failed to reach the sixty-vote minimum needed to end a filibuster).[27] A 2012 survey of gun owners and NRA members found that 87 percent of non-NRA gun owners and 74 percent of NRA members supported criminal background checks for all gun purchases.[28] As if to punctuate the point, a convicted bank robber, serving time in a maximum security prison in Colorado, wrote a letter to the editor of a Connecticut newspaper in June 2013, in which he thanked the NRA for opposing universal background checks. In part, he wrote: "As a life-long criminal . . . I'd like to take a moment to express my appreciation to the National Rifle Association for . . . protecting my ability to easily obtain them [guns] through its opposition to universal background checks."[29] Obviously, criminal Gary Bornman may be nothing more than a bored publicity hound; still, it is clear that a great many people can and do obtain guns without background checks through unregulated private sales.

Indeed, a uniform system of background checks would forestall what is reputed to be a significant gap between background check firearms transactions versus non–background check transactions. What limited studies exist suggest that, nationwide, between 30 and 40 percent of all gun sales are private—that is, occur without background checks.[30] While that figure is surely lower in New York as compared with other states with more guns and fewer regulations, even New York has encountered problems with off-the-book gun sales (gun transfers that could be later claimed as recordless private sales). In 2011, for example, the state attorney general's office conducted an undercover operation at a half-dozen gun shows around the state, where they were able to make numerous off-the-books gun purchases. In 2013 gun show organizers, working with the attorney general's office, established tighter procedures to end this problem.[31] And as for the mechanics of a New York gun owner wishing to sell a gun directly to another person, the procedure of going to a licensed dealer and paying a small fee for the background check is similar to other types of private sales where the government takes an interest in the sale. For example, a car owner in New York who wishes to sell a car to another person directly may do so through a direct transaction of the car for payment, but both buyer and seller are required to fill out and sign a simple form with an accompanying fee to be delivered to the Department of Motor Vehicles to record the sale.[32]

Finally, opponents of universal background checks often argue that such a system amounts to de facto gun registry, by virtue of the data submitted to the system. Leaving aside the fact that the national NICS background check system has already existed for decades and has not resulted in a gun registry, de facto or otherwise, the inclusion of more sales checks would simply be that—more checks. Since the NICS system was established, it always included a protocol to destroy the records of approved transfers.[33] Any change in that could only occur through the regular legislative process.

THE POLITICS OF GUNS IN NEW YORK

The passage of the SAFE Act sparked protests of many sorts throughout the state, but especially in Upstate New York. Aside from multiple rallies and demonstrations in the state capital and elsewhere, the law's opponents pressured local governments to register their opposition. Of the state's 62 counties, 52 enacted resolutions critical of the new state law within the space of about five months of the law's enactment. The 10 contrary counties included 8 downstate (including the 5 boroughs of New York City), plus Albany County (incorporating the state capital) and Tompkins County (home of the liberal college town Ithaca). Another 259 towns and villages also enacted resolutions expressing opposition to the law (this list also included three small cities). Nine cities, towns, and one county (Tompkins) approved resolutions in support of the law.[34]

These many dissenting resolutions would seem to reflect statewide repudiation of the new law, but multiple state poll numbers tell a very different story. A February 2013 Siena College poll found that 65 percent of voters statewide supported the SAFE Act, with 30 percent opposed. While support for the law was stronger downstate (New York City and surrounding suburbs), 50 percent of upstate voters reported supporting the law, with 46 percent opposed. Opposition was greater among Republicans and conservatives, with support higher among Democrats, liberals, and independents.[35] A Marist College poll taken in March reported that 41 percent of New Yorkers felt the SAFE Act was "about right," and another 19 percent felt that it did not go far enough (totaling 60 percent support), with 30 percent saying that the law went too far. Among upstaters, 46 percent reported that the law either was good as it was or should have gone further, compared to 48 percent saying it went too far.[36] A March Siena poll showed support for the law at 61 percent, with 35 percent opposed.[37] An April Quinnipiac University poll reported 63 percent in support of the law with 33 percent opposed.[38]

A revealing poll of one of the most rural, conservative, and gun-owning counties in the state was conducted in Jefferson County, located in rural northern New York (58 percent of county residents reported owning at least one gun in a 2013 survey). Fort Drum military installation is near the county's largest city, Watertown. A survey of county residents conducted in April 2013 reported that 50 percent of respondents said that the NY SAFE Act had gone too far, with 41 percent saying that it had either not gone far enough or was about right. More report opposing the law than supporting it, but the margin is surprisingly close for one of the most conservative areas in the state. When asked if they favored repealing the law, 44 percent said they opposed repealing any part of it; 28 percent favored repealing parts of the law; and 7 percent favored repealing the law entirely. Yet in the same survey, 86 percent reported support for background checks for assault weapons purchasers at gun shows. Among county gun owners, support for the measure was 79 percent and 96 percent among nonowners. Seventy-five percent favored background checks for other gun purchases at gun shows, and 81 percent favored background checks for assault weapons sales between private individuals.[39] Even as the law has taken a political battering, it has remained popular with most New Yorkers, and its specific (and most controversial) provisions are even more popular than the law itself.

The disparity between clear-cut public approval, even in conservative areas of the state, and substantial repudiation of the law by most county governments is one of many instances of the collision between interest politics

and mass politics—and is typical of gun politics dynam-
ics.[40] As is often the case at the national level, gun rights
advocates were highly motivated to engage in significant
political activism—attending meetings, writing letters and
emails, and otherwise vocally expressing their dismay in a
way to put direct pressure on local political leaders. Nearly
all those who support the law, however, lack correspond-
ing zeal and so by and large were not a presence at local
meetings with county legislatures, town boards, in com-
munications with officeholders, and at meet-your-repre-
sentative sessions around the state. Thus, local governments
responded to the pressures, knowing as well that the resul-
tant resolutions were largely symbolic and that the likelihood of the state legislature reversing course (much less the
governor) was nil.

One of the clearest expressions of this pressure group
effort was the reaction of the New York State Sheriffs'
Association (NYSSA). As noted earlier in this book, law
enforcement has generally been highly supportive of stronger gun laws, including restrictions on assault weapons and
high-capacity magazines. After passage of the new law,
NYSSA issued a statement that leveled some criticisms at
it. While immediately extolled by SAFE Act opponents
as a ringing repudiation of the law by law enforcement,
the organization's actual statement was more careful and
nuanced.

In its statement, NYSSA said that sheriffs "support
many of the provisions of the SAFE Act, and believe that
they will enhance public safety and help shield citizens
from violence." It added, however, that some parts of the
law "need clarification, and some that we think should be
reconsidered and modified. . . ."[41] The statement identified six provisions that the organization praised, including
background checks for private gun sales, beefed up mental

health background checks (this was a marked departure from the negative reaction of many in the mental health community), toughened penalties for gun crimes, and the safe storage provision. Among the six provisions NYSSA criticized were what the statement said was an overly broad definition of assault weapons and the bullet magazine reduction regulation. The other criticisms were jurisdictional or technical, such as arguing that pistol permit and assault weapons registration data should be maintained at the local level rather than by the state, that the law needed greater clarity regarding Internet ammunition sales, and that exceptions for law enforcement officers needed to be clarified or strengthened (as indeed they later were). Finally, the statement expressed concern about the bill's rapid passage and the failure to consult significantly with relevant stakeholders. The statement concluded by noting, correctly, that "Sheriffs and other law enforcement officers are not called upon by this new legislation to go door-to-door to confiscate any weapons newly classified as assault weapons, and will not do so."[42] Many of the law's critics continue to insist, erroneously, that the law requires officers to do exactly this.

NYSSA's cautious public, if partial, dissent is notable because police have as their first and most important job that of carrying out the law, regardless of their personal feelings, and thus must tread carefully in criticisms of existing law that falls to them to enforce. Yet county sheriffs are different from the rest of law enforcement at every other level in the state, because they are elected. Thus, they were and are subject to the same electoral pressures as other local officials around the state, which largely explains their public position taking on the law. Some upstate county sheriffs have been highly vocal in expressing their dismay at the law, saying, for example, that their deputies "would not go

out looking for people who failed to register certain guns"
and that "we are never going to go door-to-door in Cayuga
County . . . and take guns that were legally obtained before
Jan. 15."[43] Yet even these statements are political posturing,
because, as noted, the law does not require law enforcement to engage in the behavior decried by this and other
sheriff critics. NYSSA also submitted a brief on behalf of
those seeking to strike the law down in court.[44]

Other elements of the state criminal justice system
lined up behind the SAFE Act. Shortly after its enactment,
the state District Attorneys Association issued two statements voicing support for the new law.[45] And while the
New York State Police took no official stand on the law
(nor would they be expected to do so), state police counsel Kevin Bruen filed a brief on behalf of the law for the
lawsuit filed against it, defending in particular the assault
weapons ban and magazine limit provisions.[46]

The final key political actor on this issue, Governor
Andrew Cuomo, was the originator and chief proponent
of this legislation. It was Cuomo who seized the political
initiative in the weeks after the elementary school shooting
in nearby Connecticut, expedited the measure, and trum-
peted it as a great victory for the citizens of the state.

Since his election as governor in 2010, Cuomo has amassed
a significant record of policy accomplishment while maintaining a high degree of popularity. The son of former three-term
governor Mario Cuomo, prodigal son Andrew worked in his
father's administration as a young man in the 1980s and then
served as assistant secretary of the Department of Housing and
Urban Development in the Clinton administration from 1993
until his elevation to secretary of the department in 1997, where
he served until 2001. After a failed try at the governorship in
2002, he was elected attorney general in 2006. He swept into the
governor's mansion with 62 percent of the vote.

As governor, Cuomo has retained high popularity in large measure because of his shrewd understanding of state politics and ability to work with Republican and Democratic leaders in the state legislature, which has delivered an on-time state budget in each year of his term as governor. That accomplishment contrasts with the fact that state budgets were routinely enacted late—often months late—in the prior twenty years. While considered moderate-to-conservative on fiscal issues, Cuomo has demonstrated an aggressive social liberalism, advocating such causes as expanded women's rights, including fortifying abortion rights for women, same-sex marriage (enacted by the state legislature in 2011 largely because of his efforts), and now gun control.

In his first two years in office, Cuomo's popularity in the state remained high, fluctuating between 67 percent and 77 percent approval. In the aftermath of the SAFE Act's passage, Cuomo's statewide popularity slipped some, to the low- to mid-60 percent range.[47] Even by the fall of 2013, his approval ratings remained in that range, only once dropping below 60 percent.[48] A poll conducted at the end of 2013 reported a 62 percent approval rating statewide and a 53 percent approval rating upstate.[49]

In his 2014 reelection bid, Cuomo's chief political headaches came not from conservatives but from liberals and progressives, who felt that his economic policies favored the wealthy, who were unhappy because Cuomo had taken no position on hydrofracking (the extraction of natural gas from shale), a drilling process they largely opposed, and who were critical on his apparent abandonment of ethics reform. Liberal disaffection surfaced in the form of a primary challenge from an unknown Fordham University law professor, Zephyr Teachout, who garnered a surprising third of the primary vote. When the dust settled after the general election, Cuomo won with about 54 percent of the

vote compared with 41 percent for his Republican opponent, Rob Astorino. The liberal, pro-environment Green
Party gubernatorial candidate, Howie Hawkins, garnered
nearly 180,000 votes, a high-water mark for the party and
a further sign of liberal disaffection. Most of those who
were angered by Cuomo's advocacy of the SAFE Act
would likely not have supported him in any case. Even so,
Cuomo outpolled his opponents in ten upstate counties,
including three in the far rural northern part of the state.
Finally, overall voter turnout in 2014 was the lowest in the
state in at least four decades, and this hurt Democratic can-
didates throughout the state, including Cuomo. Cuomo's
Republican opponent, Astorino, opposed the SAFE Act,
but the gun issue proved unimportant, if not irrelevant, in
affecting the outcome of the race. In liberal-leaning New
York, Cuomo's aggressive advocacy on the gun issue (and
gay marriage) had not materially harmed either his popularity or his 2014 reelection.[50] And like it or not, his advocacy on the issue is consistent with the state's long history
related to gun regulation.

THE STATE GUN POLICY ENVIRONMENT

As noted earlier, New York has a long tradition of relatively
tough gun laws. The first modern gun law, the Sullivan
Law, was enacted in 1911. Spreading urban crime, often
involving handguns, and an attempt to assassinate New
York City Mayor William Gaynor in 1910 provided the
necessary impetus to move the state legislature to enact a
new law that not only regulated the possession and carrying of pistols and other concealable weapons but also
their sale, as handguns could only be sold to individuals
with valid permits, and gun dealers were now required to
maintain proper sales records. These regulations were not

unprecedented (see Chapter 2), but what was new was the establishment of a licensing requirement for handguns, covering both possession at home and at work. Violation of the measure was made a felony. That same year, the state also enacted a law giving the police the power to stop, search, and arrest anyone they suspected of carrying a gun illegally. No warrant was required (this came decades before the Supreme Court applied the U.S. Constitution's Fourth Amendment to the states). Police wasted no time in vigorously using this new power.[51] By one historical account, the Sullivan Law was "without precedent in the United States, since it subjected to strict regulation not only the carrying of deadly weapons, but also their sale and simple possession."[52] The idea of requiring permits for pistol possession spread to other places around the country. The law withstood legal challenges, and while it has been amended many times, it is still on the books.

As Chapter 2 made clear, the history of gun crime has been linked most directly to handguns, and that was the chief concern giving rise to the Sullivan Act. Despite a long history of crime-related problems in New York City, in the contemporary crime environment New York stands in relatively good stead in relation to most of the rest of the states, especially given that over 80 percent of firearm homicides nationwide occur in large- and medium-sized urban areas.[53] The state has the fourth lowest gun death rate on a per capita basis among the fifty states, and also rates as having the 6th strictest gun laws.[54] The overall gun death rate includes gun homicides, suicides, and fatal accidents. Focusing specifically on gun murders and nonlethal gun crimes, based on data from the FBI's Uniform Crime Reports from 2011, New York faces greater problems. New York's firearms murder rate is high—9th highest—but it also is 17th lowest in firearms murders as a percentage of all murders (notable since murder attempts with firearms are more likely to result in death than attempts using other methods, such as knives). It also ranks 19th lowest in its firearms robbery rate and 10th lowest in its firearms assault rate.[55]

Overall, these rankings are consistent with a number of recent studies that have found a strong inverse correlation between the strength of a state's gun laws and its rates of gun deaths—that is, states with tougher gun laws tend to have the lowest gun death rate, and the reverse is true for states with few or lax laws.[56] This correlation seems even stronger with respect to gun suicides compared with gun homicides[57] (nearly twice as many Americans die from gun suicides as gun homicides annually); many studies have linked gun prevalence with higher suicide rates.[58]

Aside from state laws, New York law enforcement, prosecutors, and political leaders have worked for many years to stem the flow of illegal guns into the state via the "iron pipeline," a gun trafficking pattern mostly from southern states with lax gun laws. In 2011, for example, of crime guns recovered and traced by police, the largest number came from (in order of high to low) Virginia, Pennsylvania, North Carolina, Florida, Georgia, and South Carolina. In all, of the 8793 crime guns recovered and traced that year, 82 percent came from out of state.[59] In New York City, 85 percent of crime guns came from out of state in 2009; in 2010 it was 86 percent; in 2011 it was 90 percent.[60] Over the last two decades, between 80 and 90 percent of crime guns throughout the state have been traced to outside of New York,[61] a fact that buttresses a simple proposition about gun laws.

If New York's tough gun laws (especially applicable to handguns, which compose roughly 80 percent of the guns used in crimes[62]) made no difference, why would most

crime guns come from out of state—and from places with
much more lax laws? The answer is obvious. The problem
is not that gun laws do not matter or do not work but that
the nation's system of federalism, where the vast majority
of the nation's gun laws exist at the state level, encourages such gun trafficking to circumvent tougher laws in
states that have them. For states like New York, the strategy is threefold: (1) suppress illegal sales and trafficking
within the state, thereby (2) raising the degree of difficulty,
or "opportunity costs," for those seeking weapons who
should not have them by forcing them to go elsewhere to
satisfy criminal demand, and (3) interdicting illicit interstate trafficking.

Former New York City Mayor Michael Bloomberg has
become an outspoken advocate for these and other measures, which was a primary reason for his formation, along
with former Boston Mayor Tom Menino, of Mayors against
Illegal Guns (MAIG) in 2006. MAIG has now become an
established pro–gun control group, claiming over 1000
mayor members from 45 states as of 2013.[63] From the start,
much of their effort has focused on gun trafficking patterns,
especially as they affect gun crime in large cities. As mayor,
Bloomberg relied on city law enforcement resources to
mount sting operations against rogue gun dealers in other
states found to be the source of many of the illegal guns trafficked into New York and other northeastern cities, including Boston and Philadelphia. Even in the face of a federal
law enacted in 2005 that provided special protections from
lawsuits to gun manufacturers, dealers, distributors, and
importers of firearms and ammunition,[64] Bloomberg was
able to reach settlements with the offending gun dealers to
get them to agree to strict monitoring of their sales activities. In 2013 the city reported one of its largest gun seizures
when it broke up a gun trafficking ring, arresting 19 people

and nabbing 254 guns initially obtained in North Carolina and South Carolina.[65] Studies of licensing and trafficking support the idea that these strategies can be effective in reducing the flow and availability of crime guns, especially in the absence of uniform national regulations.[66]

As noted earlier, gun owners have complained that the SAFE Act and other state laws simply make life harder for law-abiding gun owners. Of course, that is true. Yet many, many laws in many areas of life do the same thing. For example, an applicant for a driver's license in New York (and most states) must pass a written test of rules-of-the-road knowledge and take a supervised road test to demonstrate minimal knowledge and competency. Those who already possess the necessary knowledge and competency are inconvenienced and delayed in obtaining their licenses for the sake of those who do not possess those competencies in order to make sure that, before licenses are obtained, all individuals have met a minimal standard. Since laws, by their very nature, establish rules of uniform conduct to help achieve that conduct, it will always be the case that those who would walk the straight-and-narrow on their own find themselves influenced or "inconvenienced" by the laws aimed to deter or punish those who would otherwise violate the conduct proscribed by, or standards established by, the law. Thus, for example, New York's handgun-permit process takes many months because state officials are required to conduct a detailed background investigation of permit applicants on the notion that the public interest is served if those who should not have permits are weeded out in the process. Yes, it poses a notable inconvenience on those with clean records. But this information cannot be known until the investigation takes place. Thus, the investigative standards must apply to everyone. So how does the New York system work?

THE AUTHOR APPLIES FOR A PISTOL PERMIT

In August 2013 I submitted my application for a pistol permit. Herewith is my account of that experience.

New York is 1 of 10 states in the country, plus the District of Columbia, with a "may issue" pistol permit system, meaning that these states have discretion over whether to issue permits. In 36 "shall issue" states, obtaining a permit is merely a matter of applying (subject to rejection if, e.g., the applicant has a felony criminal record). Four states have dispensed with permitting entirely. In New York, applicants must offer a justification for wishing to obtain a permit, and applications can be rejected after review based on the validity of the justification. Given the relative strictness of the state's criteria, it comes as little surprise that the state is one of 9 that do not honor pistol permits from other states (19 other states honor the New York permit).[67] While Second Amendment–based challenges have been raised in court against laws with stricter may issue standards, in at least three instances they have, to date, been upheld in federal court as consistent with the Second Amendment (the Supreme Court has declined to hear appeals of these three decisions). This includes New York's may issue law and that of New Jersey.[68]

The New York pistol/revolver license application[69] offers three types of licenses: those for handgun possession on one's premises, for concealed carry (i.e., to carry in public places), and related to one's employment (such as a security guard, bank messenger, or certain government professions).[70] These are defined in the state penal law. Note also that the overall review process to merely possess a handgun is basically the same as the process to legally carry a handgun. For an applicant like me, who is not claiming a business-based justification, the critical wording in the law says:

"A license for a pistol or revolver . . . shall be issued to (a) have and possess in his dwelling by a householder" or "(f) have and carry concealed . . . by any person when proper cause exists for the issuance thereof. . . ."[71] The determination of "proper cause," and therefore whether permits are issued, is made by county judges. There are variations in county standards.

In the five boroughs of New York City, for example, permitting is subject to greater scrutiny and higher standards compared with the other counties in the state. In fact, permits obtained in any of the state's 57 non–New York City counties are not valid in the five boroughs of the Big Apple because of the city's stricter standards. As of the end of 2012, the city of 8 million had issued a total of about 37,000 permits.[72] Statewide, 1.28 million permits were listed with the state as of the end of 2011, out of a total population of about 19.5 million people. The actual number of valid current permits, however, is significantly smaller, because that count includes every pistol permit issued since 1936, as there has been no purging of these records since that date[73] (that will change with the SAFE Act, which now imposes a five-year time limit on the permit, and permits not renewed will be canceled). Whatever the number of permits, it may not equal the number of handguns, as a single permit can cover many handguns, and not all permit holders may currently own handguns. In my home county of Cortland (population 49,000), where I applied for a permit, the county clerk's office reports about 7200 permits, although this total also includes unpurged permits. By way of comparison, the upstate but more urban and suburban county of Onondaga (which includes the city of Syracuse) has a total population of about 470,000, and it reports 40,000–50,000 pistol permits.

Aside from selecting permit type, the application also requires the statement of the applicant's "reason" for the permit and asks for the names and addresses of four character references "who by their signature attest to your good moral character" (indeed, they must sign the application). The application poses a series of questions to root out those who would otherwise be disqualified from obtaining a permit in order to exclude those with a felony or other serious conviction or with a history of mental illness or who have been convicted of domestic violence or are subject to a protective court order. It also seeks other good cause to deny the application. The applicant must also be 21, except for honorably discharged military personnel or those who are involved in shooting competitions.

Unquestionably, New York's process is more demanding and discretionary than most other states. In fact, it was challenged in federal court on these and also Second Amendment grounds, but in a 2012 decision by the U.S. Court of Appeals for the Second Circuit, the law was upheld,[74] and the Supreme Court refused to hear an appeal of the ruling.[75] Still, one of the state's leading advocates of gun rights, New York State Rifle and Pistol Association President Tom King, said this about the state system: "It's an involved process, it's not an easy process, but it's certainly not an impossible process."[76] (King's organization brought the lawsuit challenging the constitutionality of the SAFE Act.) King's sentiments are similar to those of other gun enthusiasts. The owner of the Westside Rifle and Pistol Range, the only public shooting range in Manhattan, said that "when it comes to gun laws, there's the whole country, and then there's New York." Yet owner Darren Leung added that tough laws made some sense, because "you want people to realize that this [a gun] is not a toy. If you make a mistake with a firearm, there is no coming back from that."[77]

To obtain the application from the clerk's office, along with a separate form that also had to be signed by my four character references, I paid a fee of $10. I needed to obtain two passport photos to accompany my completed application taken within thirty days prior to filing it, and I needed to get fingerprinted, also within thirty days of submitting the application. I had the photos taken at the local post office for $15 and received the two pictures then and there. The fingerprinting was done at the local hospital by a private company for a fee of $102.25; I needed to bring two forms of identification. (I expected to have my hands inked Eliot Ness–style, but I was pleased to find that inking of hands had gone the way of Ness's Untouchables—my prints were electronically scanned.) My prints were then sent to the state Department of Criminal Justice, the FBI's Criminal History Record information databases, and the local county clerk's office.

I returned the completed forms and photos to the clerk's office within a week of picking up the application, signed an authorization to give my permission for "all duly authorized agencies to furnish members of" the state police, county sheriff's department, city police, and county judges with records "regarding my criminal history" (of which there are none, as far as I know). In addition, the background check process extends to the office of mental health, the Probation Department, and the county district attorney's office. I was told that the process would take at least six months and perhaps longer—in part, at least, because of a recent glut of such applications.

My four references were sent a detailed, three-page questionnaire to complete and return, which asked their relationship to me, whether they had known me to engage in any illegal activities, have any psychological problems, or demonstrate any erratic behavior. The form also asked if they knew me to associate with "persons of undesirable character," if I was of good moral character, used controlled substances, committed any acts of violence, or had any physical conditions that would "interfere with the safe and proper use of a handgun." The form also asked my references to describe my reputation in the local community and to describe my "demeanor or behavior." Finally, it asked, "from the standpoint of the safety and welfare of the community," whether they thought I should be granted the permit, following up with whether they could think of any reason why I should not be granted the permit.

One may think of these questions as subjective to a degree and the responses as obviously based on my recommenders' perceptions, which could or could not be accurate. But the larger purpose is to send up flags to local authorities to at least make further inquiries about the applicant. Think, for example, of the case of Seung Hui Cho, a Virginia graduate student who legally purchased two handguns in his home state, despite a long history of behavioral and emotional problems well known to his relatives, friends, and those with whom he had interacted at Virginia Tech. Absent any required inquiry by state or local authorities, Cho was able to use his two legally acquired guns to kill 33 people (including himself) and wound 25 others in 2007. Arizona resident Jared Lee Loughner was able to legally obtain a handgun two months before shooting Congresswoman Gabrielle Giffords and 18 other people, killing 6, in 2011. The previous year, Loughner had been suspended from college for his bizarre and threatening behavior, and had been rejected for military service, in part for flunking a drug test. James Holmes legally purchased four guns to shoot up a movie theater in Colorado in 2012, killing 12 and injuring 58. Yet people who knew him reported that, the previous year, he began to change. He dropped out of school and had what some labeled a "psychotic break."[78]

Critics of gun laws argue that people determined to commit mayhem (which Cho, Loughner, and Holmes surely were) will not be prevented by tougher laws and will simply find another way to get a gun. But how and from where, exactly? Yes, guns are trafficked illegally, but such acquisitions involve greater planning, cost, trouble, risk, and concealment, any of which could result in blocking gun acquisition. But more to the point, our entire legal system is predicated on the presumption that the law matters. Every law, of every description, is violated. That does not mean that laws do not matter or that they should simply be repealed. Laws exist to deter adverse conduct, facilitate information gathering and prosecution, and express societal standards of behavior. Had Virginia, Arizona, and Colorado had the New York kind of extensive background check process in place, there is no guarantee that the three shooters would have been thwarted, but it is equally clear that any sort of meaningful inquiry would have set off alarm bells to stop these future mass murderers.

After the reference letters are completed, they are returned to the local police and, along with the original application and information received from other agencies, are sent to one of the two Cortland County judges, who then make a determination on my application. If the local magistrate has any further questions, the judge can interview the applicant directly. While this process has been traditionally handled by the county sheriff's office, the increased number of applications prompted its office to ask the city police to handle the applications of city residents. Here in Cortland County, according to local officials, the biggest uptick in pistol permit applications occurred between 2003 and 2009. An additional applications surge occurred at the start of 2009. Since enactment of the SAFE Act at the start of 2013, however, the local application volume has changed relatively little, I was told. According to county court officials, the processing of permit applications represents a fairly small proportion of the office's time and overall workload.

On Christmas Eve day, I received a letter from the county clerk's office informing me that my permit application had been approved. I was asked to come to the clerk's office to be photographed (the picture appears on the permit) and receive my license on the spot. From application to approval, the process took almost exactly four months. The only other stipulation was that I needed to take and provide proof of successful completion of a ten-hour handgun safety course taught by an NRA-certified instructor (I need not own my own gun to complete the class) within a year of license approval. Failure to complete the course and notify the clerk's office within twelve months results in revocation of the license.

I was given a list of several instructors in the area by the clerk's office. I called one in early January, reserved a class spot, for which the fee was $65 (active military personnel and law enforcement officers are exempt from the training class). The ten-hour class I attended was held on the last two Sundays in February in two five-hour blocks at the McGraw Sportsmen's Club. The fee included $20 for a one-year membership in the club. The two instructors received no pay for their efforts.

The two began by noting that they had been giving training classes for over a decade. In our particular group, while roughly a dozen people had signed up, only six showed. This seemed odd to the instructors, they noted, as the demand for pistol safety classes had been high in recent months, and the class enrollments had been high. All of us were white males ranging in age, I figured, from our twenties to sixties.

The course curriculum was organized around a single 150-page book, *NRA Guide to the Basics of Pistol Shooting*.[79] Class instruction and the 50-question test we all took at the end hewed pretty closely to the book. Among the first points made by the instructors, in response to a question, was the funding for gun safety classes. They pointed out that a federal law enacted in 1937 (with subsequent amendments), the Pittman-Robinson Act,[80] provided funding, through excise taxes, for hunter safety courses in all fifty states. Ironically, states can decide for themselves whether to provide or require handgun safety coursework as a prerequisite for handgun ownership or the granting of carry permits, and many have no such training requirements. Among the states that do require courses, their length and content vary widely.[81]

Our instruction began with some political content (this was not in our text), as the first 45 minutes consisted of criticism of the state SAFE Act, of what was described as biased portrayals of gun owners in the media, but also the exhortations to become involved in politics and to "check things out even when they agree with your side" of the issue—certainly good advice. The rest of the first class day and much of the second focused on the basics of handgun safety, the operation and mechanisms of handguns, including information on the nature and types of ammunition, the elements of good shooting skills, and handgun maintenance. In the latter part of the second class, we inspected, handled, and "dry-fired" several handguns, including two revolvers and one semi-automatic handgun. Thereafter, we took turns on the firing range, firing fifteen rounds at a paper target from three shooting positions: five from a sitting position, five standing but holding the gun with two hands, and five one-handed shots. We concluded with our 50-question test (it was untimed and open book, consisting of half multiple choice and half true-false); a score of 90 percent was required to pass the course, as all six of us did.[82] In all, the process cost me $192.50 and took four months from application to license receipt. Adding on the time to book and complete the safety course, the total duration of the process was six months.

MY CONCLUSION

Any time the government—any government—imposes new regulations, rules, or laws, some resentment, consternation, confusion, and adjustment are an inevitable consequence.[83] Some such efforts are, of course, met with greater initial acceptance than others. For example, new, tougher laws to address the problem of drunken driving were met with general popular approval, thanks in large part to a concerted effort by Mothers against Drunk Driving (MADD), a pressure group formed in 1980 to toughen anti–drunk driving laws and educate the public. And who, after all, was anxious to speak up on behalf of inebriation behind the wheel?

In the early 1960s, states moved to require that all automobiles have safety belts as a standard feature. New York enacted such a law for all new cars as of 1962; a similar federal law was enacted in 1968. These measures met with widespread approval, although the auto industry was successful for a while in delaying and weakening new laws. As an early critical article noted at the time, "Detroit sells the pleasure of driving and the utility of the car, not the dangers of it."[84] For decades, in fact, automakers insisted that safety features did not sell cars. History eventually proved them wrong.

New York took the next step, becoming the first state to require occupants to wear belts in 1984. As of 2009, only one state, New Hampshire, had no state requirement for seat belt use by adults. In thirty-three states, police may stop and ticket drivers solely for this offense; in the other states, the police may ticket only if the vehicle is stopped for some other offense.[85] While required seat belt installation met with general approval, ticketing for failing to "buckle up" met with significant public support but also considerable resistance at the start, partly because roughly three-quarters of drivers reportedly did not regularly wear seat belts and because of questions about how monitoring and compliance would be achieved.[86] That opposition faded, however, and actual seat belt use increased dramatically, along with major reductions in automobile deaths and injuries. This was a case where behavior followed the law. Studies have consistently shown that seat belt use rose from two car occupants in ten at the time of the enactment of such laws to over 80 percent in the years after the laws' enactment.[87]

To take a different example, in 1995, California became the first state to ban smoking in public places, based on a growing scientific and medical consensus of the harm caused by secondhand smoke. New York became the third state to enact such a law in 2003. Today, most states have some kind of public place smoking restrictions; only ten states impose no uniform restrictions.[88] In New York, the public registered support for the new law, but it also engendered fierce opposition, especially from restaurant and tavern owners who feared crippling drop-offs in business. After an initial adjustment period, including some initial business drop-off, fortunes revived, business boomed and prospered, and public health improved.[89]

These and many other cases of government regulation address two related sets of complaints about government. One is the expected resentment and criticism generated any time new regulations are imposed. Such sentiments are as predictable as they are readily understandable, yet they are fundamentally an implementation problem attendant to such change. The second and related set of complaints questions the decision or policy itself. Is the policy itself fatally flawed, unwise, or defective in concept? These two sets of complaints are analytically distinct but in practice nearly inseparable.

When we apply this framework to gun regulation in New York, the intermingling of these two sets of concerns is evident. While some critics continue to argue that the new regulations are flawed in concept, the equal if not louder set of criticisms described in this chapter center on the implementation problem—the inconvenience, the complexity, the confusion, the uncertainty of parts of the SAFE Act. Part of the generalized frustration expressed by the gun community arises from comparisons with other states, most of which have significantly more lax gun laws. And despite the gun community's protestations to the contrary, most national media focus is on places with lax laws, giving rise to the impression (especially among non-Americans) that lax laws are found most everywhere. But none of this takes us to the key questions: Are New York's tougher laws, including the SAFE Act, feasible to implement? And are they, in policy terms, justifiable as public policy?

As to the first question, this chapter survey, including my own ground-level experiences, leads me to conclude that they are indeed feasible—not because the new law is not in need of amendment or change, but because its basic tenets are both relatively clear and feasible. Compliance is unlikely to be either uniform or immediate, but that is not a mark of failure; it is, rather, the frictional adjustment between new legal standards and actual behavior. Is a seat belt compliance rate of over 80 percent a success, or is it a failure because it is not 100 percent? Was the high rate of noncompliance with seat belt requirements when such laws were first enacted an indicator that the new law was doomed to failure?

As to the second question, are these measures good or justifiable public policy? Each one of the measures that compose New York law examined here has been subject to intense, protracted, and heated (in a partisan politics sense) analysis and debate. It is difficult to claim a definitive answer to the policy question—and for what policy questions do definitive conclusions exist?—but there is plenty of evidence in that debate to support New York's enactments as public policy. That does not mean that other states can or should rush to embrace the New York model (and that will not happen in any case), but it does mean that the model works.

If I were to summarize the meta-argument of this book, it would be through a series of final propositions, to wit: Gun ownership is as old as America. Gun regulation, and regulations, are also as old as America. The Second Amendment poses no obstacle to virtually any gun regulation seriously debated or enacted in America, especially in the light of the fact that, from 1791 to 2007, no federal court ever struck down a gun law as a violation of the Second Amendment. As discussed in Chapter 3, from the time of the Supreme Court's 2008 *Heller* decision and the 2010 *McDonald* decision until 2013, over 700 Second Amendment–based challenges to gun laws have been filed in federal and state courts. To date, nearly all these challenges have failed. In addition, over 60 of these cases have been appealed to the Supreme Court, but it has declined to hear any of them to date.[90]

The American gun tradition is an old and mostly honorable tradition. Guns in contemporary America, especially in the last three decades, are actually regulated less than they have been in most of our history. Indeed, guns are regulated less than most significant consumer products, a fact that has nothing to do with the fact that "arms" are mentioned in the Second Amendment. Contemporary rollbacks of gun laws, whether one agrees or disagrees with them, do not constitute a return to our past but a refutation of it, as Chapter 2 made clear. The contemporary stand your ground movement, examined in Chapter 4, is a similar refutation of our legal, political, and cultural past. The New York SAFE Act (and other state gun laws) actually reflects continuity with American gun history, law, and practices, because, as our forefathers well knew, guns without regulation equal anarchy; yet regulations without guns is not America. Like it or not, guns are and will continue to be a part of who we are.

State Gun Laws, 1607–1934

Laws grouped alphabetically within these periods: 1607–1790;
1791–1867; 1868–1899; 1900–1934

State	Year	Law

		Ban Guns
Arkansas	1881	bar handgun carry/transfer
Kansas	1901	bar handgun carry
Tennessee	1879	bar handgun carry
Tennessee	1879	bar handgun transfer/ownership
Tennessee	1883	bar pistol cartridges
Texas	1871	bar handgun carry
Wyoming	1876	bar firearms carry in towns

		Brandishing
Massachusetts	1786	weapons not to be drawn/brandished
New York	1642	weapons not to be drawn/brandished
Arizona	1867	weapons not to be drawn/brandished
Idaho	1864	weapons not to be drawn/brandished
Washington	1852	weapons not to be drawn/brandished
Washington	1859	weapons not to be drawn/brandished
Arizona	1901	weapons not to be drawn/brandished
Arkansas	1868	weapons not to be drawn/brandished
Florida	1897	weapons not to be drawn/brandished
Georgia	1880	weapons not to be drawn/brandished
Idaho	1870	weapons not to be drawn/brandished

(continued)

Appendix (continued)

State	Year	Law
Indiana	1875	weapons not to be drawn/brandished
Indiana	1883	weapons not to be drawn/brandished
Montana	1885	weapons not to be drawn/brandished
Nevada	1873	weapons not to be drawn/brandished
New Mexico	1886	weapons not to be drawn/brandished
North Carolina	1889	weapons not to be drawn/brandished
Oregon	1893	weapons not to be drawn/brandished
Washington	1869	weapons not to be drawn/brandished
Wyoming	1884	weapons not to be drawn/brandished
Arkansas	1907	weapons not to be drawn/brandished
Idaho	1909	weapons not to be drawn/brandished
Indiana	1905	weapons not to be drawn/brandished
Michigan	1931	weapons not to be drawn/brandished
Oregon	1925	weapons not to be drawn/brandished
South Carolina	1910	weapons not to be drawn/brandished
Washington	1909	weapons not to be drawn/brandished

Laws Restricting/Barring Carrying

State	Year	Law
Massachusetts	1750	unlawfully assembled
Massachusetts	1798	carry threat
New Jersey	1686/1758	carry threat
North Carolina	1792	carry crowded place
Virginia	1794	carry crowded place
Alabama	1839	bar concealed carry (CC)
Alabama	1841	CC
Arkansas	1820/1837	CC
Colorado	1862	CC
Colorado	1867	CC
Delaware	1852	carry threat
District of Columbia	1857	carry threat
Georgia	1837	CC; regulate sale
Indiana	1820	CC
Indiana	1831	CC
Kentucky	1813	CC
Louisiana	1813	CC

(continued)

State	Year	Law
Louisiana	1841	CC
Maine	1840	carry
Massachusetts	1836	carry
Massachusetts	1850	carry when committing other crime
Massachusetts	1809	carry threat
Montana	1864	CC
New Mexico	1853	CC
New Mexico	1853	CC
New Mexico	1864	CC
Ohio	1859	CC
Oregon	1853	carry
Pennsylvania	1851	carry
Pennsylvania	1861	carry
Tennessee	1837	carry
Tennessee	1838	CC
Virginia	1838	CC
Virginia	1838	CC
Virginia	1856	carry
Wisconsin	1858	carry
Alaska	1896	CC
Arizona	1889	carry
Arizona	1893	CC
Arizona	1901	CC
Colorado	1876	carry
Colorado	1881	CC
Delaware	1881	CC; sale
Florida	1887	CC; sale
Florida	1885	carry
Illinois	1881	carry
Kentucky	1871	CC
Kentucky	1880	CC; sale
Kentucky	1891	CC; regulate sale
Maryland	1872	CC
Michigan	1887	CC
Michigan	1891	CC
Michigan	1895	carry

(continued)

State	Year	Law
Minnesota	1878	carry
Mississippi	1878	CC
Missouri	1873	CC (threatening/drunk)
Missouri	1883	CC
Nebraska	1893	CC
Nebraska	1895	carry
New York	1891	CC
North Carolina	1879	CC
North Dakota	1895	CC
Oklahoma	1890	CC
Oklahoma	1903	CC
Oregon	1885	CC
Rhode Island	1893	CC
South Carolina	1880	CC
South Dakota	1877	carry
Tennessee	1870	carry
Tennessee	1871	carry
Texas	1870	carry crowded place
Virginia	1869	CC
Virginia	1877	CC
Washington	1881	CC
Washington	1881	carry; use
Washington	1883	CC; use
Washington	1883	CC; use
West Virginia	1870	CC
West Virginia	1870	carry
West Virginia	1891	carry
Wisconsin	1883	CC
Wisconsin	1883	CC
Wisconsin	1883	carry
Wyoming	1876	CC
Connecticut	1923	sale/carry permits
Florida	1927	carry regulate
Hawaii	1913	carry
Idaho	1909	CC; sale
Indiana	1905	carry

(continued)

State	Year	Law
Iowa	1929	carry in auto
Massachusetts	1927	carry/in auto
Michigan	1901	carry/sale
Michigan	1925	carry/license/auto
Nebraska	1901	CC
New Jersey	1905	CC
New York	1911	carry/sale
North Carolina	1917	CC
North Dakota	1915	CC
Oregon	1903	CC
Rhode Island	1908	CC
Rhode Island	1927	carry permits; bar auto/semi-auto
Tennessee	1907	carry
Tennessee	1929	carry
Texas	1909	carry
West Virginia	1925	carry permits

		Dangerous/Unusual Weapons
New Jersey	1771	gun trap setting
Alabama	1837	tax on Bowie knives
Georgia	1837	bar pistol sales
Massachusetts	1850	bar sale certain weapons
Tennessee	1838	bar sale certain weapons
Arkansas	1881	bar pistol sales
Illinois	1881	bar deadly weapons
Michigan	1875	gun trap setting
North Dakota	1891	protected game
Ohio	1894	discharge against hard surface
South Dakota	1877	gun trap setting
Tennessee	1879	bar pistol sales
Texas	1871	bar handguns
Vermont	1884	gun trap setting
Arkansas	1909	carry/sale pistols
California	1927	machine guns
Delaware	1931	machine guns
Florida	1901	air guns

(continued)

State	Year	Law
Florida	1931	regulate/bar pistols
Hawaii	1933	machine guns
Illinois	1931	machine guns (+8 bullets)
Indiana	1927	machine guns
Iowa	1927	machine guns
Kansas	1933	machine guns
Louisiana	1932	machine guns
Maine	1909	silencers
Massachusetts	1926	silencers
Massachusetts	1927	machine guns
Michigan	1901	air guns
Michigan	1927	machine guns (+16 bullets)
Michigan	1929	bar machine guns / silencers
Michigan	1931	gun trap setting
Minnesota	1913	silencers
Minnesota	1933	machine guns / semi-auto
Missouri	1929	machine guns
Nebraska	1929	machine guns
New Hampshire	1915	gun trap setting
New Jersey	1913	spring/air guns
New Jersey	1927	machine guns
New York	1911	pistol licensing
New York	1916	silencers
New York	1931	machine guns / sawed-off shotgun
New York	1933	machine guns
North Dakota	1931	machine guns
Ohio	1933	machine guns / semi-auto
Oregon	1925	gun trap setting
Oregon	1933	machine guns
Pennsylvania	1929	machine guns
Rhode Island	1927	machine guns
South Carolina	1931	gun trap setting
South Carolina	1934	machine guns
South Dakota	1901	air guns
South Dakota	1933	machine guns
Tennessee	1931	carry/sale firearms

(continued)

Appendix (continued)

State	Year	Law
Texas	1933	machine guns
Utah	1901	gun trap setting
Vermont	1912	gun trap setting
Vermont	1912	silencers
Virginia	1933	machine guns / semi-auto
Washington	1909	gun trap setting
Washington	1933	machine guns
West Virginia	1915	air guns
West Virginia	1925	machine guns
Wisconsin	1929	machine guns
Wisconsin	1933	machine guns
Wisconsin	1933	machine guns
Wyoming	1921	silencers

Dueling

Massachusetts	1719	dueling barred
Massachusetts	1728	dueling barred
Pennsylvania	1779	dueling barred
Idaho	1863	dueling barred
Illinois	1855	dueling barred
Michigan	1816	dueling barred
Mississippi	1837	dueling barred
Nevada	1861	dueling barred
Rhode Island	1844	dueling barred
Washington	1859	dueling barred
Idaho	1874	dueling barred
Montana	1879	dueling barred
Washington	1869	dueling barred

Felons, Foreigners, Others Deemed Dangerous

Connecticut	1723	Indians
New Jersey	1639	Indians
New York	1645	Indians
New York	1656	Indians
Pennsylvania	1763	Indians

(continued)

Appendix (continued)

State	Year	Law
Pennsylvania	1776	nonassociators
Pennsylvania	1779	nonloyals
Virginia	1619	Indians*
Virginia	1631	Indians
Virginia	1639	Indians
Virginia	1642	Indians
Missouri	1844	Indians
Oregon	1853	Indians
Florida	1885	criminals
California	1931	noncitizen, felon
Colorado	1919	unnaturalized citizen
Connecticut	1923	alien
Massachusetts	1922	unnaturalized citizen
Michigan	1921	unnaturalized citizen
Minnesota	1917	foreign-born noncitizen
Montana	1913	aliens pay gun licenses
New Hampshire	1917	noncitizens
New Jersey	1902	nonstate residents licenses
New Jersey	1903	bar guns under 15; gun sale registry
New Jersey	1915	unnaturalized citizen
New Jersey	1916	hunting intoxicated
New Mexico	1921	unnaturalized citizen hunting; bar guns
New York	1911	noncitizen guns
North Dakota	1915	noncitizen hunting
Oregon	1933	CC, machine guns, unnaturalized, felons
Pennsylvania	1903	nonresidents, aliens hunting license
Pennsylvania	1909	unnaturalized citizen hunting
Rhode Island	1927	violent criminals
Utah	1905	nonresident gun license
Utah	1917	unnaturalized citizen hunting
Washington	1911	noncitizen gun licensing
West Virginia	1925	alien guns
Wyoming	1913	nonresident gun/hunt license
Wyoming	1915	alien hunting license
Wyoming	1925	noncitizen guns

(continued)

State	Year	Law
		Firing Weapons
Connecticut	1672	alarm fire
Delaware	NA	no firing towns
Massachusetts	1697	no night firing
Massachusetts	1713	no firing near roads
Massachusetts	1746	no firing towns
Massachusetts	1785	no firing towns
New York	1665	no firing occasions
New York	1785	no firing occasions
North Carolina	1774	hunting by firelight
Pennsylvania	1750	no firing towns
Pennsylvania	1774	no firing occasions
Rhode Island	1731	gun mischief
South Carolina	1731	no fire after dark
Virginia	1631	waste gunpowder / drinking
Virginia	1632	waste gunpowder / drinking
Virginia	1642	Sabbath shooting
Virginia	1655	shooting while drinking (except weddings/funerals)
Virginia	1657	Sabbath shooting
Virginia	1657	hunting private lands
Arizona	1867	no firing towns
Connecticut	1845	no firing towns
Delaware	1812	no firing towns
Kansas	1860	no firing towns
Kentucky	1839	no firing towns
Kentucky	1855	no firing towns
Kentucky	1865	no firing towns
Maryland	1792	no firing towns
Mississippi	1833	no firing towns
New Hampshire	1823	no firing towns
North Carolina	1862	no firing towns
Ohio	1823	no firing towns
Ohio	1831	no firing towns
Rhode Island	1820	no firing towns

(continued)

State	Year	Law
Tennessee	1825	no firing towns; carry
Vermont	1818	no firing towns
Virginia	1806	no firing towns
Arizona	1901	no firing towns/buildings
California	1874	no firing towns
California	1877	no firing towns (unincorporated)
Delaware	NA	no firing towns
Georgia	1875	no firing towns
Georgia	1898	Sabbath (Sunday) shooting
Idaho	1868	no firing towns
Kentucky	1875	no firing towns
Michigan	1887	no firing towns
Montana	1873	no firing towns
Nebraska	1895	no firing towns
Nebraska	1895	no firing towns
Nevada	1891	trains
New Jersey	1872	firing on bridges
North Carolina	1891	no firing towns
Oklahoma	1890	no firing public places
Oregon	1885	no firing towns
Pennsylvania	1871	no firing towns
Wisconsin	1883	no firing towns
Connecticut	1901	no firing towns
Delaware	1901	no firing towns
Florida	1927	no firing towns
Georgia	1906	no firing towns
Indiana	1927	no firing machine guns
Iowa	1909	no firing guns
Kentucky	1924	no display or firing guns
Louisiana	1912	no firing guns
Maryland	1900	no firing guns
Maryland	1904	permits for target shooting
Minnesota	1905	gun crime
New Jersey	1907	no firing towns
New York	1900	no firing towns
North Carolina	1901	no firing towns

(continued)

State	Year	Law
Oregon	1903	no firing towns
Pennsylvania	1903	no firing towns
Tennessee	1901	no firing towns
Tennessee	1921	regulate firearms
Texas	1901	regulate firearms
Vermont	1900	regulate sale/use of guns
Virginia	1902	regulate firearm discharge
West Virginia	1905	no firing towns

Hunting

State	Year	Law
Maryland	1715	hunting on private land
Massachusetts	1710	hunting water fowl
Massachusetts	1717	hunting water fowl
New Jersey	1771	hunting preserve game
New York	1652	no hunting in city
North Carolina	1745	deer hunting season; hunting abuses
North Carolina	1768	deer hunting season; hunting abuses
Pennsylvania	1721	hunting on private land
Vermont	1777	regulate hunting
Virginia	1639	hunting on private land
Virginia	1642	hunting on private land
Delaware	NA	hunting water fowl
Delaware	NA	hunting water fowl
Delaware	NA	hunting water fowl
Florida	1828	hunting firelight at night
Florida	1852	hunting firelight at night
Maryland	1838	hunting water fowl
North Carolina	1856	hunting deer at night
Virginia	1852	hunting water fowl at night
Connecticut	1872	hunting water fowl
Delaware	NA	hunting water fowl
Georgia	1880	hunting deer firelight at night
Iowa	1894	hunting on private land
Maryland	1874	hunting water fowl at night
Maryland	1882	hunting water fowl
Michigan	1883	hunting water fowl

(continued)

State	Year	Law
Nebraska	1893	hunting water fowl
New Jersey	1874	hunting water fowl
North Carolina	1869	Sabbath hunting
North Carolina	1879	hunting water fowl
North Dakota	1899	hunting water fowl
Ohio	NA	Sabbath hunting
Ohio	1874	hunting water fowl
Oregon	1895	hunting water fowl
Pennsylvania	1876	hunting water fowl
Rhode Island	1890	hunting water fowl
South Carolina	1878	shooting fish
South Dakota	1899	hunting water fowl
Texas	1897	hunting water fowl
Utah	1899	hunting water fowl
Virginia	1875	hunting water fowl
Washington	1883	hunting water fowl
West Virginia	1889	hunting water fowl
Arizona	1931	hunting with silencers; certain weapons
Arkansas	1927	shooting fish
California	1901	shotgun hunting
Colorado	1907	hunting at night
Colorado	1931	hunting from aircraft
Connecticut	1901	game preserve
Delaware	1911	hunting guns
Delaware	1927	hunting with silencers
Florida	1911	shooting fish
Florida	1921	hunting off season
Georgia	1924	hunting with repeating shotgun
Hawaii	1925	shooting fish
Illinois	1901	hunting water fowl
Iowa	1933	hunting guns
Kansas	1921	hunting from aircraft
Kentucky	1904	wildlife preservation
Louisiana	1908	hunting water fowl
Louisiana	1918	hunting with silencers
Maine	1911	hunting deer with shotgun

(continued)

State	Year	Law
Maine	1919	hunting at night
Maryland	1900	hunting at night or snow
Massachusetts	1900	hunting water fowl
Michigan	1901	hunting water fowl
Minnesota	1903	hunting water fowl
Mississippi	1922	hunting water fowl
Missouri	1905	hunting with barred weapons
Nebraska	1901	hunting with barred weapons
New Hampshire	1905	hunting with barred weapons
New Jersey	1906	deer hunting
New Jersey	1911	hunting with silencers
New Jersey	1914	minimum gun hunting age
New Jersey	1920	hunting with silencers, certain weapons
New Mexico	1915	hunting licensing
New Mexico	1921	hunting with barred weapons
New York	1900	hunting from boat, certain weapons
North Carolina	1903	hunting water fowl
North Carolina	1917	hunting quail
North Carolina	1925	hunting with silencers
North Dakota	1901	hunting certain weapons
Ohio	1900	hunting certain weapons
Oregon	1901	hunting certain weapons
Pennsylvania	1905	hunting deer with buckshot
Pennsylvania	1923	hunting automatic weapons
Rhode Island	1907	deer hunting
Rhode Island	1914	hunting certain weapons
South Carolina	1918	hunting automatic weapons
South Dakota	1909	hunting certain weapons
Tennessee	1903	hunting certain weapons
Texas	1919	hunting licensing
Utah	1908	hunting certain weapons
Vermont	1908	hunting licensing
Vermont	1923	hunting automatic weapons
Virginia	1902	hunting at night
Washington	1913	hunting water fowl
West Virginia	1909	hunting licensing

(continued)

State	Year	Law
Wisconsin	1913	hunting with gun and dogs
Wisconsin	1921	hunting certain weapons
Wyoming	1921	shooting fish

Manufacturing, Inspection, Sale

State	Year	Law
Maryland	1757	no ammo to Indians
New Jersey	1776	bar gunpowder sale
Connecticut	1836	gunpowder storage
Indiana	1847	gunpowder storage
Iowa	1845	gunpowder storage
Massachusetts	1814	gun barrel testing
New Hampshire	1820	gunpowder inspectors/regulation
New Hampshire	1825	gunpowder sale
New Jersey	1811	gunpowder manufacture regulation
Ohio	1849	gunpowder sale
Pennsylvania	1794	gunpowder inspection
Tennessee	1867	gunpowder manufacture regulation
Vermont	1865	gunpowder manufacture regulation
California	1883	gunpowder manufacture regulation
Kentucky	1874	gunpowder manufacture regulation
Nebraska	1869	gunpowder sale
Nebraska	1895	gunpowder sale
New Hampshire	1891	gunpowder sale
New Jersey	1886	gunpowder manufacture regulation
Ohio	1889	gunpowder sale
Oklahoma	1890	gunpowder regulation
Oklahoma	1890	gunpowder regulation
Rhode Island	1885	gunpowder transport
Tennessee	1899	gunpowder regulation
Connecticut	1909	gunpowder regulation
Delaware	1913	gunpowder child labor
Florida	1923	shotgun shell regulation
Florida	1927	weapons/ammo sale
Georgia	1902	gun shop/dealer regulation
Michigan	1901	gunpowder sale
New Hampshire	1913	gunpowder transport

(*continued*)

State	Year	Law
New Hampshire	1917	firearms/gunpowder sale
New Jersey	1903	gunpowder transport
New Jersey	1927	pawnbroker firearms regulation
New Mexico	1923	gunpowder transport
New York	1911	register handgun sales
North Carolina	1905	firearm sale/use
North Carolina	1909	firearms dealer licensing
Oregon	1903	gunpowder transport
South Carolina	1903	gunpowder sale purpose
South Dakota	1913	gunpowder sale exemption
Utah	1901	gunpowder transport/marketing
Vermont	1919	gunpowder transport
West Virginia	1925	firearms dealers public display
Wisconsin	1911	gunpowder regulation
Wisconsin	1911	gunpowder child labor

Militia Regulation

State	Year	Law
Connecticut	1775	impress arms from nonmilitia members
Delaware	1782	failure to keep arms
Georgia	1770	carry arms to church
Massachusetts	1693	require gun ownership / militia drill
Massachusetts	1742	attend militia musters
Massachusetts	1757	require gun ownership / militia drill
Massachusetts	1784	require gun ownership
New Hampshire	1786	militia have firearms
New Jersey	1718	gun carry on private land
New Jersey	1778	require gun ownership
New York	1640	require gun ownership
New York	1786	require gun ownership
North Carolina	1786	require gun ownership
Rhode Island	1844	militia weapons kept unloaded
Vermont	1779	require gun ownership
Virginia	1631	travel with guns
Virginia	1632	armed to church
Virginia	1738	require gun ownership / militia drill
Virginia	1642	armed to church

(continued)

Appendix (continued)

State	Year	Law
Virginia	1755	require muster attendance
Virginia	1757	require gun ownership
Virginia	1762	militia regulation
Virginia	1785	require gun ownership / militia drill
11 state constitutions	1683– 1777	militias
Connecticut	1799	require gun ownership / militia drill
Kentucky	1799	muster attendance
Louisiana	1804	require gun ownership
Maryland	1799	maintain guns
Minnesota	NA	militia membership
Mississippi	1814	require gun ownership
Missouri	1835	require gun ownership
New Hampshire	1795	militia membership
North Carolina	1861	require gun ownership
Ohio	1836	require gun ownership
Rhode Island	1794	require gun ownership
South Carolina	1791	require gun ownership / militia drill
Tennessee	1821	require gun ownership / militia drill
Texas	1836	require gun ownership / militia drill
Vermont	1837	require gun ownership
Iowa	1878	militia membership
Missouri	1877	firearm loaded/discharge

		Sales to Minors or Others Deemed Irresponsible
Alabama	1856	pistols to minors
Kentucky	1859	pistols to minors, negroes
Delaware	NA	guns to minors
Florida	1881	guns to minors / unsound mind
Georgia	1910	guns to minors
Illinois	1911	no gun permits to minors/convicts / poor moral character
Indiana	1881	guns to minors
Kansas	1883	guns to minors / unsound mind
Kentucky	1888	guns to minors

(continued)

Appendix (continued)

State	Year	Law
Louisiana	1890	concealed weapons to minors
Michigan	1883	guns to minors
Minnesota	NA	guns to minors
Mississippi	1878	guns to minors
Nebraska	1895	guns to minors
New Jersey	1885	guns to minors
Ohio	1888	pistols to minors
Pennsylvania	1881	pistols to minors
Rhode Island	1883	ammo to minors
Tennessee	1878	pistols to minors
Texas	1897	pistols to minors
Arizona	1907	constables carry while drunk
Delaware	1918	minors hunting
Idaho	1909	guns to minors / while drunk
Indiana	1905	pistols to minors
Maryland	1904	guns to minors
Maryland	1908	guns to minors
Massachusetts	1909	guns to minors
Michigan	1931	firearms alcohol/drugs
New York	1900	gun sales to minors
New York	1911	guns to minors
North Carolina	1913	guns to minors
Ohio	1913	guns to minors
Oregon	1903	guns to minors
South Carolina	1923	guns to minors
South Dakota	1903	guns to minors
Utah	1905	guns to minors
Vermont	1912	guns to minors
Virginia	1902	guns to minors
Washington	1909	guns to minors

Registration and Taxation

New York	1652	gun trade by private persons
Virginia	1631	record of arms
Virginia	1651	arms to government
Georgia	1866	tax on more than 3 guns owned

(*continued*)

Appendix (continued)

State	Year	Law
Mississippi	1867	tax on guns owned
North Carolina	1858	tax on arms worn on the person
North Carolina	1856	tax on pistols
Pennsylvania	1795	gunpowder storage
Pennsylvania	1802	inspect gunpowder
Rhode Island	1851	tax pistol firing gallery
Virginia	1806	gun licensing for free negroes
Alabama	1898	pistol dealer tax
Florida	1898	license Winchester rifles
Hawaii	1870	license firearms
Georgia	1894	pistol dealer tax
Louisiana	1870	pistol gallery tax
Mississippi	1886	shooting gallery tax
Mississippi	1898	pistol cartridge tax
Nebraska	1895	CC licenses
Oregon	1868	right to have guns
South Carolina	1893	pistol sales licenses
Virginia	NA	CC permit
Wyoming	1899	gun license
California	1931	public/private gun sale registration
Connecticut	1923	permit for retail gun sales
Delaware	1909	nonresident gunner fee
Georgia	1921	guns' value listed on tax returns
Hawaii	1933	firearms registration/licensing / sales regulation
Illinois	1931	machine gun registration
Michigan	1913	firearms registration
Michigan	1925	firearms transfer regulation
Michigan	1927	pistol safety inspection
Mississippi	1900	county assessment number of guns +1; pistols
Mississippi	1906	pistol dealer records/fees
Montana	1918	firearms registration
North Carolina	1919	concealed weapons sale regulation
Ohio	1900	gunpowder magazine licensing
Rhode Island	1927	firearms possession regulation

(continued)

State	Year	Law
South Carolina	1923	ammo license tax
Virginia	1902	firearms tax
Wyoming	1933	firearms registration

Race- and Slavery-Based Firearms Restrictions

Maryland	1715	negroes/slaves gun carry barred
New Jersey	1750	slave gun carry barred
North Carolina	1715	slaves hunting with dogs
South Carolina	1731	slaves gun carrying/hunting
Virginia	1639	men armed except negroes
Delaware	NA	slaves gun carrying
Delaware	1827	slaves gun carrying
Delaware	NA	guns barred to negroes
Delaware	1843	repeal gun licenses for negroes
Delaware	NA	negro gun license fees
Delaware	NA	negroes barred guns
Georgia	1860	negroes barred guns
Indiana	1804	bar negro gun carrying
Kentucky	1798	bar negro gun carrying
Kentucky	1851	bar negro gun carrying
Maryland	1806	bar slave gun and dog ownership
Mississippi	1799	guns barred to negroes
Mississippi	1804	slave gun possession
Missouri	1854	license negro gun ownership
New Mexico	1858	bar weapons to slaves
North Carolina	1860	bar negro gun ownership
Tennessee	1835	no guns to slaves
Texas	1839	no slave gun carrying

Sensitive Areas and Times

Delaware	1776	no guns on election day
Maryland	1637	no guns in Assembly
Maryland	1650	no guns in Assembly
New Hampshire	1759	no gun fire after dark
New Jersey	NA	no pistols at public gatherings/schools/ churches

(continued)

Appendix (continued)

State	Year	Law
New Jersey	NA	no loaded guns during militia drill
Ohio	1790	target shooting away from buildings
Pennsylvania	1821	shooting fowl in city
Rhode Island	1636	gunplay if drinking
Rhode Island	1762	gunfire near powder house
Rhode Island	NA	gunfire near streets
Connecticut	1847	firearms discharge near cemeteries
Delaware	NA	firearms discharge within towns
Georgia	1847	firearms discharge in cemeteries
Illinois	1855	firearms discharge in cemeteries
Indiana	1855	shooting at trains
Kentucky	1866	hunting on the Sabbath
Maryland	1841	firearms discharge in cemeteries
Massachusetts	1856	firearms discharge in cemeteries
Massachusetts	1866	firearms unloaded during parade
Missouri	1840	firearms discharges in cemeteries
New Hampshire	1795	firearms discharge on muster day
New Hampshire	1820	firearms unloaded during parade
North Carolina	1868	hunting on the Sabbath
Ohio	1788	firearms discharge near towns
Ohio	1841	firearms discharge in cemeteries
Pennsylvania	1847	firearms discharge in cemeteries
Pennsylvania	1848	firearms discharge on bridge
Rhode Island	1819	firearms discharge near towns
Rhode Island	1843	firearms unloaded during parade
Rhode Island	1851	shooting ranges away from towns
Texas	1866	firearms discharge near towns
Vermont	1818	firearms discharges before parades
Washington	1859	no firearms in jails
Alabama	1898	firearms discharge on trains
Arizona	1901	no firearms carry in church, public gathering
Florida	1899	firearms discharge on trains
Georgia	1882	firearms discharge around roads at night
Georgia	1897	firearms discharge on trains or picnics
Illinois	1885	firearms discharge in cemeteries

(continued)

State	Year	Law
Iowa	1876	shoot at trains
Louisiana	1870	gun carry on election day
Louisiana	1873	firearms discharge in cemeteries
Maryland	1872	firearms discharge on bridge
Maryland	1886	gun carry on election day
Maryland	1890	no hunting or shooting on Sundays
Mississippi	1878	bar CC at schools
Missouri	1879	firearms discharge near public buildings
Nevada	1881	firearms discharge in public places
North Carolina	1868	no gun carrying on Sundays
North Carolina	1871	firearms discharge in cemeteries
North Carolina	1889	firearms discharge near churches
North Carolina	1893	firearms discharge near churches
North Carolina	1899	firearms discharge near roads
Oregon	NA	bar gun carrying on private property or shooting near highways
Pennsylvania	1874	firearms discharge near bridges
Rhode Island	1892	firearms discharge near roads
South Carolina	1899	firearms discharge while drunk
Texas	1871	firearms discharge near cities
Texas	1889	shoot at trains
Virginia	1877	no gun carry in churches or on Sundays
Virginia	1885	firearms discharge in cemeteries
Wisconsin	1883	firearms discharge in towns
Wyoming	1879	firing from or at trains
Arizona	1912	firearms discharge across highways, farmland, buildings
Connecticut	1927	allow gun club shooting affiliated with NRA
Delaware	1932	no gun carry while training dogs
Florida	1933	machine gun fire across roads, parks, etc.
Georgia	1903	no guns in penitentiaries
Georgia	1905	firing at or in train cars
Georgia	1910	shooting at dwellings
Hawaii	1927	firearms discharge across highways
Idaho	1901	regulate/bar firearms in cities

(continued)

State	Year	Law
Idaho	1917	no CC in towns, camps, public gatherings, highways
Indiana	1905	shooting at stage coaches, trains, streetcars, other conveyances
Iowa	1929	rifle shooting across public waters
Maine	1919	no loaded long guns in cars
Maryland	1908	firearms discharges near bridges
Maryland	1910	hunting on Sundays
Michigan	1925	hunting in wildlife refuges
Minnesota	1905	hunting/carrying in state parks
Minnesota	1907	shooting near cities
Mississippi	1924	hunting in bird sanctuary
Missouri	1923	carry firearms and liquor in any conveyance
Montana	1917	hunting in game preserves
New Jersey	1900	firing at train or trolly cars
New Jersey	1901	hunting on Sundays with dogs
New Jersey	1904	no guns in marshes
North Carolina	1905	firearm discharge near towns
North Carolina	1911	firearm discharge near churches
North Carolina	1921	no firearms in parks
North Dakota	1919	shotgun possession in rural areas unlawful hunting
Oregon	1913	shooting from roads
South Carolina	1900	firearm discharge while drunk near roads
Tennessee	1911	no weapons on election day
Texas	1901	firearm discharge near towns
Virginia	1916	no hunting in designated lands
West Virginia	1901	shooting near roads or grounds near dwellings
Wisconsin	1917	no firearms in parks / wildlife refuges

Sentence Enhancement for Weapons Use

State	Year	Law
Connecticut	1783	gun crimes punishable by death
Massachusetts	1717	killing waterfowl with gun
Ohio	1788	armed robbery/attack

(continued)

State	Year	Law
Mississippi	1837	dueling penalties
Nebraska	1858	armed assault
Washington	1854	assault with pistol
Florida	1888	criminal offense with weapons
Montana	1887	assault with pistol
North Carolina	1869	assault with firearm
South Carolina	1880	criminal offense with weapons
Washington	1869	assault with a pistol
Illinois	1931	serious crime with machine gun
Indiana	1921	liquor transport with gun
Indiana	1929	serious crime with gun
Kentucky	1934	robbery with gun
Maryland	1927	alcohol transport with guns
Michigan	1913	felonious assault with gun
Michigan	1925	CC firearms licensing; commit felony with gun
Minnesota	1927	commit felony with firearms
New Jersey	1934	machine/submachine gun possession / firearms permits
North Dakota	1921	liquor transport with gun
Pennsylvania	1929	commit crime with machine gun
Rhode Island	1927	commit crime with gun

Storage

State	Year	Law
Massachusetts	1782	firearms seized if improperly stored
Massachusetts	1783	no loaded firearms in houses
Connecticut	1859	inspect gun houses
Connecticut	1862	inspect gun houses
Maine	1821	search for gunpowder
Michigan	1867	firearms discharge in towns
New Hampshire	1793	gunpowder in homes
New Mexico	1851	firearms discharge
Virginia	1879	firearms discharge
Massachusetts	1919	search warrants for ownership of unreasonable number of firearms
Texas	1901	regulate/bar use of firearms

(continued)

Appendix (continued)

Source: Mark Anthony Frassetto, "Firearms and Weapons Legislation up to 1934," Georgetown University Law Center, January 15, 2013. Available at http://papers.ssrn.com/sol3/papers.cfm?abstract_id=2200991. Document data drawn from HeinOnline Session Laws Library, Yale Law School Avalon Project, digitized state archives' session laws. Most militia regulations and statutes omitted, as were duplicative statutes within states, gunpowder storage laws, many hunting regulations, and many laws pertaining to the firing of weapons.

In a few instances, the years of laws given fall outside of their designated ranges. In these instances, the laws were passed in the periods in which they are placed. The later dates given are reference years.

* "That no man do sell or give any Indians any piece, shot, or powder, or any other arms offensive or defensive, upon pain of being held a traitor to the colony and of being hanged as soon as the fact is proved, without all redemption."

Notes

Introduction

1. Saul Cornell, *A Well-Regulated Right* (New York: Oxford University Press, 2006); Adam Winkler, *Gunfight* (New York: W. W. Norton, 2011); Craig R. Whitney, *Living with Guns* (New York: Public Affairs, 2012); Saul Cornell and Nathan Kozuskanich, eds., *The Second Amendment on Trial* (Amherst: University of Massachusetts Press, 2013). An excellent, sweeping treatment of the evolution of gun policies and practices in Canada is R. Blake Brown, *Arming and Disarming: A History of Gun Control in Canada* (Toronto: University of Toronto Press, 2012).

2. Glenn H. Utter and Robert J. Spitzer, *Encyclopedia of Gun Control and Gun Rights* (Amenia, NY: Grey House, 2011), 131–33; Tom W. Smith et al., *General Social Survey, 2012* (Chicago: National Opinion Research Center, 2013). The percentage of Americans who have reported having at least one gun in their home has declined from about 50 percent in the 1970s to about 34 percent at the end of the first decade of this century.

3. Cornell, *A Well-Regulated Right*; Alexander DeConde, *Gun Violence in America* (Boston: Northeastern University Press, 2001); Winkler, *Gunfight*; Whitney, *Living with Guns*. More than any other single scholar or writer, historian Saul Cornell has been most responsible for excavating the legal and social realities of guns, laws, and practices in early America. In addition to his many articles, see his *Whose Right to Bear Arms Did the Second*

Amendment Protect? (New York: Bedford / St. Martin's, 2000); *A Well-Regulated Right*; Cornell and Kozuskanich, eds., *The Second Amendment on Trial*. The first important serious treatment of early gun laws and history is Lee Kennett and James LaVerne Anderson, *The Gun in America* (Westport, CT: Greenwood Press, 1975).

Chapter 1

1. For example, Nevada cattle rancher, Cliven Bundy, gained national attention in 2014 when he stared down government agents, thanks in large measure to hundreds of antigovernment armed men who came to his "rescue" when the federal government attempted to confiscate his cattle. For over twenty years, Bundy had grazed his cattle on federal land but refused to pay the nominal grazing fees normally charged by the government for this privilege. The Bureau of Land Management fined him $1 million in unpaid fees and interest. When agents moved to confiscate the cattle in lieu of payment, they backed down in the face of armed and angry Bundy supporters rather than risk a full-fledged armed confrontation. Bundy was interviewed in the national media and extolled as a hero on Fox News. While insisting that he was following Nevada state laws (he actually was violating Nevada's constitution), Bundy proclaimed, "I don't recognize the United States government as even existing." Max Strasser, "For Militiamen, the Fight for Cliven Bundy's Ranch Is Far from Over," *Newsweek.com*, April 23, 2014, at http://www.newsweek. com/2014/05/02/militiamen-fight-over-cliven-bundys-ranch-far-over-248354.html.

2. Herman Finer, *The Theory and Practice of Modern Government* (New York: Dial Press, 1934), 15.

3. Finer, *Theory and Practice*, 74.

4. Carl J. Friedrich, *Constitutional Government and Democracy* (Boston: Little, Brown, 1941), 18.

5. Benjamin Ginsberg et al., *We the People: Essentials Edition* (New York: W. W. Norton, 2013), 29.

6. Alexander Hamilton, James Madison, and John Jay, *The Federalist Papers* (New York: New American Library, 1961), Paper 15, 110.

7. Hamilton, Madison, and Jay, *Federalist Papers*, Paper 51, 322.

8. "Senate Judiciary Committee Hearing on Gun Violence," *Washington Post*, January 30, 2013, at http://articles.washingtonpost. com/2013-01-30/politics/36628109_1_gun-violence-gabby-giffords-senator-grassley.

9. See Joshua Horwitz and Casey Anderson, *Guns, Democracy, and the Insurrectionist Idea* (Ann Arbor: University of Michigan Press, 2009).

10. Wayne LaPierre did not come to this recently. In 1994 he wrote that "the right to arms is to enable citizens to resist a military takeover of our government" and "overthrowing tyranny." *Guns, Crime, and Freedom* (Washington, DC: Regnery, 1994), 19. Writing in 2002 with James Jay Baker, he said: "Our right to keep and bear arms . . . clearly meant for our possession of arms to be an insurance policy to make sure that the government respects our liberty." *Shooting Straight* (Washington, DC: Regnery, 2002), 109.

11. Glenn Beck, *Control: Exposing the Truth about Guns* (New York: Threshold Editions, 2013), 54–55. See also David B. Kopel, *The Truth about Gun Control* (New York: Encounter Books, 2013).

12. LaPierre and Baker, *Shooting Straight*, 110–13.

13. Greg Sargent, "Sharron Angle Floated Possibility of Armed Insurrection," *Washington Post*, June 15, 2010, at http://voices.washingtonpost.com/plum-line/2010/06/ sharron_angle_floated_possibil.html.

14. The poll was a survey of 863 registered voters nationwide conducted in late April 2013. "Beliefs about Sandy Hook Cover-up, Coming Revolution Underlie Divide on Gun Control," *Fairleigh Dickinson University's Public Mind*, May 1, 2013, at http:// www.fdu.edu/newspubs/publicmind/2013/guncontrol/final.pdf.

15. *D.C. v. Heller*, 554 U.S. 570 (2008), at 598, 600, and 613. The Court was not declaring this to be a right under the Second Amendment; it was a passing comment referred to as a "dictum."

16. For example, conservative author and commentator Ben Shapiro argues specifically for civilian assault weapons ownership in the name of resisting tyranny. "Ben Shapiro on Why Civilians Need Military Assault Weapons," *Piers Morgan Tonight*, CNN, January 10, 2013, at http://piersmorgan.blogs.cnn.com/2013/01/10/ ben-shapiro-on-why-civilians-need-military-style-assault-wea pons-for-the-perspective-possibility-of-resistance-to-tyranny/.

Fox News commentator Andrew P. Napolitano also makes this argument: "Guns and Freedom," *Foxnews.com*, January 10, 2013, at http://www.foxnews.com/opinion/2013/01/10/guns-and-freedom/. See also http://www.dailypaul.com/266890/why-do-i-need-an-assault-rifle and http://www.armedcitizensnetwork.org/our-journal/281-february-2013.

17. John Locke, *Of Civil Government, Second Treatise* (Chicago: Henry Regnery, 1955), 109.

18. William Ebenstein, *Great Political Thinkers* (New York: Holt, Rinehart and Winston, 1969), 393.

19. Robert A. Goldwin, "John Locke," in *History of Political Philosophy*, Leo Strauss and Joseph Cropsey, eds. (Chicago: Rand McNally, 1972), 480.

20. Locke, *Of Civil Government*, 170.

21. Locke, *Of Civil Government*, 184.

22. Locke, *Of Civil Government*, 170-71.

23. Locke, *Of Civil Government*, 142.

24. Locke, *Of Civil Government*, 193.

25. Locke, *Of Civil Government*, 141-42.

26. Joseph Ellis, ed., *What Did the Declaration Declare?* (Boston: Bedford / St. Martin's, 1999).

27. Pauline Maier, "Mr. Jefferson and His Editors," *What Did the Declaration Declare?*, 95-106; Garry Wills, "Jefferson and the Scottish Enlightenment," *What Did the Declaration Declare?*, 65-78.

28. Saul Cornell and Nathan DeDino, "A Well Regulated Right: The Early American Origins of Gun Control," *Fordham Law Review* 73 (November 2004): 494. See also Saul Cornell, *A Well-Regulated Militia* (New York: Oxford University Press, 2006), 27; David Hackett Fischer, *Paul Revere's Ride* (New York: Oxford University Press, 1994), xvii, 149-64.

29. 1 U.S. Stat. 264.

30. 10 U.S. Code 331-34.

31. Alexander Hamilton, James Madison, and John Jay, *The Federalist Papers* (New York: New American Library, 1961), 178-79.

32. Thomas P. Slaughter, *The Whiskey Rebellion* (New York: Oxford University Press, 1988).

33. Saul Cornell, *Whose Right to Bear Arms Did the Second Amendment Protect?* (Boston: Bedford / St. Martin's, 2000), 19-20.

34. "Letter from Lincoln to James C. Conkling, August 26, 1863," in *Abraham Lincoln: His Speeches and Writings*, Roy P. Basler, ed. (Cleveland, OH: World Publishing, 1946), 723. In his message to Congress on July 4, 1861, Lincoln said, "When ballots have fairly and constitutionally decided there can be no successful appeal back to bullets; that there can be no successful appeal except to ballots themselves at succeeding elections." James D. Richardson, *Messages and Papers of the Presidents*, 13 vols. (Washington, DC: Bureau of National Literature, 1913), vol. 5: 3231.

35. Talcott Parsons, ed., *Max Weber: The Theory of Social and Economic Organization* (New York: Macmillan, 1947), 156.

36. David C. Williams, *The Mythic Meanings of the Second Amendment* (New Haven, CT: Yale University Press, 2003), 5.

37. Kopel, *Truth about Gun Control*, 35–36.

38. Sanford Levinson, "The Embarrassing Second Amendment," *Yale Law Journal* 99 (December 1989): 650.

39. H. H. Gerth and C. Wright Mills, eds., *From Max Weber: Essays in Sociology* (New York: Oxford University Press, 1946), 78.

40. Kenneth Minogue, *Politics* (New York: Oxford University Press, 1995), 3.

41. Minogue, *Politics*, 40.

42. Jeffrey Gettleman, "Ominous Signs, Then a Cruel Attack," *New York Times Sunday Review*, September 29, 2013, 1.

43. Oscar Martinez, "Making a Deal with Murderers," *New York Times Sunday Review*, October 6, 2013, 1.

44. William Ebenstein, *Great Political Thinkers* (New York: Holt, Rinehart and Winston, 1969), 365–70, 394–99; Minogue, *Politics*, 38–42.

45. See, for example, Ebenstein, *Great Political Thinkers*, who notes that Aristotle framed the question of state authority as "moral sovereignty," reflecting his more organic view of governing in the context of Greek city-states (69). By the seventeenth century, according to Ebenstein, the state was "sharply distinguished from all other organizations because it alone possesses sovereignty, or the highest authority in a politically organized community, and the legal monopoly of enforcing such authority in its territory" (68–69).

46. Laurence Berns, "Thomas Hobbes," in *History of Political Philosophy*, Leo Strauss and Joseph Cropsey, eds. (Chicago: Rand McNally, 1972), 390.

47. Ebenstein, *Great Political Thinkers*, 354–55.
48. Arthur S. Link, ed., *The Papers of Woodrow Wilson*, 69 vols. (Princeton, NJ: Princeton University Press, 1969), vol. 6: 253–54. These quotes are from Wilson's book, *The State*, first published in 1889. Portions of the book are reprinted in Link. Wilson was a prolific scholar before entering politics and a founder of modern political science.
49. *Presser v. Illinois*, 116 U.S. 252 (1886), at 253. In *Presser*, a unanimous court ruled against Presser's claim to a Second Amendment right, saying that, under the amendment, the states could not "prohibit the people from keeping and bearing arms, so as to deprive the United States of their rightful resource for maintaining the public security, and disable the people from performing their duty to the General Government" (at 265). That is, the right to bear arms pertained to citizens' ability and "duty" to serve the government as members of the government organized and regulated militias referenced in the first half of the sentence composing the Second Amendment. For more on the case, see Robert J. Spitzer, *Gun Control: A Documentary and Reference Guide* (Westport, CT: Greenwood Press, 2009), 82–89.
50. *Presser v. Illinois*, at 265.
51. *Presser v. Illinois*, at 267.
52. *Presser v. Illinois*, at 267–68.
53. "Edelman Trust Barometer, 2013 Annual Global Study," 10, at http://edelmaneditions.com/wp-content/uploads/2013/01/EMBARGOED-2013-Edelman-Trust-Barometer-Global-Deck_FINAL.pdf.

Chapter 2

1. "1619: The Laws Enacted by the First General Assembly of Virginia," at http://oll.libertyfund.org/index.php?Itemid=264&id=1049&option=com_content&task=view.
2. This precarious dynamic is well chronicled in Nathaniel Philbrick, *Mayflower* (New York: Viking, 2006).
3. Lee Kennett and James LaVerne Anderson, *The Gun in America* (Westport, CT: Greenwood Press, 1975), 51–56.
4. Kennett and Anderson, *The Gun in America*; Saul Cornell and Nathan DeDino, "A Well Regulated Right," *Fordham Law Review* 73 (November 2004): 487–528; Saul Cornell, *A*

Well-Regulated Militia (New York: Oxford University Press, 2006); Adam Winkler, *Gunfight* (New York: W. W. Norton, 2011), 113–18; Craig R. Whitney, *Living with Guns* (New York: Public Affairs, 2012), 45–55.

5. Michael A. Bellesiles, *Arming America* (New York: Knopf, 2000). Bellesiles's book won the prestigious Bancroft Prize for history, but the prize was later withdrawn.

6. Michael A. Bellesiles, "The Origins of Gun Culture in the United States, 1760–1865," *Journal of American History* 83 (September 1996): 426–28.

7. Several critical articles appeared in the *William and Mary Quarterly* 59 (January 2002).

8. Kennett and Anderson, *The Gun in America*, 48, 249.

9. Randolph Roth, "Guns, Gun Culture, and Homicide: The Relationship between Firearms, the Uses of Firearms, and Interpersonal Violence," *William and Mary Quarterly* 59 (January 2002): 224.

10. Roth, "Guns, Gun Culture, and Homicide," 228.

11. Roth, "Guns, Gun Culture, and Homicide," 232.

12. John K. Mahon, *History of the Militia and the National Guard* (New York: Macmillan, 1983), chap. 2.

13. Kevin M. Sweeney, "Firearms, Militias, and the Second Amendment," in *The Second Amendment on Trial*, Saul Cornell and Nathan Kozuskanich, eds. (Amherst: University of Massachusetts Press, 2013), 310–82.

14. Sweeney, "Firearms, Militias, and the Second Amendment," 313.

15. Sweeney, "Firearms, Militias, and the Second Amendment," 321; also 328.

16. Sweeney, "Firearms, Militias, and the Second Amendment," 323.

17. Sweeney, "Firearms, Militias, and the Second Amendment," 322.

18. Sweeney, "Firearms, Militias, and the Second Amendment," 326. John Shy notes that, after a significant slave uprising in 1739, "the South Carolina militia became an agency to control slaves, and less an effective means of defense." *A People Numerous and Armed* (Ann Arbor: University of Michigan Press, 1990), 37.

19. Sweeney, "Firearms, Militias, and the Second Amendment," 329–30, 334. For example, evidence from Worcester County,

Massachusetts, reported that three of nineteen companies were "well" or "mostly equipped"; four were "intirely [*sic*] deficient"; another was "greatly deficient," another "a quarter fitted," three "half armed," one lacked a quarter of equipment, and another lacked a fifth (329). On the eve of the Revolution, probate records showed firearm ownership rates across the states ranging from 30 percent to 80 percent (340). In his important study, David Hackett Fischer noted that Massachusetts units on the eve of the Revolution were often short of weapons and gunpowder, were armed with "weapons not designed for war," and that some were not armed at all. *Paul Revere's Ride* (New York: Oxford University Press, 1994), 161.

20. Sweeney, "Firearms, Militias, and the Second Amendment," 316, 318–19, 321. The fact that many of the firearms in circulation during this time were broken, rusted, or inoperable is one point that Bellesiles got right. *Arming America*, 229–30.

21. Sweeney, "Firearms, Militias, and the Second Amendment," 353. See generally 349–59.

22. Sweeney, "Firearms, Militias, and the Second Amendment," 317, 342.

23. Robert J. Spitzer, *Gun Control: A Documentary and Reference Guide* (Westport, CT: Greenwood Press, 2009), 48–53.

24. Alexander DeConde, *Gun Violence in America* (Boston: Northeastern University Press, 2001), 40.

25. John K. Mahon, *The American Militia: Decade of Decision, 1789–1800* (Gainesville: University of Florida Press, 1960), 64. It is interesting to note that Mahon, an expert on historical militias, published data in 1960 highly consistent with the more recent studies cited here.

26. Robert J. Spitzer, "Upset about a Census of People? How about a Census of Guns?" *Huffington Post*, April 1, 2010, at http://www.huffingtonpost.com/robert-j-spitzer/upset-about-a-census-of-p_b_521389.html.

27. Mahon, *American Militia*, 41. See also Jerry Cooper, *The Rise of the National Guard* (Lincoln: University of Nebraska Press, 1997), 6–20; William H. Riker, *Soldiers of the States* (Washington, DC: Public Affairs Press, 1957), 21–40.

28. DeConde, *Gun Violence in America*, 59–61, 79.

29. Robert J. Spitzer, *The Politics of Gun Control*, 6th ed. (Boulder, CO: Paradigm, 2015), 30–31; Riker, *Soldiers of the States*, 21–40.

30. Saul Cornell, *A Well-Regulated Militia* (New York: Oxford University Press, 2006), 3.

31. Saul Cornell and Nathan Kozuskanich, "Introduction," in *The Second Amendment on Trial*, 5.

32. Nathaniel B. Shurtleff, ed., *Records of the Governor and Company of the Massachusetts Bay in New England*, 5 vols. (Boston: William White, 1853), vol. 2: 73–74. See also 26, 31, 82. The surveyor of arms could also sell substandard weapons and make purchases of weapons and ammunition on behalf of the colony (84).

33. Donald M. Snow and Dennis M. Drew, *From Lexington to Desert Storm* (Armonk, NY: M. E. Sharpe, 1994), 261–62.

34. Stephen Skowronek, *Building a New American State* (New York: Cambridge University Press, 1982), 315–16.

35. Sweeney, "Firearms, Militias, and the Second Amendment," 311.

36. Mark Anthony Frassetto, "Firearms and Weapons Legislation up to 1934," Georgetown University Law Center, January 15, 2013. Available at http://papers. ssrn.com/sol3/papers.cfm?abstract_id=2200991.

37. I also conducted my own spot check of a few of the laws on Frassetto's list and found them accurate and correct.

38. 1876 Wyoming Compilation of Laws, chap. 52, sec. 1.

39. 1867 Arizona Session Laws 21, sec. 1.

40. 1875 Indiana Acts 62, sec. 1.

41. This Kentucky law was struck down as a violation of the Kentucky state constitution in the case of *Bliss v. Commonwealth* (2 Littell 90; Ky. 1822). The court's decision did not involve or touch on the federal Constitution's Second Amendment but instead was based on Kentucky's more expansive right-to-bear-arms-type provision. In addition, this ruling was an anomaly, in that concealed carry laws were widely held as constitutional when challenged in other states. See Spitzer, *Gun Control*, 96–99.

42. 1821 Tennessee Public Act, chap. 13, at 16; 1837.

43. Laws of Georgia, December 25, 1837.

44. Laws of Alabama, February 1, 1839.

45. Saul Cornell, "The Right to Carry Firearms outside of the Home," *Fordham Urban Law Journal* 39 (October 2012): 1716; Dickson D. Bruce Jr., *Violence and Culture in the Antebellum South* (Austin: University of Texas Press, 1979).
46. Randolph Roth, *American Homicide* (Cambridge, MA: Belknap Press, 2012), 180–249.
47. James Wycoff, *Famous Guns That Won the West* (New York: Arco, 1968), 5–6. See also Harold F. Williamson, *Winchester: The Gun That Won the West* (Washington, DC: Combat Forces Press, 1952), 3; Martin Rywell, *The Gun That Shaped American Destiny* (Harriman, TN: Pioneer Press, 1957), 4; and James B. Trefethen and James E. Serven, *Americans and Their Guns: The National Rifle Association Story through Nearly a Century of Service to the Nation* (Harrisburg, PA: Stackpole Books, 1967).
48. Lewis Atherton, *The Cattle Kings* (Bloomington: Indiana University Press, 1961).
49. Richard Shenkman, *Legends, Lies, and Cherished Myths of American History* (New York: Morrow, 1988), 112. See also Robert R. Dykstra, *The Cattle Towns* (New York: Knopf, 1968).
50. Ray Allen Billington, *Westward Expansion: A History of the American Frontier* (New York: Macmillan, 1974), 587.
51. Joe B. Frantz and Julian Ernest Choate Jr., *The American Cowboy: The Myth and the Reality* (Norman: University of Oklahoma Press, 1955), 78.
52. Billington, *Westward Expansion*, 787. See also Frank Richard Prassal, *The Western Peace Officer* (Norman: University of Oklahoma Press, 1972), 22, and the numerous works cited by Billington.
53. W. Eugene Hollon, *Frontier Violence* (New York: Oxford University Press, 1974). Hollon notes that "of all the myths that refuse to die, the hardiest concerns the extent of the unmitigated bloodletting that occurred in the Western frontier during the closing decades of the nineteenth century" (x).
54. 1915 New Hampshire Laws 180, sec. 18.
55. 1931 South Carolina Acts 78.
56. For example, 1901 Utah Laws 97.
57. 1933 Texas General Laws 219.
58. 1927 (January Session) R.I. Public Laws 256.

59. 1927 Massachusetts Acts 413.
60. 1933 Minnesota Laws 231.
61. 1933 Ohio Laws 189.
62. 1933 South Dakota Session Laws 245.
63. 1933–1934 Virginia Acts 37.
64. 1931 Illinois Laws 452.
65. Roth, *American Homicide*, 181.
66. Winkler, *Gunfight*, 113.
67. Cornell and DeDino, "Well Regulated Right," 507. The cite for the Massachusetts law is ch. VII, 1775–1776 Mass. Acts at 31.
68. This quote is from North Carolina's 1778 version of this law, Acts of North Carolina.
69. 1768 North Carolina Session Laws 168.
70. 1878 South Carolina Acts 724.
71. 1814 Massachusetts Acts 464. Massachusetts was an important firearms manufacturer in the country's early history.
72. 1917 New Hampshire Laws 727.
73. 1925 West Virginia Acts 31.
74. Mahon, *American Militia*; Mahon, *History of the Militia and the National Guard*; H. Richard Uviller and William G. Merkel, *The Militia and the Right to Arms* (Durham, NC: Duke University Press, 2002); Cornell, *Well-Regulated Militia*.
75. 1907 Arizona Session Laws 15.
76. 1631 Virginia Acts 155, Act LVI.
77. 1651 Virginia Acts 365.
78. 1866 Georgia Law 27.
79. 1867 Mississippi Laws 327.
80. 1858 North Carolina Session Laws 34.
81. 1898 Florida Laws 71.
82. 1895 Nebraska Laws 210, sec. 6.
83. 1927 Michigan Public Acts 891, sec. 9.
84. 1918 Montana Laws 6.
85. 1868 Oregon Revised Statutes 18.
86. Cooper, *Rise of the National Guard*, 3.
87. For more on early laws and practices regarding free blacks, slaves, and guns, see Kennett and Anderson, *Gun in America*, 49–51; Cornell, *Well-Regulated Militia*, 28–29; Winkler, *Gunfight*, 115–16.
88. Quoted in Winkler, *Gunfight*, 116.

89. 1783 Connecticut Acts 633.
90. 1782 Massachusetts Acts 119, chap. 46, sec. 1.
91. 1919 Massachusetts Acts 139.
92. Spitzer, *Gun Control*, chap. 4.
93. Cornell, *Well-Regulated Militia*, 21.
94. Cornell, "Right to Carry Firearms outside of the Home," 1703, 1707. See also Nathan Kozuskanich, "Originalism in a Digital Age," in *The Second Amendment on Trial*, 289–309.
95. Spitzer, *Politics of Gun Control*, 149–55.

Chapter 3

1. "President Obama's Remarks on Trayvon Martin," *Washington Post*, July 19, 2013, at http://www.washingtonpost.com/politics/president-obamas-remarks-on-trayvon-martin-full-transcript/2013/07/19/5e33ebea-f09a-11e2-a1f9-ea873b7e0424_story.html.
2. James Arkin, "Ted Cruz: An Attack on 2nd Amendment," *Politico*, July 19, 2013, at http://www.politico.com/story/2013/07/ted-cruz-second-amendment-obama-trayvon-martin-94504.html.
3. Joseph J. Ellis, "There's No Unlimited Right to Bear Arms," *Los Angeles Times*, September 8, 2013, at http://articles.latimes.com/2013/sep/08/opinion/la-oe-ellis-gun-control-nullification-20130908.
4. Antonin Scalia, "Constitutional Interpretation the Old Fashioned Way," Remarks Delivered at the Woodrow Wilson International Center for Scholars, Washington, DC, March 14, 2005, at http://www.cfif.org/htdocs/freedomline/current/guest_commentary/scalia-constitutional-speech.htm. See also Antonin Scalia, "Originalism: The Lesser Evil," *University of Cincinnati Law Review* 57 (1989): 849–65.
5. Stephen Breyer, *Active Liberty: Interpreting Our Democratic Constitution* (New York: Knopf, 2005), 115–32.
6. Daniel A. Farber and Suzanna Sherry, *Desperately Seeking Certainty* (Chicago: University of Chicago Press, 2002), 14.
7. Farber and Sherry, *Desperately Seeking Certainty*, 10–54. See also Steven M. Teles, *The Rise of the Conservative Legal Movement* (Princeton, NJ: Princeton University Press, 2008). Jack Balkin argues that originalist and living Constitution perspectives

are compatible with each other. See *Living Originalism* (Cambridge, MA: Harvard University Press, 2011). There is, to be sure, far greater complexity to this debate than the simple originalist–living dichotomy presented here. See, for example, Corey Brettschneider, *Constitutional Law and American Democracy* (Frederick, MD: Wolters Kluwer, 2012), 135–237.

8. Jeffrey Toobin, *The Oath* (New York: Doubleday, 2012), 105–15.

9. Warren Burger, "The Right to Bear Arms," *Parade Magazine*, January 14, 1990, 5.

10. See Robert J. Spitzer, *Gun Control: A Documentary and Reference Guide* (Westport, CT: Greenwood Press, 2009), 36–43.

11. Jack Rakove, "Thoughts on *Heller* from a 'Real Historian,'" *Balkin.com*, June 27, 2008, at http://balkin.blogspot.com/2008/06/thoughts-on-heller-from-real-historian.html. Another Pulitzer Prize–winning early American historian, Joseph Ellis, referred to *Heller* as a "tour de force of legalistic legerdemain." "There's No Unlimited Right to Bear Arms."

12. Saul Cornell, *A Well-Regulated Militia* (New York: Oxford University Press, 2006), 17–18, 21–22; Saul Cornell, "The Right to Carry Firearms outside of the Home," *Fordham Urban Law Journal* 39 (October 2012): 1703, 1707; Craig R. Whitney, *Living with Guns* (New York: Public Affairs, 2012), 74–75.

13. 116 U.S. 252 (1886).

14. 307 U.S. 174 (1939).

15. Robert J. Spitzer, *The Right to Bear Arms* (Santa Barbara, CA: ABC-CLIO, 2001), 13–84; Robert J. Spitzer, *The Politics of Gun Control*, 6th ed. (Boulder, CO: Paradigm, 2015), 38–39, 213. Before *Heller*, only one federal case had ever embraced the individual-rights view: *U.S. v. Emerson* (270 F.3d 203; 5th Cir. 2001). Yet even in this case, the court did not strike down the federal gun law in question, and its ruling that the Second Amendment protected an individual right was of no help to the person in the case claiming such a right.

16. For example, legal historian David Thomas Konig wrote that *Heller* "has rewritten the past to provide a comforting and simplistic vehicle for the transformation of the 'right of the people to keep and bear arms' from a collective civic model to an individual one." "Heller, Guns, and History,"

Northeastern University Law Journal 3 (May 2012): 176. Historian Jack Rakove said that "the private keeping of firearms was manifestly not the right that the Framers of the Bill of Rights guaranteed in 1789." Quoted in Toobin, *The Oath*, 113.

17. For example, see *D.C. v. Heller*, at 578–80, 604–5. See also Neil H. Cogan, ed., *The Complete Bill of Rights* (New York: Oxford University Press, 1997), 181–82.

18. Saul Cornell, "New Originalism: A Constitutional Scam," *Dissent*, May 3, 2011, at http://www.dissentmagazine.org/online_articles/new-originalism-a-constitutional-scam; Rakove, "Thoughts on Heller from a 'Real Historian.'"

19. For more on this, see Robert J. Spitzer, *Saving the Constitution from Lawyers: How Legal Training and Law Reviews Distort Constitutional Meaning* (New York: Cambridge University Press, 2008), 27–29, 41–44.

20. Richard A. Posner, "In Defense of Looseness," *New Republic*, August 27, 2008, at www.tnr.com/article/books/defense-looseness. For more on "law office history" and the Second Amendment, see Spitzer, *Saving the Constitution from Lawyers*, chap. 5.

21. Posner, "In Defense of Looseness"; J. Harvie Wilkinson III, "Of Guns, Abortions, and the Unraveling Rule of Law," *Virginia Law Review* 95 (April 2009): 253–323; Douglas Kmiec, "Guns and the Supreme Court: Dead Wrong," *Tidings Online*, July 11, 2008, at http://www.the-tidings.com/2008/071108/kmiec_text.htm. Douglas Kmiec, "What the Heller?" *Slate Magazine*, July 8, 2008, at http://www.slate.com/blogs/blogs/convictions/archive/2008/07/08/what-the-heller-is-only-the-supreme-court-s-liberty-enhanced.aspx.

22. Toobin, *The Oath*, 104. Toobin describes this history, arising from conservative, gun rights activists, on 97–104. For more on the provenance of this history, including the key role of the National Rifle Association and its allies in promoting the individualist view, see Robert J. Spitzer, "Lost and Found: Researching the Second Amendment," *Chicago-Kent Law Review* 76 (2000): 349–401.

23. Stuart R. Hays, "The Right to Bear Arms, a Study in Judicial Misinterpretation," *William and Mary Law Review* 2 (1960): 381–406. Hays was a law student at William

and Mary at the time and a life member of the National
Rifle Association. Spitzer, "Lost and Found," 367.

24. See Spitzer, "Lost and Found"; Spitzer, *Right to Bear Arms*, 72.

25. Toobin, *The Oath*, 114.

26. Adam Winkler, *Gunfight* (New York: W. W. Norton,
2011), 287. See also Reva B. Siegel, "Dead or Alive:
Originalism as Popular Constitutionalism in *Heller*,"
Harvard Law Review 122 (November 2008): 191–245.

27. Cornell, "New Originalism: A Constitutional Scam."

28. 561 U.S. 3025 (2010).

29. The Court did this through the process of "incorporation,"
whereby it has applied parts of the Bill of Rights over
time to the states through the Fourteenth Amendment.
Robert J. Spitzer, "Why Gun Ruling Is a Teachable
Moment," *CNN.com*, June 30, 2010, at http://www.
cnn.com/2010/OPINION/06/29/spitzer.guns.
supreme.court/index.html?iref=storysearch.

30. *D.C. v. Heller*, at 628.

31. *D.C. v. Heller*, at 626.

32. *D.C. v. Heller*, at 627.

33. *D.C. v. Heller*, at 626–27.

34. *D.C. v. Heller*, at 632.

35. *D.C. v. Heller*, at 625.

36. *D.C. v. Heller*, at 582.

37. Stephen Breyer, "On Handguns and the Law," *New
York Review of Books*, August 19, 2010, 18.

38. "Post-*Heller* Litigation Summary," *Law Center to
Prevent Gun Violence*, August 2, 2013, at http://smart-
gunlaws.org/post-heller-litigation-summary/.

39. "Post-*Heller* Litigation Summary." From least strict to most
strict, the three levels of scrutiny are a "rational basis" test, that
is, asking simply whether there is a rational basis for the regulation in question; "intermediate scrutiny," asking whether the
law is reasonably related to a significant interest of the government; and "strict scrutiny," which sets the highest bar to
accepting a law's constitutionality, asking whether the law in
question serves a compelling state interest (e.g., laws restricting
free speech are subject to strict scrutiny, given speech's overriding importance to society). Most lower courts have applied
intermediate scrutiny, but some have adopted a lower level.

40. *Moore v. Madigan* (702 F.3d 933; 7th Cir. 2012).

41. The Illinois law falls into the "shall issue" category, meaning
that as long as the concealed carry permit applicant is not a
felon or mentally unbalanced and completes a 16-hour training course, the permit is granted. The system was to be up and
running in 2014; roughly 300,000 applicants were expected.
The law, which allows concealed and "mostly concealed"
carry, included a lengthy list of places where guns could not
be carried, including schools, parks, government buildings,
buses, trains, bars and restaurants with significant alcohol sales,
and other public places. Stores and malls can also exclude
gun carrying if they post signs. David Heinzmann et al.,
"How Gun Law Works: Likely 2014 before Permits Issued,"
Chicago Tribune, July 10, 2013, at http://www.chicagotribune.
com/news/local/ct-met-illinois-concealed-carry-whats-
next-0709-2-20130710,0,5978206.story. At least two other
Courts of Appeal, the Second and Tenth, have ruled that concealed carry is not protected as a right under the Second
Amendment.

42. For example, *Kachalsky v. County of Westchester*,
701 F.3d 81 (2nd Cir. 2012).

43. *Moore v. Madigan*, at 937.

44. *Moore v. Madigan*, at 941.

45. Vivian S. Chu, "Federal Assault Weapons Ban: Legal
Issues," *CRS Report for Congress*, Congressional
Research Service, February 14, 2013, 3.

46. Chu, "Federal Assault Weapons Ban"; Spitzer,
Politics of Gun Control, 149–55.

47. Chu, "Federal Assault Weapons Ban," 7–12.

48. Chu, "Federal Assault Weapons Ban," 6–7.

49. Dave Altimari et al., "Adam Lanza Researched Mass
Murderers, Sources Say," *Hartford Courant*, March 13,
2013, at http://articles.courant.com/2013-03-13/news/
hc-newtown-lanza-mass-murderers-20130313_1_adam-
lanza-nancy-lanza-mary-scherlach; Justin Peters, "Everyone Who Claims Adam Lanza Didn't Use an AR-15-Style
Rifle Is Wrong, Wrong, Wrong," *Slate.com*, March 22,
2013, at http://www.slate.com/blogs/crime/2013/03/22/

ar_15_sandy_hook_everyone_who_claims_adam_lanza_
didn_t_use_an_ar_15_style.html; Erica Goode, "Rifle Used
in Killings, America's Most Popular, Highlights Regulation
Debate," *New York Times*, December 17, 2012, A22.

50. Jonathan Weisman, "Gun Control Drive Blocked in Senate;
Obama, in Defeat, Sees 'Shameful Day,'" *New York Times*,
April 18, 2013, A1.

51. Adam Weinstein, "A Non-Gun-Owner's Guide to Guns,"
Mother Jones, December 21, 2012, at http://www.motherjones.
com/politics/2012/12/semi-automatic-gun-assault-weapon-
definitions.

52. Spitzer, *Politics of Gun Control*, 138–40, 145–49.

53. For example, "Background Information on So-Called
'Assault Weapons,'" National Shooting Sports Foundation,
at http://www.nssf.org/factsheets/semi-auto.cfm.

54. "Assault Weapons and Accessories in America,"
Violence Policy Center, 1988, at http://www.vpc.org/
studies/awaconc.htm; Canis Aureus, "Firearms 101,"
Daily Kos, July 22, 2012, at http://www.dailykos.com/
story/2012/07/22/1112659/-Firearms-101-the-Assaul
t-Rifle-Capabilities-and-the-Militia-Concept#.

55. Peter Ferrara, "'Assault Weapon' Is Just a PR Stunt
Meant to Fool the Gullible," *Forbes*, December 28, 2012,
at http://www.forbes.com/sites/peterferrara/2012/12/28/
assault-weapon-is-just-a-pr-stunt-meant-to-fool-the-gullible/.

56. Tom Diaz, *Making a Killing* (New York: New Press, 1999),
124–28, 230–31.

57. Phillip Peterson, *Buyer's Guide to Assault Weapons* (Iola, WI:
Gun Digest Books, 2008), 11.

58. Tom Diaz, *The Last Gun* (New York: New Press, 2013), 144.

59. See http://www.nssf.org/msr/.

60. John Haughey, "Five Things You Need to Know about
'Assault Weapons,'" *Outdoor Life*, March 19, 2013, at
http://www.outdoorlife.com/blogs/gun-shots/2013/03/
five-things-you-need-know-about-assault-weapons.

61. Diaz, *The Last Gun*, 156–59.

62. Larry Kahaner, *AK-47: The Weapon That Changed
the Face of War* (New York: Wiley, 2007).

63. The first assault weapon marketed to civilians was the Colt AR-15, introduced in 1964. Peterson, *Buyer's Guide to Assault Weapons*, 4. Peterson says that the poor sales of these weapons, along with imported versions, was attributable at least in part to the fact that they were "too expensive to appeal to the average shooter."

64. Jay Mathews, "AK47 Rifles Flood into U.S. from Chinese Sales War," *Washington Post*, February 2, 1989, A1.

65. Diaz, *Making a Killing*, 71–73.

66. Diaz, *Making a Killing*, 125.

67. Iola, WI: Gun Digest Books, 2008.

68. Erica Goode, "Even Defining 'Assault Rifles' Is Complicated," *New York Times*, January 17, 2013, A1.

69. Iola, WI: Gun Digest Books, 2010.

70. Peterson, *Buyer's Guide to Assault Weapons*, 11.

71. Diaz, *The Last Gun*, 156–57.

72. Dan Baum, *Gun Guys* (New York: Knopf, 2013), 61.

73. Spitzer, *Politics of Gun Control*, 54–56.

74. Christopher S. Koper et al., "An Updated Assessment of the Federal Assault Weapons Ban: Impacts on Gun Markets and Gun Violence, 1994–2003," Report to the National Institute of Justice, U.S. Department of Justice, Jerry Lee Center of Criminology, University of Pennsylvania, June 2004, 1.

75. Alex Seitz-Wald, "Fact Check: LaPierre's Big Fib," *Salon.com*, January 30, 2013, at http://www.salon.com/2013/01/30/wayne_lapierre_hopes_you_dont_read_that_study_he_mentioned/. The comments were made by NRA vice president Wayne LaPierre and David Kopel, a conservative think tank writer.

76. Koper et al., "Updated Assessment of the Federal Assault Weapons Ban," 1. An earlier version of this study from 1997 found similar, if tentative, trends. Jeffrey A. Roth et al., "Impact Evaluation of the Public Safety and Recreational Firearms Use Protection Act of 1994," *Urban Institute*, March 13, 1997.

77. Koper et al., "Updated Assessment of the Federal Assault Weapons Ban," 2–3.

78. Christopher S. Koper, "Disassembling the Assault-Gun Ban," *Baltimore Sun*, September 13, 2004, at http://articles.baltimoresun.com/2004-09-13/news/0409130079_1_ban-guns-gun-crimes-magazines.

79. Statement by John F. Walsh, U.S. Attorney for the District of Colorado, testimony before the U.S. Senate Committee on the Judiciary, Washington, DC, February 27, 2013, 3. See also Police Executive Research Forum, *Guns and Crime: Breaking New Ground by Focusing on the Local Impact*, May 2010; "Target: Law Enforcement," *Violence Policy Center*, February 2010. This latter study chronicles 235 incidents involving a total of 333 weapons identified as assault weapons in news reports and/or by police during a two-year period, from 2005 to 2007, when assault weapons were involved in crimes.

80. Arindrajit Dube, Oeindrila Dube, and Omar Garcia-Ponce, "Cross-Border Spillover: U.S. Gun Laws and Violence in Mexico," *American Political Science Review* 107 (August 2013): 397–417.

81. "Officer Down," *Violence Policy Center*, May 2003.

82. Lori Robertson, "Biden Wrong on Police Deaths," *FactCheck. org*, January 30, 2013, at http://www.factcheck.org/2013/01/biden-wrong-on-police-deaths/. The FBI data categorize gun shootings by types of guns (handguns, rifles, shotguns) but do not include a separate category for assault weapons, meaning that the data must be reanalyzed or obtained in some other way.

83. The *New York Times* studied 100 such shootings. See Ford Fessenden, "They Threaten, Seethe and Unhinge, Then Kill in Quantity," *New York Times*, April 9, 2000, at http://www.nytimes.com/2000/04/09/us/they-threaten-seethe-and-unhinge-then-kill-in-quantity.html?pagewanted=all&src=pm; Mark Follman, "More Guns, More Mass Shootings— Coincidence?" *Mother Jones*, December 15, 2012, at http://www.motherjones.com/politics/2012/09/mass-shootings-investigation. A study of 84 "active shooter events" from 2000 to 2010 by researchers at Texas State University found an increase in such shootings during that period. J. Pete Blair and M. Hunter Martaindale, "United States Active Shooter Events from 2000 to 2010: Training and Equipment Implications," Texas State University, March 2013, at http://alerrt.org/files/research/ActiveShooterEvents.pdf. A study by the U.S. Department of Justice, from 2000 to 2008, shows that the nation averaged 5 mass shootings per year. During this period, these shooting incidents resulted in 324 people shot

and 145 killed. From 2009 to 2012, 404 people were shot and 207 killed, resulting in a tripling of such events. In the past ten years, the Justice Department has provided training to 50,000 police officers, 7000 local commanders, and 3000 federal, state, and local agency heads on active shooter response techniques, as well as information on how to detect and disrupt such events. Associated Press, "Mass Shootings Have Tripled," *Seattle Times*, October 21, 2013, at http://seattletimes.com/html/nationworld/2022097500_massshootingsxml.html.

84. Criminologist James Alan Fox disputes some of *Mother Jones*'s methodology as to which cases are included or excluded. By Fox's analysis, which includes more cases, the number of mass shootings has remained roughly constant from 1976 to 2010, at roughly twenty events per year. In any case, even Fox's numbers do not show a decline over that time, nor do they follow overall crime trends. See James Alan Fox, "Mass Shootings Not Trending," *Boston Globe*, January 23, 2013, at http://boston.com/community/blogs/crime_punishment/2013/01/mass_shootings_not_trending.html. *The New Republic* reanalyzed the *Mother Jones* data and also concluded that such shootings are on the rise. Amy Sullivan, "Mass Shootings Are on the Rise—and 2012 Has Been Deadlier Than Ever Before," *New Republic*, December 14, 2012, at http://www.newrepublic.com/article/111149/mass-shootings-are-rise-and-2012-has-been-deadlier-ever. A Congressional Research Service study of mass shootings discusses the criteria for mass shootings. See Jerome P. Bjelopera et al., *Public Mass Shootings in the United States*, CRS Report for Congress, March 18, 2013.

85. D'Vera Cohn et al., "Gun Homicide Rate Down 49 percent since 1993 Peak," *Pew Research*, May 7, 2013, at http://www.pewsocialtrends.org/2013/05/07/gun-homicide-rate-down-49-since-1993-peak-public-unaware/.

86. Michael S. Schmidt, "F.B.I. Report Confirms a Sharp Rise in Mass Shootings," *New York Times*, September 25, 2014, A17; U.S. Department of Justice, *A Study of Active Shooter Incidents in the United States Between 2000 and 2013*, 2014, at http://www.fbi.gov/news/stories/2014/september/fbi-releases-study-on-active-shooter-incidents/pdfs/a-study-of-active-shooter-incidents-in-the-u.s.-between-2000-and-2013.

87. Mark Follman, "Why Mass Shootings Deserve Deeper Investigation," *Mother Jones*, January 30, 2013, at http://www. motherjones.com/politics/2013/01/mass-shootings-james-alan-fox; Follman, "More Guns, More Mass Shootings." A Congressional Research Service study identified seventy-eight mass shootings in the U.S. between 1983 and 2012, although the study deliberately avoided the gun control issue. See Bjelopera et al., *Public Mass Shootings in the United States*.

88. The Blair and Martaindale study of active shooting events found that handguns were used in 60 percent of the incidents. "United States Active Shooter Events from 2000 to 2010."

89. Mark Follman and Gavin Aronsen, " 'A Killing Machine': Half of All Mass Shooters Used High-Capacity Magazines," *Mother Jones*, January 30, 2013, at http://www.motherjones.com/ politics/2013/01/high-capacity-magazines-mass-shootings.

90. Mark Follman, "Mass Shootings: Maybe What We Need Is a Better Mental-Health Policy," *Mother Jones*, November 9, 2012, at http://www.motherjones.com/politics/ 2012/11/jared-loughner-mass-shootings-mental-illness; Fessenden, "They Threaten, Seethe and Unhinge."

91. *People v. James*, 94 Cal. Rptr. 3d 576 (Cal. Ct. App. 2009).

92. *Heller v. District of Columbia*, 670 F.3d 1244 (D.C. Cir. 2011). The case is also referred to as *Heller II*.

93. *Wilson v. Cook County*, 968 N.E.2d 641 (Ill. 2012).

94. The primary sidearm for military use is the Beretta M9 semi-automatic pistol and successors, which come with a fifteen-round magazine. The Beretta has been issued to troops since 1990, and the company's current contract with the government extends through 2015. See http://www. berettausa.com/usarmyawardsnewberettam9pistolcontract/.

95. Justin Peters, "How Many Assault Weapons Are There in America?" *Slate.com*, December 20, 2012, at http:// www.slate.com/blogs/crime/2012/12/20/assault_rifle_ stats_how_many_assault_rifles_are_there_in_america. html; "Assault Weapons," *GunCite*, October 24, 2010, at http://www.guncite.com/gun_control_gcassaul.html; Paul Whitefield, "4 Million Assault Weapons in America," March 14, 2013, at http://articles.latimes.com/2013/mar/14/news/ la-ol-feinstein-assault-weapons-ban-good-start-20130314.

96. This metric—recent sales—is often used by opponents of assault weapons regulation. See, for example, "U.S. Senate Judiciary Committee Passes Semi-Auto and Private Sales Ban," *NRA-ILA*, March 15, 2013, at http://www.nraila.org/legislation/federal-legislation/2013/3/us-senate-judiciary-committee-passes-semi-auto-and-private-sales-bans.aspx?s=%22David+Kopel%22&st=&ps=; Charles Cooper, "Proposals to Reduce Gun Violence," Statement before the Senate Committee on the Judiciary, Subcommittee on the Constitution, Civil Rights and Human Rights, February 12, 2013, at http://www.judiciary.senate.gov/imo/media/doc/2-12-13CooperTestimony.pdf.

97. Adam Winkler, "Did the Assault-Weapons Ban Kill Gun Control?" *Daily Beast*, March 20, 2013, at http://www.thedailybeast.com/articles/2013/03/20/did-the-assault-weapons-ban-kill-gun-control.html.

98. 1927 Michigan Public Acts 888; 1933 Minnesota Laws 231.

99. Mark Almonte, "Why Does Anyone Need a High-Capacity Magazine?" *American Thinker*, March 4, 2013, at http://www.americanthinker.com/2013/03/why_does_anyone_need_a_high-capacity_magazine.html.

100. Erik Voeten, "Why the Second Amendment Rulings May Make a Ban on Assault Weapons More Likely," *Monkey Cage*, December 15, 2012, at http://themonkeycage.org/2012/12/15/why-the-second-amendment-rulings-may-make-a-ban-on-assault-weapons-more-likely/.

101. Quoted in Trip Gabriel, "Many Owners Say Semiautomatic Weapons Are Just Another Hobby," *New York Times*, December 19, 2012, at http://www.nytimes.com/2012/12/20/us/owners-of-assault-weapons-dismiss-idea-of-federal-ban.html?pagewanted=1&_r=1.

102. Quoted in Joshua Horwitz and Casey Anderson, *Guns, Democracy, and the Insurrectionist Idea* (Ann Arbor: University of Michigan Press, 2009), 71.

103. Zumbo is hardly the only gun writer to be banished for offering even the mildest suggestion that some gun regulation might be allowable, or even beneficial. In 2013 one of the most well-known and highly respected gun journalists, Dick Metcalf, was literally banished from gun media for writing in his column for

the magazine *Guns & Ammo* that "all constitutional rights are regulated, always have been, and need to be." The one regulation he spoke up for in his column was Illinois's recently enacted sixteen hours of training to obtain a concealed carry license. As a result of this column, Metcalf's column was pulled, his television appearances ended, and gun manufacturers said that they would have nothing more to do with him. In addition, death threats "poured in" via email, and the magazine that ran his column apologized, even though its editorial staff had approved the column before publication. According to Metcalf, "I've been vanished, disappeared." Ravi Somaiya, "Banished for Questioning the Gospel of Guns," *New York Times*, January 5, 2014, A1.

104. Tim Catts, "Smith & Wesson, Gunmakers Rally after Obama Re-Elected," *Business Weekly*, November 7, 2012, at http://www.businessweek.com/news/2012-11-07/smith-and-wesson-gunmakers-rally-after-obama-re-elected; Aaron Smith, "Obama's Re-election Drives Gun Sales," *CNN.com*, November 9, 2012, at http://money.cnn.com/2012/11/09/news/economy/gun-control-obama/index.html; Tony Rizzo, "U.S. Gun Sales Hit a Record High since Obama's Reelection," *McClatchy News*, January 11, 2013, at http://www.mcclatchydc.com/2013/01/11/179551/us-gun-sales-hit-a-record-high.html.

105. Meghan Lisson, "Run on Guns: AR-15 Sales Soar," *CNBC*, April 25, 2013, at http://www.cnbc.com/id/100673826.

106. The Internet is awash with accounts from gun enthusiasts of the fun associated with the ownership and use of assault weapons.

107. Gabriel, "Many Owners Say Semiautomatic Weapons Are Just Another Hobby."

108. Terry Greene Sterling, "Fire in the Hole!" *Slate.com*, July 30, 2013, at http://www.slate.com/articles/health_and_science/science/2013/07/big_sandy_machine_gun_shoot_arizona_s_gun_lovers_and_gun_control.html.

109. Dan Baum's book on gun owners and users is rife both with prolific accounts of guns as fun—especially assault weapons—and as sexual objects. One of his chapters begins with this quote: "I *am* compensating. If I could kill stuff with my dick from 200 yards I would not need a firearm, would I?" *Gun Guys*, 11.

110. Eric Lach, "A History of the Rifle Used in the Sandy Hook Massacre," *Talking Points Memo*, December 20, 2012, at http://talkingpointsmemo.com/muckraker/a-history-of-the-rifle-used-in-the-sandy-hook-massacre.

111. Winkler, "Did the Assault-Weapons Ban Kill Gun Control?"

112. Whitney, *Living with Guns*, 245.

113. Elspeth Reeve, "A GIF Guide to the Most Bannable Semi-Automatic Weapons," *Atlantic Wire*, January 8, 2013, at http://www.theatlanticwire.com/politics/2013/01/gif-guide-most-bannable-semi-automatic-weapons/60728/. See also Baum, *Gun Guys*, 11–24.

114. Spitzer, *The Politics of Gun Control*, xv–xvi. Former Representative Gaby Giffords's husband, Mark Kelly, also pointed this out during congressional testimony in early 2013.

115. "Senate Judiciary Committee Hearing on Gun Violence," January 30, 2013, at http://articles.washingtonpost.com/2013-01-30/politics/36628109_1_gun-violence-gabby-giffords-senator-grassley.

116. Jim Barrett, "Assault Weapons Bans: Are You Ready?" *TheTruth AboutGuns.com*, June 8, 2012, at http://www.thetruthaboutguns.com/2012/06/jim-barrett/assault-weapons-bans-are-you-ready/.

117. Gabriel, "Many Owners Say Semiautomatic Weapons Are Just Another Hobby."

118. Paul Barrett, "Semi-Automatic Thinking on Gun Control," *Business Week*, August 7, 2012, at http://www.businessweek.com/articles/2012-08-07/semi-automatic-thinking-on-gun-control.

Chapter 4

1. Michele McPhee, " 'Whitey' Bulger Hitman Says He Was a 'Vigilante, Not a Serial Killer,' " *ABC News*, June 18, 2013, at http://abcnews.go.com/US/whitey-bulger-hitman-vigilante-serial-killer/story?id=19430619.

2. Shelley Murphy, "Defense Attacks Credibility of Bulger's Accuser," *Boston Globe*, June 18, 2013, at http://www.bostonglobe.com/metro/2013/06/18/confessed-killer-john-martorano-says-whitey-bulger-murdered-dorchester-man/pAwShMkfFOzRvb3RIn2LfL/story.html.

3. "The Trial of Bernhard Goetz: Goetz's Videotaped Confession," transcript of December 31, 1984, interview with New York City police, at http://law2.umkc.edu/faculty/projects/ftrials/goetz/goetzconfession.html.

4. Steve Kroft, "John Martorano: The Executioner," *60 Minutes*, CBS News, January 6, 2008, at http://www.cbsnews.com/8301-18560_162-3672273.html.

5. Erin Fuchs, "1980s 'Subway Vigilante' Shot Four Black Teens Who Asked Him for $5, and He Got Off, Too," *Business Insider*, July 15, 2013, at http://www.businessinsider.com/is-george-zimmerman-like-bernhard-goetz-2013-7; Richard Maxwell Brown, *No Duty to Retreat* (Norman: University of Oklahoma Press, 1994), 129–30, 134–39.

6. Harry Siegel and Filipa Ioannou, "Bernhard Goetz on George Zimmerman: 'The Same Thing Is Happening,' " *Daily Beast*, July 12, 2013, at http://www.thedailybeast.com/articles/2013/07/12/bernhard-goetz-on-george-zimmerman-the-same-thing-is-happening.html.

7. The FBI's Uniform Crime Reporting (UCR) Program defines murder and nonnegligent manslaughter as the willful (nonnegligent) killing of one human being by another.

8. The legal scholar H. L. A. Hart referred specifically to "Thou shalt not kill" as "the most characteristic provision of law and morals." *The Concept of Law* (New York: Oxford University Press, 1961), 190.

9. William C. Sprague, *Abridgment of Blackstone's Commentaries* (Detroit: Sprague School of Law, 1899), 480.

10. Donald L. Carper et al., *Understanding the Law* (Minneapolis: West, 1995), 237.

11. See, for example, Thomas Hobbes, *Leviathan* (New York: Macmillan, 1962). As Hobbes notes, governments are formed to bring order from the chaos of the state of nature. When people form or join a society, they relinquish some rights in order to receive the benefits of an ordered society where fundamental rights, including that of life, can be protected. Thus, "when a man hath . . . granted away his right [to the "freedom" of the state of nature]; then he is said to be OBLIGED, or BOUND, not to hinder those, to whom such right is granted . . . from the benefit of it . . ." (104).

12. H. H. Gerth and C. Wright Mills, eds., *From Max Weber: Essays in Sociology* (New York: Oxford University Press, 1946), 78. Italics in original.

13. Henry C. Black, *Black's Law Dictionary* (St. Paul, MN: West, 1991), 801.

14. H. L. A. Hart, *Punishment and Responsibility: Essays in the Philosophy of Law* (New York: Oxford University Press, 1968), 13. See also Fiona Leverick, *Killing in Self-Defence* (New York: Oxford University Press, 2007). The distinction between a killing that occurs as an extension of the state and that which is committed by an individual, even if justified, evolved from the British distinction made between a killing that is justifiable versus one that is excusable. See Sprague, *Abridgment of Blackstone's Commentaries*, 472–73; Joseph H. Beale Jr., "Retreat from a Murderous Assault," *Harvard Law Review* 16 (June 1903): 567–82.

15. Beale, "Retreat from a Murderous Assault," 567.

16. Sprague, *Abridgment of Blackstone's Commentaries*, 472–73.

17. Quoted in Garrett Epps, "Any Which Way but Loose: Interpretive Strategies and Attitudes toward Violence in the Evolution of the Anglo-American 'Retreat Rule,'" *Law and Contemporary Problems* 55 (Winter 1992): 309.

18. Epps, "Any Which Way but Loose," 309.

19. Brown, *No Duty to Retreat*, 3–4.

20. Beale, "Retreat from a Murderous Assault," 574–75; Catherine L. Carpenter, "Of the Enemy Within, the Castle Doctrine, and Self-Defense," *Marquette Law Review* 86 (Spring 2003): 655–57.

21. Quoted in Elizabeth B. Megale, "Deadly Combinations: How Self-Defense Laws Pairing Immunity with a Presumption of Fear Allow Criminals to 'Get Away with Murder,'" *American Journal of Trial Advocacy* 34 (Summer 2010): 112.

22. Christine Catalfamo, "Stand Your Ground: Florida's Castle Doctrine for the Twenty-First Century," *Rutgers Journal of Law and Public Policy* 4 (Fall 2007): 506–7.

23. *Seyman's Case*, 5 Co. Rep. 91a, 91b, 77 Eng. Rep. 194, at 195 (K. B. 1603). The decision was authored by the eminent British jurist and legal scholar Sir Edward Coke.

24. Epps, "Any Which Way but Loose," 313. The phrase "true man" appears in William Shakespeare's play *The First Part of*

Henry IV, when the character Falstaff is describing a hill on the road to Canterbury called Gadshill, widely known for the many robberies that occurred there, and then says: "This is the most omnipotent villain that ever cried 'Stand' to a true man" (Act I, scene 2).

25. NRA Executive Director Wayne LaPierre captured this sentiment in the press conference he held a week after a gunman shot and killed twenty schoolchildren and six teachers at Sandy Hook Elementary School in Connecticut in December 2012. Arguing against any new gun laws, LaPierre said that "the only thing that stops a bad guy with a gun is a good guy with a gun." Eric Lichtblau and Motoko Rich, "N.R.A. Envisions a 'Good Guy with a Gun' in Every School," *New York Times*, December 21, 2012, at http://www.nytimes.com/2012/12/22/us/nra-calls-for-armed-guards-at-schools.html?pagewanted=all&_r=0.

26. Jeannie Suk, "The True Woman: Scenes from the Law of Self-Defense," *Harvard Journal of Law and Gender* 31 (Summer 2008): 239. Key early cases that upheld a stand your ground defense were *Erwin v. State*, 29 Ohio St. 186 (1876), and *Runyan v. State*, 57 Ind. 80 (1877).

27. Brown, *No Duty to Retreat*, 5. Much of Brown's book is a close examination of key cases, mostly from the late nineteenth and early twentieth centuries, that produced the no duty to retreat principle.

28. State rulings are found in Beale, "Retreat from a Murderous Assault," and Suk, "The True Woman."

29. 158 U.S. 550 (1895).

30. 164 U.S. 492 (1896).

31. 164 U.S. 492, at 497.

32. *Allen v. U.S.*, 164 U.S. 492 (1896); *Alberty v. U.S.*, 162 U.S. 499 (1896); *Rowe v. U.S.*, 164 U.S. 546 (1896).

33. 256 U.S. 335 (1921).

34. 256 U.S. 335, at 343.

35. 256 U.S. 335, at 344.

36. Brown, *No Duty to Retreat*, 17. Brown argues persuasively that Holmes's jurisprudence on this issue was shaped by his experiences in the Civil War, which imbued him with a deep personal distaste for behavior he viewed as cowardly and admiration for manly bravery in the face of danger. See 31–36.

37. Ronald S. Sullivan Jr., testimony at hearing on stand your ground laws, before Committee on the Judiciary, Subcommittee on the Constitution, Civil Rights, and Human Rights, U.S. Senate, September 17, 2013, 4.

38. Epps, "Any Which Way but Loose," 305.

39. "Guns in Public Places," *Law Center to Prevent Gun Violence*, July 1, 2011, at http://smartgunlaws.org/guns-in-public -places-the-increasing-threat-of-hidden-guns-in-america/.

40. Zachary L. Weaver, "Florida's 'Stand Your Ground' Law: The Actual Effects and the Need for Clarification," *University of Miami Law Review* 63 (October 2008): 401–3.

41. Manual Roig-Franzia, "Florida Gun Law to Expand Leeway for Self-Defense," *Washington Post*, April 26, 2005, A1.

42. Marc Fisher and Dan Eggen, "Stand Your Ground Laws Coincide with Jump in Justifiable-Homicide Cases," *Washington Post*, April 7, 2012, A1; Adam Weinstein, "How the NRA and Its Allies Helped Spread a Radical Gun Law Nationwide," *Mother Jones*, June 7, 2012, at http://www. motherjones.com/politics/2012/06/nra-alec-stand-your- ground; Ben Montgomery, "Florida's 'Stand Your Ground Law' Was Born of 2004 Case, but Story Has Been Distorted," *Tampa Bay Times*, April 14, 2012, at http://www.tampabay. com/news/publicsafety/floridas-stand-your-ground-law- was-born-of-2004-case-but-story-has-been/1225164.

43. Abby Goodnough, "Florida Expands Right to Use Deadly Force in Self-Defense," *New York Times*, April 27, 2005, A18.

44. Marion P. Hammer, "At Last, a Balance Shifts Away from Criminals," *Atlanta Journal-Constitution*, May 2, 2005, 11A.

45. Goodnough, "Florida Expands Right to Use Deadly Force in Self-Defense."

46. Toluse Olorunnipa, "Florida: Fertile Ground for Pro-Gun Laws," *Miami Herald*, March 31, 2012, at http://www. miamiherald.com/2012/03/27/2725483/florida-fertile- ground-for-pro.html#storylink=cpy.

47. Michelle Cottle, "Shoot First, Regret Legislation Later," *Time*, May 9, 2005, 80.

48. Susan Ferriss, "NRA Helped Spread 'Stand Your Ground' Laws across the Nation," *Center for Public Integrity*, March 26, 2012, at http://www.publicintegrity.org/2012/03/26/8508/

nra-pushed-stand-your-ground-laws-across-nation. Of the 26 states, 4 (Missouri, North Dakota, Ohio, and Wisconsin) confine the "shoot-first" policy (as it is called by critics) to shooters in motor vehicles. An additional 7 states have approximations of the stand your ground principle based on court rulings, laws, and jury instructions but apply these standards under narrower circumstances, such as during a criminal trial (as opposed to earlier in the criminal justice process), and law enforcement is not restricted from conducting an initial criminal investigation. See "Shoot First Laws." The full list of states that adopted some version of stand your ground laws since 2005 includes Alabama, Alaska, Arizona, Florida, Georgia, Indiana, Kansas, Kentucky, Louisiana, Michigan, Mississippi, Missouri, Montana, Nevada, New Hampshire, North Carolina, North Dakota, Ohio, Oklahoma, Pennsylvania, South Carolina, South Dakota, Tennessee, Texas, West Virginia, Wisconsin. Utah adopted such a law in 1994, making a total of 27 states with such laws. "Shoot First Laws Policy Summary," *Law Center to Prevent Gun Violence*, July 18, 2013, at http://smartgunlaws.org/shoot-first-laws-policy-summary/.

49. Tim Dickinson, "The NRA vs. America," *Rolling Stone*, January 31, 2013, at http://www.rollingstone.com/politics/news/the-nra-vs-america-20130131.

50. Of the five "Whereas" statements that preface the legislation, three reference the right of people to defend themselves in their homes or cars; one cites the state constitution's "right of the people to bear arms," and one says that "nor should a person or victim be required to needlessly retreat in the face of an intrusion or attack. . . ." Quoted in Weaver, "Florida's 'Stand Your Ground' Law," 398–99.

51. Megale, "Deadly Combinations," 107.

52. Quoted in "Shoot First Laws Policy Summary."

53. Kris Hundley et al., "Florida 'Stand Your Ground' Law Yields Some Shocking Outcomes Depending on How the Law Is Applied," *Tampa Bay Times*, June 1, 2012, at http://www.tampabay.com/news/publicsafety/crime/florida-stand-your-ground-law-yields-some-shocking-outcomes-depending-on/1233133.

54. Hundley, "Florida 'Stand-Your-Ground' Law Yields Some Shocking Outcomes."

55. Quoted in Weaver, "Florida's 'Stand Your Ground' Law," 406–7.

56. Weaver, "Florida's 'Stand Your Ground' Law," 407–9.

57. William N. Meggs, testimony at hearing on stand your ground laws, before Committee on the Judiciary, Subcommittee on the Constitution, Civil Rights, and Human Rights, U.S. Senate, September 17, 2013, 2.

58. Marc Fisher and Dan Eggen, "Stand Your Ground Laws Coincide with Jump in Justifiable-Homicide Cases," *Washington Post*, April 7, 2012, at http://articles.washingtonpost.com/2012-04-07/national/35452643_1_new-law-american-law-justice-system.

59. Elizabeth Berenguer Megale, "Disaster Unaverted: Reconciling the Desire for a Safe and Secure State with the Grim Realities of Stand Your Ground," *American Journal of Trial Advocacy* 37 (2013): 286.

60. These arguments are fully examined in Daniel Michael, "Florida's Protection of Persons Bill," *Harvard Journal on Legislation* 43 (Winter 2006): 199–212; Weaver, "Florida's 'Stand Your Ground' Law," 395–429; Megale, "Deadly Combinations," 105–34.

61. For more on the case and its consequences, see Lisa Bloom, *Suspicion Nation: The Inside Story of the Trayvon Martin Injustice and Why We Continue to Repeat It* (Berkeley, CA: Counterpoint Press, 2014).

62. Dan Barry et al., "In the Eye of a Firestorm," *New York Times*, April 2, 2012, A1.

63. Lizette Alvarez, "Self-Defense, Hard to Topple," *New York Times*, July 15, 2013, A1.

64. Judge H. Lee Sarokin, "What Are the Real Issues Now That George Zimmerman Has Been Arrested and Charged?" *Huffington Post*, April 12, 2012, at http://www.huffingtonpost.com/judge-h-lee-sarokin/what-are-the-real-issues-_b_1421817.html.

65. Alvarez, "Self-Defense, Hard to Topple"; Lizette Alvarez, "Zimmerman Forgoes Pretrial Hearing, Taking Issue of Immunity to a Jury," *New York Times*, May 1, 2013, A12.

66. Quoted in Jonathan Turley, "The Stand Your Ground Law and the Zimmerman Trial," July 20, 2013, at http://jonathanturley.org/2013/07/20/the-stand-your-ground-law-and-the-zimmerman-trial/.

67. Quoted in Timothy Johnson, "Media Neglect That 'Stand Your Ground' Is Centerpiece of Florida's Self-Defense Law," *Media Matters*, July 16, 2013, at http://mediamatters.org/research/2013/07/16/media-neglect-that-stand-your-ground-is-centerp/194916.

68. Marc Caputo, "Juror: We Talked Stand Your Ground before Not-Guilty Zimmerman Verdict," *Miami Herald*, July 18, 2013, at http://www.miamiherald.com/2013/07/16/3502481/juror-we-talked-stand-your-ground.html.

69. Quoted in Matt Gertz, "Stand Your Ground and the Zimmerman Defense," *Media Matters*, July 15, 2013, at http://mediamatters.org/blog/2013/07/15/stand-your-ground-and-the-zimmerman-defense/194870.

70. Joseph Kennedy, "Why It Was Too Easy for George Zimmerman to Get Off for Self-Defense," *Slate.com*, July 16, 2013, at http://www.slate.com/articles/news_and_politics/jurisprudence/2013/07/george_zimmerman_and_self_defense_why_it_was_too_easy_for_him_to_get_off.html.

71. Emily Bazelon, "Why George Zimmerman, Trayvon Martin's Killer, Hasn't Been Prosecuted," *Slate.com*, March 19, 2012, at http://www.slate.com/articles/news_and_politics/crime/2012/03/why_george_zimmerman_trayvon_martin_s_killer_hasn_t_been_prosecuted_.html.

72. Lizette Alvarez, "Weapon in Slaying of Florida Teenager Figures Again in Court," *New York Times*, February 13, 2014, A15; Greg Botelho and Sunny Hostin, "Dunn Convicted of Attempted Murder; Hung Jury on Murder in 'Loud Music' Trial," *CNN.com*, February 16, 2014, at http://www.cnn.com/2014/02/15/justice/florida-loud-music-trial/; Lizette Alvarez, "Florida Man Gets Life Term in Fatal Dispute over Music," *New York Times*, October 18, 2014, A18.

73. Arielle Stevenson, "Bond Hearing Is Held in Killing at Theater," *New York Times*, February 6, 2014, A16; Arielle Stevenson, "Florida Man Is Denied Bail in Killing at a Movie Theater," *New York Times*, February 8, 2014, A8.

74. Jack Healy, "A Boy Shot, and Regret on Montana 'Castle' Law," *New York Times*, May 8, 2014, A1.

75. Susan Taylor Martin, "Race Plays Complex Role in Florida's 'Stand Your Ground' Law," *Tampa Bay Times*, June 2, 2012, at http://www.tampabay.com/news/courts/criminal/race-plays-complex-role-in-florid as-stand-your-ground-law/1233152.

76. Kameel Stanley et al., "Many Killers Who Go Free with 'Stand Your Ground' Law Have History of Violence," *Tampa Bay Times*, July 21, 2012, at http://www.tampabay.com/news/courts/criminal/many-killers-who-go-free-with-florida-stand-your-ground-law-have-history/1241378.

77. Anton Strezhnev, "Some More Evidence That Florida's 'Stand Your Ground' Law Increased Firearm Homicide Rates," *Causal Loop*, July 16, 2013, at http://causalloop.blogspot.nl/2013/07/some-more-evidence-that-floridas-stand.html.

78. Charles C. Branas et al., "Investigating the Link between Gun Possession and Gun Assault," *American Journal of Public Health* (November 2009): 2034–40. Quotes appear on 2034.

79. Joe Palazzolo and Rob Barry, "More Killings Called Self-Defense," *Wall Street Journal*, March 31, 2012. The paper's analysis was based on data obtained from the FBI and Florida.

80. Cheng Cheng and Mark Hoekstra, "Does Strengthening Self-Defense Law Deter Crime or Escalate Violence?" NBER Working Paper No. w18134, June 2012. Available at SSRN: http://ssrn.com/abstract=2079878, 26.

81. Chandler McCellan and Erdal Tekin, "Stand Your Ground Laws, Homicides, and Injuries," National Bureau of Economic Research, Working Paper 18187, http://www.nber.org/papers/w18187, June 2012, 23–24.

82. "Shoot First: 'Stand Your Ground' Laws and Their Effect on Violent Crime and the Criminal Justice System," Mayors against Illegal Guns, September, 2013, 6–7.

83. Herbert H. Haines, *Against Capital Punishment: The Anti-Death Penalty Movement in America: 1972–1994* (New York: Oxford University Press, 1996), 76–79; "Illegal Race Discrimination in Jury Selection: A Continuing Legacy," *Equal Justice Initiative*, June 2010; Mona Lynch, "Institutionalizing Bias: The Death Penalty, Federal Drug Prosecutions, and Mechanisms of Disparate Punishment," *American Journal of Criminal Law* 41 (Winter 2013): 91–132; Death Penalty Information Center at

http://www.deathpenaltyinfo.org/race-and-death-penalty.
My thanks to Haines for his thoughtful assistance.

84. One author who has persistently extolled the value of civilian gun carrying has been John Lott. In various articles and in his book *More Guns, Less Crime*, 3rd ed. (Chicago: University of Chicago Press, 2010), he argues that gun carrying has reduced murder rates and violent crimes from 1977 to 2006. But there are numerous problems with Lott's claims and evidence. First, his period of study in the third edition of this book (published in 2010) ends the year Florida enacted its stand your ground law. Second, others who have analyzed his data have concluded that it not only does not support his more-guns-less-crime thesis but in fact reveals opposite trends. According to researchers Aneja, Donohue, and Zhang, examining the impact of right to carry laws on crime in seven categories, of 56 statistical estimates, 23 were negative—that is, in the direction of decreasing crime—but none was statistically significant at the .01 level, and only 1 was significant at the .05 level. On the other hand, 33 were positive—that is, in the direction of increasing crime associated with the enactment of right to carry laws, with 3 significant at the .01 level and 8 significant at the .05 level. See Abhay Aneja, John J. Donohue III, and Alexandria Zhang, "The Impact of Right to Carry Laws and the NRC Report: The Latest Lessons for the Empirical Evaluation of Law and Policy," September 4, 2014; Stanford Law and Economics Olin Working Paper no. 461. Available at SSRN: http://ssrn.com/abstract=2443681. Aside from these problems, Lott has engaged in a series of problematic behaviors, including making up a fictional person who extolled his work on the Internet (using the name "Mary Rosh"), referring to study findings that he could not produce, and other problems. See Robert J. Spitzer, *The Politics of Gun Control*, 6th ed. (Boulder, CO: Paradigm, 2015), 70–74.

85. A. V. Dicey, *Introduction to the Study of the Law of the Constitution* (Indianapolis: Liberty Fund, 1982), 341. Originally published 1885.

86. Michael Planty and Jennifer L. Truman, *Firearm Violence, 1993–2011*, Bureau of Justice Statistics, U.S. Department of Justice, May 2013; Joelle Anne Moreno, "Perils of 'Stand Your

Ground,'" *Los Angeles Times*, July 21, 2013, at http://articles. latimes.com/2013/jul/21/opinion/la-oe-moreno-florida-stand-your-ground-laws-20130722.

87. "Guns," *Gallup.com*, n.d., at http://www.gallup.com/poll/ 1645/guns.aspx.

88. "Why Own a Gun? Protection Is Now Top Reason," *Pew Research Center for the People and the Press*, March 12, 2013, at http://www.people-press.org/2013/03/12/ why-own-a-gun-protection-is-now-top-reason/.

89. Robert J. Spitzer, "The NRA's Silent Motive," *Salon*, April 3, 2012, at http://www.salon.com/2012/04/03/the_nras_silent_ motive/; Sabrina Tavernise and Robert Gebeloff, "Share of Homes with Guns Shows 4-Decade Decline," *New York Times*, March 10, 2013, A1; Tom W. Smith et al., *General Social Survey 2012* (Chicago: National Opinion Research Center, 2013).

90. The Gallup polling organization has reported higher gun ownership rates over this period of time but also shows gun ownership decline. The NORC surveys have asked gun ownership questions longer and more frequently, compared to Gallup, and interviews larger samples. Gallup has also proven to be an outlier in its results in recent years compared with other polling organizations, which suggests that its results may be less reliable than those of NORC on the gun issue. See Nate Silver, "Gallup vs. the World," *New York Times*, October 18, 2012, at http://fivethirtyeight.blogs. nytimes.com/2012/10/18/gallup-vs-the-world/#more-36284.

91. Tavernise and Gebeloff, "Share of Homes with Guns Shows 4-Decade Decline."

92. News stories and anecdotes have reported an increased interest in guns among women in recent years. While there probably has been an uptick in women acquiring guns, taking gun-training classes, and forming women's shooting clubs, based in part on the argument that women need guns for protection from abusive partners and other predatory men, the aggregate statistical change is small. As early as 1989, Smith and Wesson produced a line of handguns marketed specifically to women, called the "Lady Smith" line. Other manufacturers followed suit, but these efforts had little aggregate effect on the proportion of women owning guns in

America. Erica Goode, "Rising Voice of Gun Ownership Is Female," *New York Times*, February 11, 2013, A9.

93. "Threatened by long-term declining participation in shooting sports, the firearms industry has poured millions of dollars into a broad campaign to ensure its future by getting guns into the hands of more, and younger, children." Mike McIntire, "Selling a New Generation on Guns," *New York Times*, January 27, 2013, 1; Katie McDonough, "Inside the Kiddie Gun Market," *Salon.com*, May 3, 2013, at http://www.salon.com/2013/05/03/inside_the_kiddie_gun_market/.

94. Spitzer, *Politics of Gun Control*, 164–67.

95. Peter H. Stone and Ben Hallman, "NRA Gun Control Crusade Reflects Firearms Industry Financial Ties," *Huffington Post*, January 11, 2013, at http://www.huffingtonpost.com/2013/01/11/nra-gun-control-firearms-industry-ties_n_2434142.html; Natasha Singer, "The Most Wanted Gun in America," *New York Times*, February 3, 2013, Business Section, 1; "Blood Money: How the Gun Industry Bankrolls the NRA," *Violence Policy Center*, April 2011.

96. Hundley et al., "Florida 'Stand Your Ground' Law Yields Some Shocking Outcomes."

97. Jack Nicas and Ashby Jones, "Permits Soar to Allow More Concealed Guns," *Wall Street Journal*, July 4, 2013, A3.

98. Megale, "Disaster Unaverted," 61.

99. Brown, *No Duty to Retreat*, 157.

Chapter 5

1. "America's Gun—the Rise of the AR-15," *CNBC*, April 25, 2013, at http://www.youtube.com/watch?v=OCvjoFPD5Kg.

2. Dan Haar, "America's Rifle: Rise of the AR-15," *Hartford Courant*, March 9, 2013, at http://articles.courant.com/2013-03-09/business/hc-haar-ar-15-it-gun-20130308_1_ar-15-rifle-new-rifle-the-ar-15.

3. Ailsa Chang, "Why the AR-15 Is More Than Just a Gun," *NPR.org*, June 24, 2013, at http://www.npr.org/2013/06/24/194228925/why-the-ar-15-is-more-than-just-a-gun.

4. The stock can be modified to make its position permanent rather than adjustable by inserting a simple pin that cannot be then pulled out, as the pin expands when inserted in the hole.

5. Katherine Lagrave, "Step-by-Step Heart Surgery," *Popular Mechanics*, n.d., at http://www.popularmechanics.com/science/health/med-tech/step-by-step-heart-surgery#slide-1.

6. Peter Squires, *Gun Culture or Gun Control?* (London: Routledge, 2000), 19. Squires finds that "the idea that firearms might be used by people to shoot and kill other people seems hardly worth a mention in many of the texts examining the history of firearms development" (20).

7. The Brady Campaign, a pro–gun control organization, ranks New York in the top five among states with the strictest gun laws. In its 2011 rankings, New York ranks fourth, behind California, New Jersey, and Massachusetts. See "Brady Campaign 2011 Scorecards," at http://www.bradycampaign.org/sites/default/files/2011_Brady_Campaign_State_Scorecard_Rankings.pdf.

8. Michelle Breidenbach, "The Safe Act 'Emergency,'" *Syracuse Post-Standard*, March 13, 2013, at http://www.syracuse.com/news/index.ssf/2013/03/state_emergency_gun_law.html.

9. A legal challenge was mounted against the SAFE Act based on the argument that the governor had abused the message of necessity power, but it was dismissed.

10. "2012 Legislative Session Analysis," NYPIRG, July 2, 2012, at http://www.nypirg.org/media/releases/goodgov/NYPIRG%202012%20Session%20Analysis.pdf; Karen DeWitt, "What the Record Says about the NYS Legislature's Spring," *North Country Public Radio*, July 4, 2013, at http://www.northcountrypublicradio.org/news/story/22296/what-the-record-says-about-the-nys-legislature-s-spring.

11. This summary is drawn from *Guide to the New York SAFE Act for Members of the Division of (New York) State Police*, Office of Division Counsel, September 2013, and from interviews with local public and law enforcement officials.

12. When I posed the ammunition question to a representative responding on the SAFE Act hotline operated by the state, I was told that private ammunition exchanges would not be subject to state scrutiny.

13. K. C. Maas and Josh Levs, "Newspaper Sparks Outrage for Publishing Names, Addresses of Gun Permit Holders," *CNN. com,* December 27, 2012, at http://edition.cnn.com/2012/12/25/us/new-york-gun-permit-map/; Patrik Jonsson, "New York Paper That Published Gun-Owners Map Sues County for Names," *Christian Science Monitor,* October 4, 2013, at http://www.csmonitor.com/USA/Justice/2013/1004/New-York-paper-that-published-gun-owners-map-sues-county-for-names.

14. Quoted in *Guide to The New York Safe Act,* 13.

15. Reid Wilson, "Gun-Control Advocates Losing Ground in the States despite Mass Shootings," *Washington Post,* September 21, 2013, at http://articles.washingtonpost.com/2013-09-21/politics/42269255_1_gun-control-advocates-federal-gun-legislation-private-gun-sales; "State Gun Laws Enacted in Year Since Newtown," *New York Times,* December 11, 2013, A16.

16. Tamer El-Ghobashy, "Gun Law's Mental-Health Provision Draws Ire," *Wall Street Journal,* January 15, 2013, at http://online.wsj.com/article/SB10001424127887324235104578244224056908126.html; James Mulder, "Mental Health Advocates: State Gun Law Is Unfair and Misguided," *Syracuse Post-Standard,* March 17, 2013, A1; Jessica Bakeman, "Mental-Health Officials Clash on N.Y. Gun Law Reporting," *USA Today,* March 24, 2013, at http://www.usatoday.com/story/news/nation/2013/03/24/mental-health-new-york-gun-law/2011399/.

17. Anemona Hartocollis, "Mental Reports Put Thousands on New York's No-Guns List," *New York Times,* October 19, 2014, 1; Thomas Kaplan, "Cuomo's Gun Law Plays Well Downstate but Alienates Upstate," *New York Times,* October 25, 2014, 1.

18. Jesse McKinley, "Upset over Gun Limits, Group Plans Upstate Concert," *New York Times,* April 11, 2013, A21.

19. Opponents of the law filed suit against it in *New York State Rifle and Pistol Association, Inc. v. Cuomo,* 990 F. Supp. 2d 349 (2013), U.S. District Court, Western District of New York (Buffalo). In a ruling handed down on the last day of 2013, a federal judge largely upheld the law but did strike down four specific provisions. Concluding that the law's seven-bullet limit for magazines was "a largely arbitrary number" that the state failed to explain or justify, the court concluded that it could adversely affect a citizen's Second Amendment self-protection

rights and therefore struck it down (leaving the preexisting ten-bullet standard in place). Three other minor provisions of the law were struck down by the judge on the grounds of vagueness: an ambiguous "and if" clause that followed wording barring the possession of large-capacity bullet-feeding devices; references to "muzzle breaks" in the law, erroneously spelled "break" instead of the correct "brake" (a device to minimize recoil and barrel rising during rapid fire); and language referencing "semiautomatic versions[s] of an automatic rifle, shotgun or firearm." In each instance, however, elimination of the language in question did not affect the law's regulations (except for the elimination of muzzle brakes as a listed trait identifying assault weapons). The ruling was appealed to the U.S. Court of Appeals for the Second Circuit.

20. I have heard this objection personally from gun owners on numerous, numerous occasions, but especially in recent months. Prolific sources replicate these grievances; see, for example, Mark Boshnack, "NY Sheriffs: We Won't Enforce Gun Laws, Magazine Limits," *Daily Star*, September 17, 2013, at http://www.policeone.com/chiefs-sheriffs/articles/6435415-NY-sheriffs-We-wont-enforce-gun-laws-magazine-limits/.

21. Robert J. Spitzer, *The Politics of Gun Control*, 6th ed. (Boulder, CO: Paradigm, 2015), 100–11, 137–41, 159–66; Robert J. Spitzer, "Government Can Improve Gun Records," *The Hill*, January 14, 2013, at http://thehill.com/opinion/op-ed/277099-government-can-improve-gun-records; Erica Goode and Sheryl Gay Stolberg, "Legal Curbs Said to Hamper A.T.F. in Gun Inquiries," *New York Times*, December 26, 2013, A1.

22. Freeman Klopott, "Cuomo's 7 Bullet Limit to Be Suspended Indefinitely," *Bloomberg News*, March 24, 2013, at http://www.bloomberg.com/news/2013-03-25/cuomo-s-7-bullet-limit-to-be-suspended-indefinitely-skelos-says.html.

23. Jacob Sullum, "Andrew Cuomo Realizes He Mandated Gun Magazines That Don't Exist," *Reason.com*, March 21, 2013, at http://reason.com/blog/2013/03/21/cuomo-realizes-he-mandated-gun-magazines.

24. Under regulations of the state's Department of Environmental Conservation, hunters are restricted from bringing into the field firearms loaded with more than six rounds (see http://www.

dec.ny.gov/outdoor/8305.html). Also, up until 1991, the federal assault weapons ban, eventually enacted in 1994, included a magazine round limit of seven. See Paul M. Barrett, *Glock: The Rise of America's Gun* (New York: Broadway Books, 2013), 108.

25. This is actually a fairly routine alteration. For example, an NRA competitive shooting manual stipulates at one point that a "reduced capacity magazine" is allowable for use in shooting competitions where a variety of stipulations are imposed for the weapons used. See "NRA High Power Rifle Rules" (Fairfax, VA: National Rifle Association, 2012), 11.

26. 990 F. Supp. 2d 349, 2013.

27. Tom Hamburger and Ed O'Keefe, "Gun Rights Group Endorses Manchin-Toomey Background-Check Bill," *Washington Post*, April 15, 2013, A1; forty-six senators voted against the bill. The NRA played both sides of the fence on this measure: while publicly vilifying the bill and working for its defeat, it also helped write the bill behind the scenes. The bill was also endorsed by another gun group, the Independent Firearm Owners Association.

28. "Gun Owners' Poll," Luntz Polling, July 2012. The poll was conducted at the behest of Mayors against Illegal Guns, a pro–gun control group. See also William Saletan, "Don't Regulate Guns. Regulate Who Can Get Them," *Slate.com*, January 11, 2013, at http://www.slate.com/articles/health_and_science/human_nature/2013/01/guns_don_t_kill_people_people_kill_people_so_keep_dangerous_people_away.html.

29. Justin Peters, "Felon Pens a 'Heartfelt Thank You to the NRA' for Opposing Universal Background Checks," *Slate.com*, June 13, 2013, at http://www.slate.com/blogs/crime/2013/06/13/gary_w_bornman_felon_pens_a_heartfelt_thank_you_to_the_nra_for_opposing.html.

30. Timothy Johnson, "Discredited Gun Researcher John Lott's Failed Attempt to Correct Obama's Gun Statistic," *MediaMatters*, January 25, 2013, at http://mediamatters.org/blog/2013/01/25/discredited-gun-researcher-john-lotts-failed-at/192391.

31. Thomas Kaplan, "New York Deal Adds Controls at Gun Shows," *New York Times*, March 15, 2013, A1.

32. Having both bought and sold cars in this manner over the years, I can attest to the relative simplicity and utility of this process.

33. Benjamin Hayes, "Stop Lying about Universal Background Checks," *Crime Report*, June 20, 2013, at http://www.thecrimereport.org/news/articles/2013-06-stop-lying-about-universal-background-checks.

34. See New York SAFE Resolutions, at http://www.nysaferesolutions.com/.

35. "NY and Southern Tier Voters Nearly Evenly Divided on Fracking," *Siena Research Institute*, February 4, 2013, at http://www.siena.edu/uploadedfiles/home/parents_and_community/community_page/sri/sny_poll/SNY%20February%202013%20Poll%20Release%20--%20FINAL.pdf.

36. Jimmy Vielkind, "Poll: Upstate Support for Gun Law," *Albany Times-Union*, March 7, 2013, at http://blog.timesunion.com/capitol/archives/180916/poll-upstate-support-for-gun-law-at-36/.

37. "Cuomo's Favorability Rating," *Siena Research Institute*, March 11, 2013, at http://www.siena.edu/uploadedfiles/home/parents_and_community/community_page/sri/sny_poll/SNY%20March%202013%20Poll%20Release%20--%20FINAL.pdf.

38. Robert Harding, "Quinnipiac Poll," *The Citizen*, April 17, 2013, at http://auburnpub.com/blogs/eye_on_ny/quinnipiac-poll-strong-support-for-ny-safe-act-majority-approve/article_8abebeea-a76d-11e2-8fd9-001a4bcf887a.html.

39. The survey of Jefferson County residents was conducted by the Center for Community Studies at Jefferson Community College in April 2013, based on a telephone survey of 400 county residents. My thanks to center director Dr. Raymond Petersen for sharing the results. The center has conducted county surveys annually since 2000. See the full results at http://www.sunyjefferson.edu/sites/default/files/Jefferson_Survey_Report_2013.pdf; and Gordon Block and Daniel Flatley, "JCC Survey Reveals Residents Like Quality of Life," *Watertown Daily Times*, June 12, 2013, at http://www.watertowndailytimes.com/article/20130612/NEWS03/706119746.

40. Spitzer, *Politics of Gun Control*, 87–128.

41. "New York State Sheriffs' Association Responds to SAFE Act," January 26, 2013, at http://www.wktv.com/news/local/New-York-State-Sheriffs-Associati

ons-Offical-Response-to-NY-SAFE-Act-188504611.
html?video=YHI.

42. "New York State Sheriffs' Association Responds to SAFE Act."
43. Teri Weaver, "Sheriffs Choose Gun Law Targets," *Syracuse Post-Standard*, October 10, 2013, A1.
44. "Amici Curiae Brief of New York State Sheriffs' Association," filed May 29, 2013, *New York State Rifle and Pistol Association, Inc. v. Cuomo*, at http://michellawyers.com/wp-content/uploads/2013/04/NY-v.-Cuomo_Amici-Curiae-Brief-of-New-York-State-Sheriffs-Association-et-al.__.pdf.
45. "Statement Regarding Passage of NY SAFE Act," January 15, 2013, at http://www.daasny.org/1.15.13%20DAASNY%20-%20Passage%20of%20Safe%20Act.pdf; "Statement of DAASNY President," January 22, 2013, at http://www.daasny.org/1%2022%2013%20Statement%20re%20Governor%27s%20Budget%20%282%29.pdf. See also Teri Weaver, "State DA's Group Proposes Gun Rules," *Syracuse Post-Standard*, January 9, 2013, A4. Onondaga County District Attorney William Fitzpatrick, a conservative upstate Republican, said in an interview that he believed the law's seven-bullet magazine maximum was unconstitutional (as a federal judge had earlier ruled) but that "military weapons should not be in the hands of civilians" and that "the last thing we would need to do would be to 'loosen up' gun laws." "DA: 7-Shot Maximum Clip Is Unconstitutional," *Syracuse Post-Standard*, May 9, 2014, A3.
46. See Declaration of Kevin Bruen, filed June 21, 2013, *New York State Rifle and Pistol Association, Inc. v. Cuomo*, at http://michellawyers.com/wp-content/uploads/2013/04/Cuomo_Declaration-of-Kevin-Bruen-re-Cross-Motion-for-Summary-Judgment.pdf.
47. "Cuomo's Favorability Rating."
48. Teri Weaver, "Siena Poll: New Low for Cuomo," *Syracuse Post-Standard*, October 1, 2013, A8.
49. Michelle Breidenbach, "Cuomo Approval Rating High Heading into '14 Election," *Syracuse Post-Standard*, December 2, 2013, A3. The poll was conducted by Quinnipiac.
50. Thomas Kaplan, "Cuomo: Obama Hurt Democrats at Polls," *Syracuse Post-Standard*, November 9, 2014, A24;

Teri Weaver, "How Upstate New York Won and the Gun Lobby Lost," *Syracuse Post-Standard,* November 9, 2014, A5; Carl Campanile, "NY Breaks Lowest Voter Turnout Record in Governor's Race," *New York Post,* November 6, 2014, at http://nypost.com/2014/11/06/ny-breaks-lowest-voter-turnout-record-in-governors-race/.

51. Alexander DeConde, *Gun Violence in America* (Boston: Northeastern University Press, 2001), 109–10.

52. Lee Kennett and James LaVerne Anderson, *The Gun in America* (Westport, CT: Greenwood Press, 1975), 175.

53. Daniel W. Webster et al., "Effects of State-Level Firearm Seller Accountability Policies on Firearm Trafficking," *Journal of Urban Health* 86 (July 2009): 525–37.

54. "Gun Laws Matter 2012," *Law Center to Prevent Gun Violence,* November 14, 2012, at http://smartgunlaws.org/gun-laws-matter-2012-understanding-the-link-between-weak-laws-and-gun-violence/; "States with Weak Gun Laws and Higher Gun Ownership Lead Nation in Gun Deaths, New Data for 2012 Confirms," *Violence Policy Center,* October 23, 2014 at http://www.vpc.org/press/1410gundeath.htm.

55. Simon Rogers, "Gun Crime Statistics by US State," *The Guardian,* December 17, 2012, at http://www.theguardian.com/news/datablog/2011/jan/10/gun-crime-us-state.

56. Eric W. Fleegler et al., "Firearm Legislation and Firearm-Related Fatalities in the United States," *JAMA Internal Medicine* 173 (May 13, 2013): 732–40; Michael Siegel et al., "The Relationship between Gun Ownership and Firearm Homicide Rates in the United States, 1981–2010," *American Journal of Public Health* 103 (November 2013): 2098–105.

57. Richard Florida, "The Hidden Geography of America's Surging Suicide Rate," *Atlantic Cities,* May 8, 2013, at http://www.theatlanticcities.com/neighborhoods/2013/05/hidden-geography-americas-surging-suicide-rate/5489/.

58. Spitzer, *Politics of Gun Control,* 58–61.

59. "Federal Report Tracks New York Crime Guns to Many States," *Syracuse Post Standard,* July 30, 2012, at http://www.syracuse.com/news/index.ssf/2012/07/federal_report_tracks_new_york.html.

60. Tina Moore, "Guns from Out-of-State Make Up the Grand Majority of City Crimes," *New York Daily News*, July 31, 2013, at http://www.nydailynews.com/new-york/out-of-state-guns-ny-gun-crimes-article-1.1414139.

61. Spitzer, *Politics of Gun Control*, 184–85.

62. "ATF New York," Department of Justice, Bureau of Alcohol, Tobacco, Firearms and Explosives, January 1, 2011–December 31, 2011.

63. Barnini Chakraborty, "Bloomberg Gun Control Group Facing Internal Backlash amid Growing Profile," *foxnews.com*, July 29, 2013, at http://www.foxnews.com/politics/2013/07/29/bloomberg-anti-gun-group-backlash/. Some mayors have reportedly left the group, unhappy with some of its recent political efforts.

64. Spitzer, *Politics of Gun Control*, 164–67.

65. Tom Hays, "Authorities: Men Smuggled Guns to NYC on Buses," *AP*, August 19, 2013, at http://bigstory.ap.org/article/authorities-men-smuggled-guns-nyc-buses.

66. Webster et al., "Effects of State-Level Firearm Seller Accountability Policies"; Daniel W. Webster et al., "Relationship between Licensing, Registration, and Other Gun Sales Laws and the Source State of Crime Guns," *Injury Prevention* 7 (September 2001): 184–89; Philip J. Cook and Jens Ludwig, "Principles for Effective Gun Policy," *Fordham Law Review* 73 (November 2004): 589–613.

67. http://www.usacarry.com/new_york_concealed_carry_permit_information.html.

68. "U.S. Supreme Court Rejects NJ Man's Appeal of Gun-Carry Suit," *New Jersey Star-Ledger*, May 6, 2014, at http://www.nj.com/sussex-county/index.ssf/2014/05/us_supreme_court_rejects_nj_mans_appeal_on_carrying_a_gun_in_public.html. The challenge to New Jersey's may issue law was rejected by the U.S. Court of Appeals for the Third Circuit in *Drake v. Jerejian*, 724 F.3d 426 (2013), and the Supreme Court declined to hear an appeal in 2014. New York's may issue law was upheld in the Court of Appeals for the Second Circuit in *Kachalsky v. County of Westchester*, 701 F.3d 81 (2012). The Supreme Court denied the appeal of that case in 2013.

69. The New York pistol permit application is available at the state police website at http://troopers.ny.gov/firearms/PPB-3.pdf.
70. New York Penal Law, sec. 400(2), at http://ypdcrime.com/penal.law/article400.htm. Special consideration is also cited in sec. 400(2) (g) for collectors of antique handguns.
71. New York Penal Law, sec. 400(2).
72. Monique Garcia, "On Concealed Carry Issue, Illinois Looks to N.Y. Gun Laws," *Chicago Tribune*, December 30, 2012, at http://articles.chicagotribune.com/2012-12-30/news/ct-met-illinois-concealed-carry-models-20121230_1_gun-laws-gun-issue-typical-gun-owner.
73. "Gun Control: States' Laws and Requirements for Concealed Carry Permits Vary across the Nation," *Government Accountability Office*, July 2012, 76–77.
74. *Kachalsky v. County of Westchester*, 701 F.3d 81 (2nd Cir. 2012).
75. Cert. denied, *Kachalsky v. Cacace*, 2013 U.S. LEXIS 3132 (U.S., April 15, 2013).
76. Garcia, "On Concealed Carry Issue."
77. Daniel Krieger, "Home on the Range—in New York City," *Salon.com*, June 23, 2013, at http://www.salon.com/2013/06/23/home_on_the_range_in_new_york_city_partner/.
78. Spitzer, *Politics of Gun Control*, xvii.
79. The book was "Produced by the Education and Training Division of the NRA" and published in 2009.
80. The law's formal title is the Federal Aid in Wildlife Restoration Act (16 U.S.C. 669–669i; 50 Stat. 917).
81. "Gun Safety and Public Health," *Law Center to Prevent Gun Violence*, September 25, 2013, at http://smartgunlaws.org/gun-safety-public-health-policy-recommendations-for-a-more-secure-america/.
82. For the record, I scored 100 percent on my exam.
83. Among the many types of government policies, regulatory policies are invariably the most controversial, and social regulatory policies (of which gun control is an exemplar) even more controversial. See Spitzer, *Politics of Gun Control*, 2–7.
84. Charles Leedham, "Vision of a Crashproof Car," *New York Times Sunday Magazine*, October 25, 1964, 121.

85. "Safety Belt Use Laws," *Insurance Institute for Highway Safety*, October 2009, at http://www.iihs.org/iihs/topics/laws/safetybeltuse?topicName=safety-belts.
86. Suzette Morelock et al., "Mandatory Seatbelt Law Support and Opposition in New England," *Public Health Reports* 100 (July–August 1985): 357–63.
87. For example, "High Belt Use Rates?," *Status Report*, Insurance Institute for Highway Safety 22 (November 21, 1987), 1; "Seat Belt Use Laws: What to Expect," *Status Report*, Insurance Institute for Highway Safety 19 (September 8, 1984).
88. "Overview List: How Many Smokefree Laws?," *American Nonsmokers' Rights Foundation*, October 1, 2013, at http://www.no-smoke.org/pdf/mediaordlist.pdf.
89. Robert J. Spitzer, "Clearing the Air," *Syracuse Post-Standard*, August 4, 2004, A16.
90. "Post-*Heller* Litigation Summary," *Law Center to Prevent Gun Violence*, August 2, 2013, at http://smartgunlaws.org/post-heller-litigation-summary/; also http://smartgunlaws.org/wp-content/uploads/2012/07/2014-for-web.pdf.

About the Author

Robert J. Spitzer (PhD, Cornell, 1980) is Distinguished Service
Professor and Chair of the Political Science Department at the State
University of New York, College at Cortland. He is the author of
fifteen books, including *The Presidency and Public Policy, The Right
to Life Movement and Third Party Politics, The Presidential Veto, The
Bicentennial of the U.S. Constitution, President and Congress, Media and
Public Policy, Politics and Constitutionalism, The Right to Bear Arms, The
Presidency and the Constitution, Saving the Constitution from Lawyers, Gun
Control, The Encyclopedia of Gun Control and Gun Rights, We the People:
Essentials Edition*, and *The Politics of Gun Control* (6th edition). He is
also series editor for the American Constitutionalism book series for
SUNY Press. He is a recipient of the SUNY Chancellor's Award for
Excellence in Scholarship. Spitzer is the author of over 600 articles
and papers appearing in many books, journals, newspapers, and web-
sites on a variety of American politics subjects. He served as president
of the Presidency Research Group of the American Political Science
Association from 2001 to 2003 and as a member of the New York
State Commission on the Bicentennial of the U.S. Constitution. He
has testified before Congress on several occasions. Spitzer is often
quoted and interviewed by American and international news outlets,
including *The Today Show, Good Morning America, ABC Nightly News*,
PBS's *News Hour with Jim Lehrer*, MSNBC's *All In with Chris Hayes*,
CNN, NPR's *Fresh Air with Terry Gross, The Diane Rehm Show*, the
BBC, CBC, NHK, *Der Spiegel*, the *New York Times*, the *Los Angeles
Times*, the *Wall Street Journal, USA Today, TIME Magazine, Newsweek*,
Slate, and Politico, among others. He is also a regular contributor
to the *Huffington Post* and has been a visiting professor at Cornell
University for over twenty years.

Index

Note: Italicized letter *n* designates footnotes. Italicized letter *t* designates tables. Headings which appear periodically throughout the page range are designated with *passim*.